WHAT INVESTORS REALLY WANT

Discover What Drives Investor Behavior
and Make Smarter Financial Decisions

MEIR STATMAN

New York   Chicago   San Francisco   Lisbon   London   Madrid   Mexico City
Milan   New Delhi   San Juan   Seoul   Singapore   Sydney   Toronto

This publication is designed to provide accurate and authoritative information in regard to the subject matter covered. It is sold with the understanding that neither the author nor the publisher is engaged in rendering legal, accounting, securities trading, or other professional services. If legal advice or other expert assistance is required, the services of a competent professional person should be sought.
—*From a Declaration of Principles Jointly Adopted by a Committee of the American Bar Association and a Committee of Publishers and Associations*

McGraw-Hill books are available at special quantity discounts to use as premiums and sales promotions or for use in corporate training programs. To contact a representative, please e-mail us at bulksales@mcgraw-hill.com.

This book is printed on acid-free paper.

To the memory
of my beloved parents,
Tova and Mordechai Statman

Contents

We want more than high profits from our investments. We want to be number 1 and beat the market. We want to nurture hope for riches and banish fear of poverty. We want to feel the pride of profits and avoid the regret of losses. We want the sophistication of hedge funds and the virtue of socially responsible funds. And we want to leave a legacy for our children.

Investments with profits equal to their risks are as easy to find as good lunches at fair prices. But we want free lunches, not fair ones, and we are always searching for investments with profits higher than risks.

Cognitive errors mislead us into thinking that investments with profits higher than risks are easy to find. Hindsight errors are one example, misleading us into thinking that we have seen investment winners in foresight when, in truth, we have seen them only in hindsight.

Emotions, like cognitive errors, draw us into promises of profits higher than risks. Exuberance highlights profits and obscures risks; fear highlights risks and obscures profits; and unrealistic optimism exaggerates our investment skills and chances.

The game of finding investments with profits higher than risks is tempting, even when we know that it is difficult to win. Playing the game makes us feel alive, in the groove, in control, and in the flow. And winning is exhilarating.

CHAPTER 5: **We Join Herds and Inflate Bubbles**   67

We stampede into investments in exuberance and stampede out in fear. We inflate bubbles and deflate them. Our herding instinct also opens the door to frauds, where early fools pull in late fools, and all turn into losers.

CHAPTER 6: **We Want Self-Control and**
Mental Accounts   81

We do not spend dollars from "hard-earned" mental accounts as easily as we spend dollars won in lotteries. Mental accounting facilitates self-control, stopping us from buying a shiny new car today when we need the money for retirement tomorrow.

CHAPTER 7: **We Want to Save for Tomorrow and**
Spend It Today   93

We try to strike a balance between saving too little and saving too much. Mental accounting helps us distinguish what we are permitted to spend from what we must save. Self-control helps us manage our conflicting desires to spend and save.

CHAPTER 8: **We Want Hope for Riches and**
Freedom from the Fear of Poverty   107

Investors who hate risk buy insurance policies, while investors who love risk buy lottery tickets. Yet most of us buy both, just as we buy both safe bonds and risky stocks. We are motivated by our twin desires of hope for riches and freedom from the fear of poverty.

CHAPTER 9: **We Have Similar Wants and**
Different Ones   119

Some investors are passionate about hope, while others care more about freedom from fear. Our personalities, life experiences, and cultures weigh on the balance we strike between hope and freedom from fear.

CHAPTER 10: **We Want to Face No Losses**   **133**

Profits bring pride while losses inflict regret. Realizing losses is especially painful because we give up hope of recouping our losses. So we realize gains quickly and procrastinate in the realization of losses.

CHAPTER 11: **We Want to Pay No Taxes**   **151**

Some investors greet taxes with acceptance or resignation. Some feel smart and savvy when they avoid taxes. Some are angry that taxes are wasted by politicians. And some are willing to forego $5,000 in profits to avoid paying $4,000 in taxes.

CHAPTER 12: **We Want High Status and Proper Respect**   **161**

Hedge funds open their doors only to the rich, making it easy to brag about riches without appearing to brag. Yet wealth does not always bring respect. Women investors resented disrespect a century ago, and they resent condescending attitudes today.

CHAPTER 13: **We Want to Stay True to Our Values**   **177**

Some socially responsible investors are willing to sacrifice investment profits for human rights and others are willing to sacrifice profits for a clean environment. Values extend beyond social responsibility to religion, ideology, patriotism, and philanthropy.

CHAPTER 14: **We Want Fairness**   **195**

We want to play on level playing fields in sports, investments, and every other field. We boycott stores that treat their employees unfairly, protest unfair investment practices, and forego profits to avoid money managers whose fairness we suspect.

CHAPTER 15: **We Want to Invest in Our Children and Families**   **209**

We prod our children to do well in school and we save for their college expenses. Middle-class parents worry that they might not have enough for their children's education. Rich parents worry that their children would feel entitled to spend what they do not earn.

CHAPTER 16: **We Want Education, Advice, and Protection**   **223**

We are increasingly responsible for our financial futures. We seek information, protection, and advice from financial advisors, the Internet, the government, and other investors. Some advice is good and some is bad. Some sticks with us and some washes away.

CONCLUSION: **What We Have**   **237**

Some trade investments because they have a true advantage over other traders. Others trade investments because cognitive errors mislead them. Yet others trade because they want to enjoy the thrill of trading. Still, it is important to distinguish truth from cognitive errors and cognitive errors from wants. And it is important to remember that investments are about life beyond money.

What We Want

At a dinner party some years ago, a fellow guest, an engineer who had learned that I am a professor of finance, wanted to know where he can buy Japanese yen. "Why do you want to buy Japanese yen," I asked. "Because its value is sure to zoom past the American dollar," he said, and proceeded to list the American budget deficit, its trade deficit, and other indicators of the advantage of the Japanese yen over the American dollar.

I wanted to tell my fellow guest quickly and gently that while his thinking is quite normal, it is not very smart. "Buying and selling Japanese yen, American stocks, French bonds, and all other investments," I said, "is not like playing tennis against a practice wall, where you can watch the ball hit the wall and place yourself at just the right spot to hit it back when it bounces. It is like playing tennis against an opponent you've never met before. Are you faster than your opponent? Will your opponent fool you by pretending to hit the ball to the left side, only to hit it to the right?"

"Think for a moment," I said to my fellow guest. "You are on one side of the net, thinking that the yen will go up. Your opponent is on the other side, thinking that it will go down. One of you must be the slow one. Have you considered the possibility that the yen seller might be Goldman Sachs, Barclays, Bank of Tokyo-Mitsubishi UFJ, or another of many traders in the yen market who have offices in both Tokyo and New York and know more about both the Japanese and American economies than you can learn from your morning's *Wall Street Journal*?"

Yet there is more to investing and tennis than faulty thinking. My fellow guest wanted to make money on his yen trade, but he also wanted to feel the thrill of winning when the yen zooms. He wanted to express himself as a player in financial markets, not one who stands at the market's sideline. And he wanted to be a member of the investing community, the community of people who observe financial markets, trade in them, and share their experiences with one another.

This book is about what we want from our investments. It is about how we think about our investments, how we feel about them, and how investment markets drive us crazy as we try to cajole them into giving us what we want. This book is about normal investors like you, me, and my fellow guest. We are intelligent people, neither irrational nor insane. We are "normal smart" at times and "normal stupid" at other times. We do our best to increase the ratio of smart behavior to stupid behavior, but we do not have computers for brains and we want benefits computers cannot comprehend.

We want high returns from our investments, but we want much more. We want to nurture hope for riches and banish fear of poverty. We want to be number 1 and beat the market. We want to feel pride when our investments bring gains and avoid the regret that comes with losses. We want the status and esteem of hedge funds, the warm glow and virtue of socially responsible funds, and the patriotism of investing in our own country. We want good advice from financial advisors, magazines, and the Internet. We want to be free from government regulations yet be protected by regulators. We want financial markets to be fair but search for an edge that would let us win, sometimes fair and at other times not. We want to leave a legacy for our children when we are gone. And we want to leave nothing for the tax man. The sum of our wants and behaviors makes financial markets go up or down as we herd together or go our separate ways, sometimes inflating bubbles and at other times popping them.

WHAT DO WE WANT? UTILITARIAN, EXPRESSIVE, AND EMOTIONAL BENEFITS

Tennis is a job for the likes of the Williams sisters who play at Wimbledon and the United States Open. Professional players earn money from prizes and endorsements, but the benefits of their tennis jobs extend beyond money. Tennis makes up much of the expressive life of professional players, expressed in their identity as tennis players when they are cheered on the court and asked for autographs off the court. And tennis makes much of the emotional life of professional players, hoping for the thrills of victory and dreading the agony of defeat.

Most of us have jobs, even if not professional tennis jobs. We want to earn money from our jobs, but we want much more. Our jobs encompass much of our expressive and emotional life. We want to express our identity, whether that of a professor, policeman, technician, or physician. We want pride in a job well done, satisfaction in a contribution to society, and a sense of belonging to a community of colleagues and friends. When we lose a job we lose more than money, we lose part of our identities, pride in our accomplishments, and membership in our communities.

The benefits of a job come in packages and we face trade-offs as we choose among them. A lawyer who wants to earn money but is also passionate about public advocacy can choose a public advocacy package with little money and much passion or a corporate law package with more money but less passion. Moreover, the money we earn in our jobs is only a station on the way to the benefits of spending it on food, shelter, and perhaps tennis. While professionals earn money from tennis, amateurs pay money for it, money for tennis rackets, balls, and court fees. Amateurs pay because tennis is enjoyable exercise, because it affords us time with friends, because we hope for the thrill of victory, and because we want to express our membership in the tennis community.

Investments are like jobs, and their benefits extend beyond money. Investments express parts of our identity, whether that of a trader, a gold accumulator, or a fan of hedge funds. Investments are a game to many of us, like tennis. We may not admit it, and we may not even know it, but our actions show that we are willing to pay money for the investment game. This is money we pay in trading commissions, mutual fund fees, and software that promises to tell us where the stock market is headed. And investments are about what we would do with the money we make and how it makes us feel. Investments are about a sense of security in retirement, the hope of riches, joy and pride of raising our children, and paying for the college education of our grandchildren.

Investments, jobs, products and services have benefits that enhance wealth, well-being, or both. These include utilitarian benefits, expressive benefits, and emotional benefits. Utilitarian benefits are the answer to the question, What does it do for me and my pocketbook? The utilitarian benefits of watches include time telling, the utilitarian benefits of restaurants include nutritious calories, and the utilitarian benefits of investments are mostly wealth, enhanced by high investment returns.

Expressive benefits convey to us and to others our values, tastes, and status. They answer the question, What does it say about me to others and to me? Private banking expresses status and esteem. One private bank advertised its services along with a chauffeured vintage Rolls-Royce and the tag line "Once you've earned exclusive service, there's no turning back."

A stock picker says, "I am smart, able to pick winning stocks." An options trader says, "I'm sophisticated, willing to take risk and knowing how to control it."

Emotional benefits are the answer to the question, How does it make me feel? The best tables at prestigious restaurants make us feel proud, insurance policies make us feel safe, lottery tickets and speculative stocks give us hope, and stock trading is exciting. Gerald Tsai, Jr. was a fund manager who pioneered the go-go performance funds in the 1960s. "He loved doing transactions," said Christopher Tsai, recalling his father's enthusiasm about the stock market. "He loved the excitement of it."[1]

Investment professionals are often uncomfortable with the commingling of utilitarian, expressive, and emotional benefits. Many financial advisors are puzzled by the desire of some investors to exclude from their portfolios stocks of tobacco companies. Why not invest in stocks of tobacco companies if they produce the highest returns and then use these returns for anti-smoking campaigns? As Rob Moody, a financial advisor at Compass Advisors in Atlanta said, "Those investors who are interested in social or ethical investing would be ahead if they invested in anything else, including "unethical" companies, and then donate their profits to the charities of their choice."[2]

Moody's suggestion makes as much sense to socially responsible investors as a suggestion to Orthodox Jews that they forgo kosher beef for cheaper and perhaps tastier pork and donate the savings to their synagogues. A member of the Church of the Brethren said, "I occasionally see articles by investment columnists on the sin funds that invest primarily in tobacco and alcohol, etc., advising people to take their profits from these funds and do good with them. That argument seems completely backwards to me, because the money is already out there supporting bad things."[3]

Advising socially responsible investors to separate their social goals from their financial goals is symptomatic of a more general tendency among investment professionals to separate the utilitarian benefits of investments from their expressive and emotional benefits. Reathel Geary, a financial advisor with IMHO Investments understands that the benefits of socially responsible investments extend beyond utilitarian returns. He said: "We like to call it "opinionated investing"—helping our clients to invest in firms that share their views on what's important."

OUR WANTS, THOUGHTS, COGNITIVE ERRORS, AND EMOTIONS

Have you noticed that most movies are fiction? Of course you have. You know that the people you see on the movie screen are actors, only pretending to be who they are not. You know that the movements you see on the screen are cognitive errors, optical illusions caused by fast projection of still images. And sometimes you wear funny glasses that fool you into seeing 3-D images on a flat screen. So why are we willing to pay money for movie tickets, sacrificing wealth for fiction and truth for exploitation of cognitive errors? The answer is obvious. Movies touch our emotions and add to our well-being. They make us laugh and cry and help us enjoy the company of dates, spouses, children, and friends. Indeed, we enjoy movies more when we share expressions and emotions with our companions.[4]

The world of investments is different from the world of the movies because it offers no clear boundary between fact and fiction. Lights are rarely turned on in the world of investments, so it is hard to distinguish fact from fiction and truth from cognitive errors. But the world of investments is also similar to the world of the movies because movies offer benefits that go beyond the utilitarian benefits of facts, and investments offer benefits that go beyond the utilitarian benefits of wealth. We know that most investors who trade frequently sacrifice wealth. But frequent traders might be receiving good value for the wealth they sacrifice, enjoying hope for enormous wealth as lottery buyers enjoy hope for giant prizes. Traders also add to their well-being as they play the trading game, tracking the stocks displayed on their computer screens as video game players track heroes and villains. And traders enjoy the community of fellow traders, meeting at investment clubs, sipping coffee or beer, and swapping stories.

I tried to dissuade my fellow dinner guest from trading Japanese yen but I have probably failed. Perhaps I failed to help my fellow dinner guest overcome his cognitive error, learn that trading should be framed as playing tennis against a possibly better player, and refrain from trading. Or I might have succeeded in helping my fellow guest overcome his cognitive error and yet failed to dissuade him from trading because he wanted the expressive and emotional benefits of the trading game, the fun of playing and the thrill of winning.

Emotional benefits come with positive emotions such as exuberance, hope, or pride. Negative emotions such as fear, despair, and regret, detract from benefits in some ways and add to them in others. We are often advised to use reason, not emotions, when we make investment decisions. But this advice is neither feasible nor smart. Emotions complement reason more often than they interfere with it, and the interaction between emotions and reason is mostly beneficial, often critically so. Emotions prevent us from being lost in thought when it is time to act, and emotions reinforce lessons we must learn.

Regret is a painful emotion but it is also an effective teacher. Regret over unwise choices teaches us to make better ones. Patients with orbitofrontal cortex lesions do not feel the pain of regret, but they are also deprived of the good lessons we learn from it.[5] Yet sometimes emotions interact with cognitive errors, reinforcing poor lessons. Cognitive errors dispose us to hold on losing investments even when selling them would add to our wealth. These cognitive errors are reinforced by regret. Reflection on losing investments brings a gnawing pain of regret, but realizing losses by selling losing investments brings a searing pain of regret. It is no wonder that we are reluctant to realize losses.

Computers want nothing. They only execute the wants of their human masters, whether programmers or users. IBM programmers wanted to win when they got Deep Blue ready for a chess match with the world's champion Gary Kasparov. Kasparov wanted to win no less than IBM's programmers and called the match unfair when he lost. He demanded a rematch and secured a draw against another version of Deep Blue.

Computers are immune to cognitive errors and emotions, and they never jump to conclusions, but we often do. The computers at the supermarket's checkout counter do not jump to the total bill. They add the prices of our groceries one at a time, methodically but very fast, before they reach their conclusion and display the total bill. We, however, might add the prices of a few groceries in our brains, perhaps those of the most expensive groceries, and jump to a conclusion, approximating our total bill. Outside the supermarket, we look at a series of stock prices, those of Google or those of Ford, detect a rising pattern or a falling one, and jump to conclusions about where stock prices will go next.

We are fortunate to have brains that jump to conclusions. Indeed, jumping to the right conclusions is the essence of intelligence. This is what we do when we swerve our cars quickly to avoid mattresses that just fell off the truck in front of us. There is no computer today that can rival our driving ability. But sometimes we crash as we jump to conclusions. A lightning-quick combination of thoughts and emotions prompts us to slam on the brakes when the cars ahead of us stop suddenly, but we are unable to coordinate our thoughts, emotions, and foot movements fast enough to pump the brakes, as instructed in driving school. Computers are better at the braking task. The computers onboard today's cars let us jump to our own conclusions, slamming the brakes, while they pump the brakes fast enough to avoid a crash.

Rational investors know instantly, like the computers that pump our brakes, how to frame a trade. Faulty framing is one cognitive error that afflicts normal investors, but it is not the only one. Other cognitive errors include hindsight, which misleads us into thinking that we could have seen winning investments with foresight when in truth we have seen them only with hindsight; overconfidence, which leads us to overestimate our investment skills; and availability, which leads us to exaggerate the likelihood that we will pick top-performing mutual funds because mutual fund companies advertise such funds, making them available to our memory. Daniel Kahneman and Amos Tversky articulated these and other cognitive errors. The Nobel Prize committee awarded Kahneman the Nobel Prize in economics in 2002 for his contributions, in collaboration with Amos Tversky, to our understanding of human cognition. These contributions underlie much of behavioral finance and much of this book.

Human nature changes very slowly. We are more rapidly informed than our predecessors a century ago, but we are neither better informed nor better behaved. The *World's Work* magazine summed it up a century ago: "Human nature is human nature." The magazine initiated an advice column for individual investors in 1906 and its editor wrote in 1911: "In these five years of close and often intimate intercourse with investors of all sorts and descriptions the editor of this department has learned a great many things about the habits and state of mind of the individual investor. . . . One minor conclusion from all this data and experience is that the very small investor is the most inveterate bargain hunter in the world. . . . It is the small investor who always wants 100 percent cent on his money and who is willing to take the most astounding chances to get it."[6]

WHAT WE WANT AND WHAT WE SHOULD

We are not embarrassed to admit that we want our investments to support us during our years in retirement. Neither are we embarrassed to admit that we want our investments to support our children or favorite charities. But some of what we want from our investments is embarrassing, such as our wanting status. We might want to mention our investments in hedge funds, knowing that hedge funds signal high status because they are available only to the wealthy. But a loud expression of status, like a loud display of an oversized logo on a Gucci bag, can bring embarrassment rather than an acknowledgment of status.

"Wants" are also difficult to acknowledge because they often conflict with "shoulds." The voice of wants says, "I want this new red sports car," but the voice of shoulds says, "You should buy a used sedan and add the difference in price to your retirement account." Investment advice is full of shoulds: save more, spend less, diversify, buy-and-hold. Wants are visceral while shoulds are reasoned. Wants emphasize the expressive and emotional benefits of investments while shoulds emphasize the utilitarian ones. Wants often drive us into stupid investment choices, while shoulds drive us mostly into smart ones.

The visceral voice of wants is especially loud and the reasoned voice of shoulds is especially muted when our reasoning is weak and our minds are overloaded. The conflict between the visceral and the reasoned in on display in a choice between a chocolate cake we want and a fruit salad we should. In one experiment, people were brought to a room, one at a time. Some were asked to memorize a two-digit number, a task unlikely to overload their minds. Others were asked to memorize a seven-digit number, a task more likely to overload their minds. Next, each person was asked to go to another room. On their way, each could choose chocolate cake or fruit salad. People overloaded with memorizing the seven-digit number were more likely to listen to their visceral voice than to their reasoned one and choose the chocolate cake over the fruit salad.[7]

Dot-com stocks were the chocolate cakes of the Internet bubble of the late 1990s, raising their visceral voice. Some companies with fruit-salad-like names turned them into chocolate-cake-like names. Computer Literacy, Inc., was turned into FatBrain.com. Prices of newly named stocks zoomed as investors rushed to grab them as they would grab a slice of chocolate cake.[8]

Indulgence, impulsive spending, and lack of self-control are the norm, testifying to the tempting voice of wants and evident in the mountains of debt we accumulate. But we can go too far in restraining indulgence and tightening self-control. Spendthrifts would do better with a little less indulgence, but tightwads would do better with a little more. The reasoned voice encourages well-off tightwads to splurge on a great dinner at a fine restaurant. They can surely afford that dinner without hampering their retirement prospects. But the visceral voice dissuades tightwads from enjoying their meal, as their thoughts drift to the pain of the restaurant tab. Years later spendthrifts regret excessive indulgence and insufficient self-control, while tightwads regret insufficient indulgence and excessive self-control. One financial advisor told me of a tightwad client who lived in a dilapidated house and deprived his family of necessities only to leave them $3 million when he died.

HERDS AND BUBBLES

We are similar to one another in our wants, thoughts, cognitive errors, and emotions, but we are not identical. Some of us are more likely than others to be fooled by hindsight, some are more fearful, and some find special joy in trading. Our wants, thoughts, cognitive errors, and emotions affect our own behavior. But what is the sum of our behaviors?

The total number of shares of stocks changing hands as we trade is one sum of our behaviors. High returns on stocks we have chosen increase our confidence in our ability to pick winning stocks, so we trade more, overconfident in our ability to replace great winners with greater winners. A rising stock market multiplies the number of our winning stocks, and cognitive errors blind us to the distinction between winning stocks we can credit to our special stock-picking skills and those we must credit to the rising market. Conversely, a falling stock market saps our confidence in our ability to find winners. Moreover, anticipated regret deters us from selling stocks whose prices have declined. Indeed, more shares are traded after the market has risen and fewer are traded after the market has fallen.[9]

Sometimes our behaviors compound rather than merely sum. We read the same investment reports on the Internet and listen to the same investment news on television. We speak with one another and influence one another, moving as herds. Herds inflate bubbles, pumping stock prices far above their values, and herds deflate bubbles faster than they have inflated them. Managers of mutual funds influence one another, moving as herds into some stocks and out of others.[10] Investors who care about status inflate bubbles. Investors competing for status herd into similar investments, afraid that they would lose the status race if their investments trail those of the herd.[11] In the process, they pump the prices of the investments they herd into, inflating bubbles.

Sometimes our behaviors balance one another rather than compound or merely sum. Some investors shy away from risk, preferring safe bonds over risky stocks. Other investors seek risk, preferring risky stocks to safe bonds. The two balance each other, but the fact that stock returns over long periods exceeded bond returns indicates that the desire to avoid risk is greater than the desire to seek it. Similarly, some investors shun stocks of tobacco, alcohol, and gambling companies, branding them as "sin companies," while others are quite ready to buy such stocks if their returns are high. The fact that the returns of stocks of sin companies exceeded the returns of stocks of virtuous companies indicates that the choices of investors who shun stocks of sin companies exert power on stock prices, a power that is not fully balanced by the choices of investors who seek nothing but high returns.

In the following chapters we will reflect on what we really want from our investments as we reflect on our thoughts, emotions, wants, and behaviors.

We Want Profits Higher than Risks

In late 2008, Bernard Madoff confessed that his investment company was nothing but a Ponzi scheme, where longtime investors were paid from the money deposited by new investors. Madoff was sentenced to 150 years in prison, but his investors were calling on God to punish him some more. "May God spare you no mercy," cried Tom FitzMaurice, a sixty-three-year-old defrauded Madoff investor. "I am financially ruined and will worry every day how I will take care of my wife."[1] Madoff himself "was God," said Elie Wiesel, the Nobel Peace Prize winner. Wiesel's foundation lost more than $15 million in Madoff's fraud, and he and his wife lost their personal fortune.[2]

Madoff's investors were not unreasonable, surely not in their own eyes. The account statements mailed to George Rautenberg, one of Madoff's longtime investors, showed annual profits no higher than 14 percent.[3] "They weren't outrageous compared with what Harvard was telling you they were doing and what all those other smart guys were doing," said Rautenberg. "He wasn't winning big at all in the good years. He stayed fairly stable."

Madoff's reported returns might not qualify as outrageous, but "winning" and "stable" do not reasonably go together, surely not for individual investors such as Rautenberg. We can invest in stocks, reasonably expecting high returns with high risk, or we can invest in bonds, reasonably expecting low returns with low risk. But Rautenberg wanted investments with returns higher than their risks—attractive combinations we all want but cannot reasonably expect. Madoff's reported returns exceeded the returns of stocks in all but two of the seven years from 2001 through 2007,[4] they exceeded the returns of long-term bonds for all but one year,[5] and they exceeded the returns of short-term bonds each and every year.[6] Harvard

Endowment had higher returns than those reported by Madoff in five of the seven years, but it lost money in 2001 and 2002, two very bad stock market years, while Madoff reported gains.[7] Ponzi schemes like Madoff's are always fueled by the desire for investments with returns higher than their risks.

INDEX INVESTORS AND BEAT-THE-MARKET INVESTORS

The utilitarian benefits of investments center on high returns and low risk. Some investors are index investors, satisfied when they find investments with returns equal to their risks. Other investors are beat-the-market investors, searching for investments with returns higher than their risks. Beat-the-market investors among us do not expect something for nothing. They are willing to work hard to find investments with returns higher than their risks. They spend weekends analyzing financial statements of companies, distinguishing leading companies from laggards. They spend hours examining charts of the ups and downs of stock prices. They ask friends for names of winning money managers. They read financial magazines recommending mutual funds and watch television programs recommending stocks, bonds, gold, and oil. But cognitive errors and emotions mislead many beat-the-market investors into the belief that investments with returns higher than their risks are readily available when, in truth, they are not.

Think of stocks as ingredients of a stew, some with fat returns and some with lean. Now think of the stock market as a giant well-mixed vat of stew that contains all stocks. Some investors dip their ladles into the stew and fill them with fat and lean in proportions equal to the proportions in the market vat. These are index investors who buy index funds that contain all stocks. Index investors pay the expenses of their funds, but they can easily find index funds whose expenses are very low, equivalent to a few teaspoons of stew taken out of their ladles. Index investors tend to be buy-and-hold investors who trade only infrequently, as when they invest savings from their paychecks into index funds during their working years and withdraw them in retirement. While index investors are satisfied with returns equal to risks, beat-the-market investors search for returns higher than risks. Some beat-the-market investors choose handfuls of stocks and trade them frequently, hoping to fill their ladles with more fat returns than in the ladles of index investors. Others buy beat-the-market mutual funds, exchange traded funds, or hedge funds, hoping that their managers would find stocks with fat returns. But not all beat-the-market investors can be above average. The ladles of index investors are filled with average amounts of fat returns. If some beat-the-market investors fill their ladles with above-average fat returns, other beat-the-market investors are left with below-average fat returns in their ladles. Moreover, the expenses of beat-the-market investors are higher than those of index investors because beat-the-market investors pay higher costs of trading and the higher costs of beat-the-market managers. Beat-the-market costs are substantial. By one estimate, the annual cost of mutual funds is $100 billion. Hedge funds add $45 billion, and brokers add more billions.[8]

Yesterday's Pursuit of Profits Higher than Risks

Beat-the-market investors have always been searching for investments with returns higher than risks. The *World's Work*, a magazine published a century ago, warned investors away from the belief that they can easily find such investments. "Why should I invest money at $4\frac{1}{2}$ percent when I can get 6 percent with the same security?" asked a reader in 1911.[9] Because the six percent bond is likely to be riskier than the $4\frac{1}{2}$ percent bond, answered the *World's Work*.

A New York bonds broker wrote to the *World's Work* in 1910 to say that he was unable to sell the bonds of a city in upstate New York because bonds sold by Philadelphia brokers offered higher returns. The story was simple, wrote the *World's Work*. The New York broker was selling bonds on a rail line. The Philadelphia brokers, however, were selling bonds on an airline that was to connect New York and Philadelphia. The *World's Work* followed the bonds' story to its conclusion. Three years later, the bonds offered by the New York broker earned a profit, while the Philadelphia bonds were worthless. The Philadelphia property was sold at a bankruptcy sale for a price that left nothing for its bondholders.[10]

Stocks were less common in the portfolios of individual investors a century ago than in today's portfolios, and they were considered more risky than they are considered today. The *World's Work* did not seek to discourage investment in stocks whose returns equaled their risks but added that "it is unalterably opposed to the investment of savings by inexperienced people in new, untried, poorly-backed or wildly-financed enterprises."

Mining enterprises constituted a large proportion of poorly-backed and wildly-financed enterprises a century ago and the failure of one precipitated the Panic of 1907. The *World's Work* was beset by inquiries from investors asking for advice on mining stocks and its advice was unequivocal. "To one and all, the reply has been that the small investor should by no means purchase mining stocks. We shall make no exception to this statement. . . . The old adage that a Western mine is 'a hole in the ground with a liar at the top' holds good in a remarkably large proportion of cases. Emotion plays too large a part in the business of mining stocks. Enthusiasm, lust for gain, gullibility are the real bases of this trading. The sober common-sense of the intelligent business man has no part in such investment."[11] The *World's Work* punctuated its warning with a story about a man, the son of a country doctor, who reached adulthood and was about to go into business. His father took him into the little back office, swung open the door of the rusty old safe, and took out a thick bundle of stock certificates. "My son," he said, "you are going into business, and, I hope, will make some money. . . . When the time comes you will wish to buy some mining stock. Everyone does. When that time arrives come to see me. I will sell you some of mine. They are just as good, and will keep the money in the family.'"[12]

Today's Pursuits of Profits Higher than Risks

Lessons from a century ago need repeating because we fail to learn. Almost half a million Italian retirees bought Argentine bonds in the 1990s because they offered higher interest rates than Italian bonds. The word *default* became an Italian word in 2001 when Argentina defaulted on its bonds. In 2005 Nestor Kirchner, Argentina's president at the time, offered to pay bondholders less than a third of their investment. When Rodrigo de Rato of the International Monetary Fund called on Argentina to be respectful to bondholders, Kirchner mocked him, "It's pathetic to listen to them sometimes." "Enter now," said Kirchner to the bondholders, "or it will be your problem."[13] In 2010 Cristina Fernández de Kirchner, who succeeded her husband as Argentina's president, offered bondholders a deal no better than the one offered by her husband five years before. "At this point they could accept anything," said Lucio Golino, who works with a consumer protection group in Rome. "A lot of people are tired and have had enough." But Egidio Rolich, who bought Argentine bonds with the proceeds from the sale of an apartment and his wife's severance pay, was not ready to accept Argentina's offer. "Investors were shafted the first time with the default," he said, "the second time with the 2005 swap and this time is going to be the third."[14]

The desire for returns higher than risks also fuels the Nigerian 419 scams we know from e-mails of the kind I received from Mrs. Catharina Kitty Sies from the Netherlands, addressed to "Dearly beloved in Christ." Mrs. Sies was married to the late James Davis "of blessed memory" who worked with the South African Embassy before he died. While at the embassy, Mr. Davis deposited $25 million with a company in Europe. Now Mrs. Sies is ill with cancer and fibroid problems and her doctor told her that she has no more than three months to live. "Having known my condition," wrote Mrs. Sies, "I decided to donate this find to either a charity organization, devoted Christian individual, or God-fearing person who will utilize this money the way I am going to give instruction with all sincerity to fund churches, orphanages homes, widows and also propagating the word of God." Mrs. Sies promised to send me the $25 million "luggage" as soon as she receives my reply.

Nigerian 419 scams seem easy to detect yet prove irresistible to those looking for returns higher than risks. The United States Secret Service estimates that such scams cost Americans more than $100 million each year. Yet Americans are not alone as scam targets. Australians make good targets as well according to a report by the Australian Securities Investments Commission (ASIC). Australians are targeted, wrote ASIC, because their interest in investments is not matched by knowledge. Men are by far more gullible than women, accounting for more than nine out of ten scam victims.[15]

Banks sold $7 billion of reverse convertibles in 2008, promising returns higher than risks and collecting fees in the process. Reverse convertibles are bonds linked to stocks such as Apple and Johnson & Johnson. Investors were promised high interest rates during the life of the bonds in addition to their invested money when the bonds mature. Yet if the prices of the stocks to which the bonds are linked fall, investors get the stocks rather than their invested money. The high interest rates of reverse convertibles were enticing, but not all investors were aware of their risks. Lawrence Batlan, an 85-year-old retired radiologist, invested $400,000 in reverse convertibles linked to stocks such as Yahoo! and SanDisk. He lost $75,000 of it when stock prices declined. "I had no idea this could happen," said Dr. Batlan. "I have no desire to own Yahoo! stock or the others."[16]

The "accumulator" was also an investment that was too good to be true, but this one was offered mainly to investors in Hong Kong. Accumulators obliged investors to buy shares of a stock at a fixed price. Investors profited if the price of the shares increased but lost if the price decreased. Yet the profit potential of investors was limited by a condition mandating that they sell their shares back to the issuer if their price increases to a specified level. The year 2008 was bad for investors in accumulators as stock prices declined and investors nicknamed accumulators "I kill you later." The fundamental flaw . . . is something that I learned from my grandmother," said Kathryn Matthews, an investment professional. "You get nothing for free."[17]

The trading records of thousands of investors at an American broker reveal that the returns of the heaviest trading beat-the-market investors trailed those of index investors by more than seven percentage points each year on average, while the lightest trading investors trailed by only one-quarter of a percentage point.[18] The trading records of thousands of investors at a Swedish broker reveal that, on average, the losses of heavy traders amounted to almost 4 percent of their total financial wealth each year.[19]

Beat-the-market investors trail further behind index investors because they tend to buy high and sell low, reversing the investment maxim of buying low and selling high. Investors who switched stocks frequently in 19 major international stock markets trailed index investors by an average 1.5 percentage points each year.[20] Investors who switched mutual funds frequently trailed buy-and-hold mutual fund investors by less than one percentage point if they switched among mutual funds dedicated to stocks of large-value companies, but the lag increased to more than three percentage points if they switched among mutual funds dedicated to stocks of small-growth companies, and to an astonishing 13 percentage points if they switched among mutual funds dedicated to stocks of technology companies.[21] Switching-hedge-fund investors did no better than switching-mutual-fund investors. Hedge fund investors who switched among funds trailed those who bought and held hedge funds by approximately four percentage points each year. Those who switched among "star" funds with the highest returns trailed by approximately nine percentage points.[22]

BEAT-THE-MARKET INVESTORS EXPLAINED

Why don't beat-the-market investors abandon their game and join index investors? One part of the answer is easy. While average beat-the-market investors cannot beat the market, some beat-the-market investors are above average. Professional investors, such as mutual fund and hedge fund managers, regularly beat the market. Stocks bought by beat-the-market mutual fund managers had higher returns than stocks sold by them.[23] And hedge fund managers are famous for the billion-dollar paychecks they earn by beating the market. But investors in beat-the-market mutual funds trail investors in index funds because the costs of beat-the-market mutual funds detract from the returns passed on to investors more than managers add to them.[24] Hedge funds are riskier than investors believe and the returns they pass on to investors are lower than investors believe.[25] Tom Perkins, a wealthy venture capitalist, tells about Harry, one of his investors, who asked him how Perkins can live with the risk of his investments. "Well, Harry," laughed Perkins, "it's your money!"[26]

Military service is mandatory in Finland so that nearly every Finnish male of draft age undergoes extensive intelligence tests. Intelligence promotes investment success. Finns who score highly on intelligence at draft age are better at picking stocks in the following years than their less intelligent brethren.[27] Germans who score highly on cognitive skills resist cognitive errors better than their less intelligent brethren.[28] Highly intelligent investors might be able to beat the market, but their success is far from assured because intelligent investors are not always wise. Harvard staff members are intelligent and so are Harvard undergraduate students with SAT scores in the 99th percentile and Wharton MBA students with SAT scores at the 98th percentile.[29] Staff and students received information about past performance and fees of index funds that track the S&P 500 Index. But the information about the funds varied by the dates when the funds were established and the dates when the funds' prospectuses were published.

Wise investors faced with a choice among index funds following the S&P 500 Index choose the index fund with the lowest fees since these index funds are otherwise as identical as identical cereal boxes. But nine out of ten staff and college students chose index funds with higher fees and so did eight out of ten MBA students. Staff and students chased returns instead, choosing funds with the highest historical returns, apparently assuming that these offer returns higher than risks. Staff ranked fees as the fifth most important factor in their choice of funds, out of eleven factors, and students ranked it eighth. Staff chose funds whose annual fees exceeded the minimum fee by more than two percentage points on average, and students chose funds whose fees exceeded the minimum fee by more than one percentage point.

Insiders Deepen the Beat-the-Market Puzzle

Some investors have access to inside information, such as information about mergers being negotiated or disappointing earnings about to be revealed. Investors with inside information include corporate executives and investors with links to executives, including investment bankers and hedge fund managers. Members of Congress have inside information as well. Only one-third of American senators bought or sold stocks in any one year during the boom years of the 1990s but trading senators did very well. While corporate insiders beat the market by six percentage points each year on average, trading senators beat it by 12 percentage points. "I don't think you need much of an imagination to realize that they're in the know," said Alan Ziobrowski, one of the authors of the study.[30]

Insiders can beat the market without crossing the legal line, but sometimes they cross it. Some are comical in their incompetence. Bonnie Jean Hoxie, a Walt Disney administrative assistant, and Yonni Sebbag, her boyfriend, offered inside information about Disney's earnings in a letter to almost two dozen hedge funds. The letter said: "Hi, I have access to Disney (DIS) quarterly earnings report before its release on 5/03/10. I am willing to share this information for a fee that we can determine later. . . . My e-mail is XXX. I count on your discretion as you can count on mine." One of the hedge funds was not discrete, notifying the authorities. FBI agents pretended to be representatives of a hedge fund and paid Sebbag $15,000 for the information before arresting him and his confederate.

Still, most of those who cross the insider trading line are more competent than the Disney couple, even if not always lucky. Arthur Samberg, founder of hedge fund Pequot Capital Management, agreed to pay $28 million to settle allegations of insider trading. Samberg also closed his hedge fund and was barred from serving as an investment advisor. Samberg's insider trading started when he agreed to hire David Zilkha, a product manager at Microsoft, and asked him for inside information on the company's coming earnings report. Samberg wrote to Zilkha that while Pequot's analysts did a good job in covering high-tech stocks, "I'm not as impressed with our research on msft. do you have any current views that could be helpful? Might as well pick your brain before you go on the payroll!" Zilkha responded that "the worst is over for Microsoft," and Samberg bought call options on Microsoft and sold put options in the expectation that Microsoft's stock price would increase. Zilkha received a congratulatory e-mail from a managing director at Pequot when Microsoft's stock prices increased. The director wrote, "I am sitting here with 'the great one' aka art [Samberg]; who says we've made more money in msft in the last month than in the entire seven years before that!" Samberg himself wrote to Zilkha, "I shouldn't say this, but you have probably paid for yourself already!"[31]

The success of insiders in the beat-the-market game only deepens its puzzle. Insiders fill their stock market ladles with above-average proportions of fat returns, while index investors fill their ladles with average proportions of fat returns. This leaves below-average proportions of fat returns in the ladles of outsiders in the beat-the-market game, even if we set aside the cost of playing the game. So why don't outsiders quit the beat-the-market game? Perhaps they are as skilled as mutual fund managers, hedge fund managers, or investment bankers. Or perhaps they are as smart as the intelligent traders in Finland. Or perhaps they have specialized knowledge that provides a trading edge without crossing the line into inside information.

Medical scientists might well know the potential of drugs under development earlier and more precisely than other investors. Electrical engineers might well understand that the price of a stock is surging because the company introduced a new cell phone that is selling briskly now but will soon be surpassed by another phone from another company. But the knowledge of medical scientists, engineers, and other professionals does not give them much of an investment edge. A study of Finnish investors reveals that professionals concentrate their portfolios in the stocks of professionally close companies, as if they have special knowledge about these companies. But these stocks bring them losses more often than they bring gains.[32]

THE MARKET EFFICIENCY PUZZLE

The puzzle of the beat-the-market game is the market efficiency puzzle. There are two main definitions of efficient markets, one ambitious and the other modest. The ambitious definition is better called *rational markets*. Rational markets are markets where investments with returns higher than risks do not exist. More modest is the definition of "efficient markets" as *unbeatable markets*. Unbeatable markets are markets where investments with returns higher than risks exist, but most investors are unable find them.

Warren Buffett illustrated the distinction between rational markets and unbeatable markets and the confusion that arises when they are lumped together. Buffett was considering buying bonds of Citizens Insurance, established by the state of Florida to cover hurricane damage and backed by state taxes. Berkshire Hathaway, his company, received offers from three sellers of these bonds at three different prices, one at a price that would yield Berkshire Hathaway a 11.33 percent return, one at 9.87 percent and one at 6.0 percent. "It's the same bond, the same time, the same dealer. And a big issue," said Buffett. "This is not some little anomaly, as they like to say in academic circles every time they find something that disagrees with their [efficient market] theory."[33]

Buffett used the term "'efficient market'" where the term "'rational market'" would have been more precise. The story of the Citizens Insurance bonds is, as Buffett noted, an anomaly, contradicting the claim that the market for these bonds is rational. If investors in the 6.0 percent bond are receiving returns equal to risks then investors in the 9.87 percent and 11.33 percent bonds receive returns higher than risks. Yet Buffett cautioned investors not to jump too fast from evidence that markets are not rational to a conclusion that they are easily beatable. When asked for advice Buffett said: "Well, if they're not going to be an active [beat-the-market] investor—and very few should try that—then they should just stay with index funds. Any low-cost index fund. . . . They're not going to be able to pick the right price and the right time."

We know from Buffett's bond story and much other evidence that markets are not rational; investments with returns higher than risks do exist. Moreover, we know that markets are not unbeatable for insiders and skillful investors such as Buffett. But we should not jump from the conclusion that markets are beatable by some to the conclusion that they are beatable by all. Indeed, markets are beatable by some because they are not beatable by all. The extra returns of Buffett and his brethren over the returns of index fund investors come from diminished returns of beat-the-market investors who find themselves on the other side of the net from Buffett and his brethren. Markets are often irrational, even crazy, but crazy markets do not turn all investors into psychiatrists. Buffett followed his words with deeds. On January 1, 2008, Buffett placed roughly $320,000 on a bet that the S&P 500 Index would outperform a portfolio of hedge funds over the following ten-year period. On the other side is Protégé Partners, LLC, a hedge fund company, whose people placed an identical amount on a bet that the hedge funds they have chosen would beat the S&P 500 Index. All the money is now in a zero-coupon bond that would grow to $1 million by December 31, 2017, and go to charity, to Absolute Returns for Kids if Protégé wins, and to Girls Inc. if Buffett does.[34]

Protégé argued that "Funds of [hedge] funds with the ability to sort the wheat from the chaff will earn returns that amply compensate for the extra layer of fees their clients pay," and noted that Paulson & Co. hedge fund is among its investments. John Paulson made billions in profits by selling short investments linked to subprime mortgages. But Buffett said, "A lot of very smart people set out to do better than average in investment markets. Call them active [beat-the-market] investors. Their opposites, passive [index] investors, will by definition do about average." But investors in hedge funds are unlikely to overcome their costs. "Investors, on average and over time," concluded Buffett, "will do better with a low-cost index fund than with a group of fund of [hedge] funds."

Ben Stein, an author and investor, lamented the clobbering administered to many stocks in his portfolio.[35] "Unless you are a thorough genius like Warren E. Buffett," he concluded, "buying individual stocks is risky. . . . " Stein resolved to stick to index funds with one exception, the stock of

Berkshire Hathaway, Buffett's company. Buffett himself would likely have advised Stein to stick with index funds exclusively. Millions of investors, including Stein, admire Warren Buffett, as Stein does, but many try to beat the market by running in his footsteps rather than adopting his index-fund advice. Buffett's Berkshire Hathaway bought convertible bonds of Level 3 Communications, Inc., and their prices increased when other investors followed. But two months passed before investors learned that Buffett converted his bonds into stocks and sold them. Unscrupulous boiler-room brokers employ Buffett's name to lure investors into losses. John Clancy is one such broker and Robert Gaddis is one such investor. Gaddis was about to put the phone down when he heard Clancy's voice on a cold call, but changed his mind when he heard Buffett's name. Buffett, said Clancy, owns shares of UST Inc., the maker of smokeless tobacco products, and he is buying more. "We're looking for a major announcement literally any day," said Clancy. "Hold this stock through the announcement of Buffett's additional investments in UST. I think your percentage gain here looks to be staggering." Gaddis was persuaded to invest and, in time, lost almost all of his investment.[36]

Even Great Investors Stumble

Beating the Street and *One Up on Wall Street* were both written by Peter Lynch, who beat the market decisively as manager of Fidelity's Magellan mutual fund. His investors beat the market right along with him. Those who placed $1,000 in Magellan's shares on May 31, 1977, when Lynch took over as its manager, and held their shares until May 31, 1990, when Lynch stepped down, would have accumulated approximately $28,000. Investors who placed their $1,000 in the S&P 500 Index would have accumulated approximately $6,700.

Lynch worked hard to beat the market. He visited over 200 companies every year and added to his knowledge by observing what people bought in malls. Lynch was also smart about using this knowledge in the selection of stocks.[37] Walking in a shopping mall, Lynch reminisced about his winning stock picks: "Well . . . right over here we have a Kentucky Fried Chicken, the old colonel. . . . When I started at Fidelity, this was one of the single most exciting stocks. . . . It was more exciting than Microsoft. It was *it*. . . . And then, right next to it, we have one of my great companies of all time, Dunkin' Donuts. Amazing company. Made great coffee and they put it in a china cup. They didn't serve it in a crummy paper cup."

But even great investors stumble on occasion and not all investors coached by Lynch succeed at beating the market. Charles Glasgow, a sixty-six-year-old former college professor, idolized Lynch. When Glasgow heard that Lynch bought shares of SafeScript Pharmacies he jumped in, buying $498,000 worth of the stock and sharing his insights with relatives. "He is the most brilliant investor ever," said Glasgow, "I would not have touched this little company with a 10-foot pole except for his involvement." SafeScript's stock reached $5.66 a share on January 27, 2004, and a week later Eddie Minton, another SafeScript investor, got a panicky call from his wife Rosemary. "Did you see the price of SafeScript?" The $28,000 invested in SafeScript by Eddie Minton, his wife, and his mother had plunged some 60 percent.[38]

Lynch lost money on his SafeScript investment but he had an advantage over ordinary investors such as Glasgow and Minton. Lynch bought some of his shares directly from SafeScript at a discount, paying $1.25 per share while ordinary investors who bought SafeScript shares when information about Lynch's investment became public paid $1.75 or more. And along with his $1.25 shares, Lynch also received options to buy additional shares at $1.50 a share.

Trying to Win with War and Jet Stocks

Early in World War I, investors tried to beat the market with "war stocks," stock of companies that might profit from the war. The *World's Work* wrote about them in 1915: "When two busy Americans meet nowadays, after discussing the progress of the war and perhaps personalities, one is pretty sure to ask the other: 'What do you think of the market?' The question has reference, of course to the stock market—or more specifically to that part of the market in which the so-called "war stocks" are being bought and sold." The *World's Work* was astonished by the rush to war stocks. "The most striking fact about the war stocks is that the speculative increase in their value equals the sum of all the war orders that have been placed in this country. In other words, the public has already discounted not only all the profits in these orders but their gross value as well."[39]

The most recent war stocks are stocks of companies that might profit from the war in Afghanistan. One investor wrote on Morningstar's Web site: "With 30,000 more troops going to Afghanistan, they will obviously need more armor vehicles. Force Protection FRPT manufactured and sold 3,000 ambush-protected armor vehicles and during the past year had over $1B in revenue. . . . Does anyone have an opinion on this stock or a suggestion of some other company in the same industry?"[40]

Another investor responded, "What about Oshkosh Corp. (OSK)? He quoted Morningstar's assessment: "Despite a burdensome acquisition, we think specialty vehicle manufacturer Oshkosh has cemented itself as a leading supplier for the United States military by securing the government's mine-resistant, ambush-protected, all-terrain vehicle (M-ATV) and the Family of Medium Tactical Vehicles (FMTV) contracts."[41]

"Turn $10,000 into $50,000 in weeks!" screamed a flyer shoved into my mailbox. "The sky is the limit with this stock!" it continued, displaying a jet streaking upward and a man with arms up in the air in a victory salute. The small print said, in small part:

> "This informational mailer does not purport to provide an
> analysis of any company's financial position, operations or
> prospectus . . . Connect-a-Jet ("CAJT") . . . appears as paid
> advertising by Wynn Holdings, LLC (WHL). . . . WHL has
> received 10 million shares of CAJT stock that may be sold into
> the market at any time, without notice. . . ."

While most recipients of the flyer likely tossed it away, not all did. The number of CAJT shares traded jumped from zero on August 21, 2007, to more than 2.5 million on August 22, and to more than double that number on the day after that. The price of CAJT shares fluctuated between a low of $1 to a high of $2 on August 22, and ended the day at $1.25. By September 10, the price of share increased by 138 percent, but by September 2, it declined by almost half. By June 9, 2008 the price was at 3 cents. I could not find the stock when I checked most recently in 2010.

The flyer disclosed all facts and violated no law. The flyer even provided the addresses of the regulatory agencies. Anyone reading the small print was put on notice that the people of WHL, the advertiser, and perhaps the people of CAJT as well, are likely to be the ones selling the shares to readers of the flyer who were enticed to buy. It is easy to see how the people of WHL and CAJT would gain by turning readers into buyers. But why would readers choose to be turned into buyers?

Why do so many investors with average intelligence and no special information play the beat-the-market game? Why do we ignore Buffett's advice to stick with index funds? One part of the answer is in cognitive errors and emotions that mislead us. In the next chapter I begin with cognitive errors.

CHAPTER 2

We Have Thoughts, Some Erroneous

A couple in a TV commercial is rushing into their car.
"I have something to tell you," they say in unison.
"You go first," he says.
"No, you go first."
"I'm not ready to get married . . . "
"OK," she says after a pause, sad and resigned.
"So what's your news," he asks
"I won the lottery," she says, flashing her winning lottery ticket.

Cut to the man at a pool hall with friends holding bottles of beer.

"63 million dollars," says the man, still incredulous.
"Think about it this way, man," says his friend, "After taxes it's only like 28 to 30 million dollars."
"Yeah," says the man, brightening up a bit.
"Life is better told over a great tasting [beer]," says the announcer.

This is a beer commercial, extolling friendship lubricated by beer, but it's also a lesson about framing. The man frames his misfortune as a $63 million loss, while his friend places it into an after-tax frame, diminishing the loss and its pain. Framing is everywhere in investments. We can frame a 10 percent return on a stock as a 10 percent gain, or we can frame it as a 20 percent loss relative to our neighbor's 30 percent return. We can frame selling our house for $600,000 as a gain, knowing we paid $400,000 for it a decade ago, or we can frame it as a loss relative to the $800,000 offer we turned down a year ago.

17

FRAMING ERRORS

Some frames are quick and intuitive, but frames that come to mind quickly and intuitively are not always correct. The $63 million before-tax frame comes to mind quickly and intuitively, but the $28 to $30 million after-tax frame is correct. The beat-the-market frame that comes to mind quickly and intuitively is that of tennis played against a practice wall, but the correct frame is tennis played against a possibly better player. Incorrect framing of the beat-the-market game is one cognitive error that fools us into believing that beating the market is easy.

It is natural for us to adopt the frame of the beat-the-market game as tennis played against a practice wall because that frame is generally correct in our daily work. We gain competence at our work as surgeons, lawyers, or teachers by study and practice, as we gain competence playing tennis against a practice wall. At first we fail to hit the ball with our racket, so the ball falls to the floor rather than flies to the wall. Then we hit the ball too high or too low and fail to position ourselves right to hit it back when it bounces. In time, with practice, we get it right, hitting most balls as they bounce from the wall.

We cannot be competent surgeons with little knowledge of the human body, we cannot be competent lawyers with little knowledge of the law, and we cannot be competent teachers with little knowledge of the subject matter we teach. Yet we can be competent investors with virtually no knowledge of the companies whose stocks we buy. S&P 500 Index mutual funds contain 500 stocks, and more comprehensive index funds contain thousands of stocks. Rare are the index fund investors who can name more than a few dozen of these stocks. Rarer still are index fund investors who know something about these companies beyond their names. Surgeons, lawyers, and teachers with no knowledge of their fields cannot hope to earn average incomes. Yet investors with no knowledge of stocks earn average returns by nothing more than investing in index funds.

Divergence of stock prices from their values is a prerequisite for beating the market. All we need to do now is sell stocks whose prices exceed their values and buy stocks whose prices fall short of their values. Most investors believe that stock prices often diverge from stock values. Moreover, investors name their own studies of the companies as the most important reason to buy or sell stocks.[1] These beliefs make it natural for investors to jump to the conclusion that they can beat the market by study and practice just as surgeons learn to perform competent surgeries. But the conclusion of such investors is wrong because they fail to grasp the difference between surgery and investing. The human body does not change as surgeons become more competent. The human body does not compete against surgeons. In that, the human body is like a practice wall. But investors always meet competing investors on the other side of the net. Investors who frame the beat-the-market game as a game of tennis against a practice wall lose when insiders and skilled professionals shoot fast and surprising balls from their side of the net.

Successful entrepreneurs, unlike most investors, are keenly aware that they are playing tennis against fellow entrepreneurs rather than against a practice wall, so they choose to compete in tennis courts where they have advantages that serve as the equivalent of outsize tennis rackets. These advantages might be patented chemical technologies or established relations with buyers of chemicals. But these entrepreneurs have no advantage in the court of the beat-the-market game. Successful entrepreneurs in the chemicals business often fail when they expand into the restaurant business because the advantages that helped them win in the chemicals game do them little good against better players in the restaurant game. Entrepreneurs in the chemicals business commit a similar framing error when they conclude that they can easily win the beat-the-market game when they are blind to the fact that their skills at the chemicals game give them no advantage in the beat-the-market game.

A stock market expert might opine on a television program that a particular stock is worth $40, and therefore a bargain at $35. But, even if the expert is right, the posted $35 sale price might turn to $40 as throngs of viewers rush into the stock exchange. Even worse, the prices of stocks of companies featured on television programs often spike as investors rush in, only to fall later, turning buyers into losers. CNBC interviews of chief executive officers of companies were generally followed by increases in the prices of their stocks on the day of the interview. But over the next few days the prices of these stocks usually proceeded to decline by more than they have increased on the interview day.[2] Similarly, stock-touting spam e-mails bring gains to spammers but losses to the investors they attract. The volume of trading goes up significantly when spammers tout stocks. But investors who buy stocks when they are most heavily touted and sell them two days after touting ends lose more than 5 percent on average. Trading costs only compound losses.[3]

Some traders hope to be as clever as spammers by jumping into the spammers' side of the tennis court. One wrote in the Wired.com blog:

> If the spam e-mails are truly causing the penny stock to rise a few cents, then it actually would be wise to buy the stock as the e-mail suggests. You could sell the next day and have a tidy profit. :)

But another trader lamented on spamstocktracker.com the losses he had incurred when seduced by spam e-mail:

> I received the 'tip' . . . that FPPL (First Petroleum and Pipeline) was about to go 'big time.' So I looked at the stock on my Ameritrade Web site, saw that it was indeed on the upswing, and bought 2000 shares at a total cost of 510.00 (not a HUGE investment . . . but hey, 500 skins can buy some cool stuff . . . mountain bike, stereo, etc.). Well today that stock is worth about 12 bucks . . . a net change of –97%.
>
> I'm pissed at myself, mostly . . . but more ticked off at the company itself and the email promoters, whoever they are/were. I'm holding the stock now, because it would be foolish to sell it for 12 dollars, in the hope that I might get at least a few bucks back on it.

Investment tips and touts enticing us into the beat-the-market game have always been with us. A 1931 advertisement by Investors Research Bureau bragged about an 88 percent profit in three weeks on Chrysler's stock.[4] Then it offered an even better stock. "It is a stock in which you might, in the months ahead, double your money and then double it again. It is the stock that we have chosen as a premier money-maker of 1931. Send for a free analysis of this issue—without obligation, of course." Recommendations for market-beating investments abound today in magazines, television, and the Internet. The cover of a recent Special Investor's issue of a magazine displayed a handsome couple on a yacht, gazing at an island in the distance. "Retire Rich," it says, and promises to name "50 Great Stocks and Funds."[5] Investors fail to frame the beat-the-market game as a game of tennis against opponents on the other side of the net even when they are alerted to that frame. Joseph Goodman touted "stocks with possibilities" in 1939 in his *Forbes* magazine column.[6] Goodman provided fair warning that he was placing players with bigger rackets on the other side of the beat-the-market net. Indeed, he was offering to sell these bigger rackets to interested readers. He wrote: "Advance release by airmail, or a telegraphic summary of this regular article, will be sent to interested readers on the day of its writing. Rates on request." Readers of the magazine who failed to receive Goodman's recommendations by airmail and failed to frame the beat-the-market game correctly as tennis against opponents on the other side of the net, likely lost when they followed Goodman's recommendations when they were published in the magazine.

More recently, Goldman Sachs alerted its clients to the true frame of the beat-the-market game, echoing Joseph Goodman's warning in *Forbes* decades earlier. Goldman Sachs wrote:

> Dear client . . .
> We may trade, and may have existing positions, based on Trading Ideas before we have discussed those Trading Ideas with you.
> We may continue to act on Trading Ideas, and may trade out of any position, based on Trading Ideas, at any time after we have discussed them with you. We will also discuss Trading Ideas with other clients, both before and after we have discussed them with you . . .
> Kind Regards . . .[7]

It is not difficult to overcome the framing error. All we need to do is install an app in our minds as we install apps on our iPhones. When we are ready to trade it would pipe in, asking, "Who is the idiot on the other side of the trade? Have you considered the likelihood that the idiot is you?"

REPRESENTATIVENESS ERRORS

The "law of large numbers" is an important law of science. It teaches us, for instance, that that the percentage of heads in a sequence of coin tosses is likely to be closer to 50 percent when we toss a coin a large number of times, say 600, than when we toss it a small number of times, say six. Rational investors know the law of large numbers, even if they have never attended a statistics course. But we, normal investors, use intuition in place of formal statistics. We believe that a random sequence, such as a coin toss, will generate close to 50 percent heads not only when we toss the coin a large number of times but also when we toss it a small number of times. We know this belief as the "belief in the law of small numbers," a tongue-in-cheek play of the robust law of large numbers.[8]

One manifestation of belief in the law of small numbers is that five good years of returns out of six are interpreted as a representation of the skill of a mutual fund manager rather than as a representation of luck. So we are forever chasing hot funds and sage gurus in our quest to beat the market, never pausing to ask whether the size of the sample is indeed large enough to warrant the guru designation. Mutual fund managers often argue that the standards set by statisticians for distinguishing skill from luck are un-fair. "How can I convince you that my investment results are due to skill, not luck," ask fund managers, "if it takes fifty years of performance to do so?" Fund managers often also object to studies that judge them as a group. As one asked me: "Is it fair to judge me not only by my own performance but also by performance of other fund managers?"

Fund managers, like the rest of us, do not hesitate to say "no, thank you," and put down the telephone when a solicitor calls. We do not feel obliged to listen to an entire sales pitch. As we make our decision to listen or quit, we properly take into account two pieces of information. First is "similarity" or "representativeness" information—how similar is the particular solicitor on the telephone right now to solicitors who were worth listening to. Second is "base rate" information—the proportion of the many telephone solicitors who have interrupted our dinners yet were worth listening to. We put down the telephone because base-rate information tells us that most sales pitches are not worth listening to, even though the voice of this particular solicitor is attractive. The same rule is properly applied to managers of beat-the-market funds. If we make a mistake, it is in giving too much consideration to the performance of particular beat-the-market funds and too little consideration to the average performance of all such funds relative to index funds.

Judging a fund in isolation from the overall group of mutual funds, we might be tempted to conclude that fund managers who beat their index fund benchmarks six years in a row provide clear evidence of skill. After all, the chance of getting six heads in six tosses of a coin is only one in sixty-four. But once we note that this fund manager is one among thousands of fund managers we understand that it is highly likely that there would be lucky coin tossers who get six heads in a row and lucky fund managers who beat index fund benchmarks six times in a row.

We can see the tendency to focus on similarity information and neglect base-rate information in the story of David Pearl, a mutual fund manager and winner during one year.[9] Pearl prefers stocks that are followed by few analysts. "When there's less research, I get to know the companies personally," he said. "That's the way you make money—finding good stocks that few companies know about." Pearl's performance that year was phenomenal, and his strategy makes sense. Does Pearl have characteristics that make him similar to the stereotype of a future winner? Surely, and we should properly consider similarity information. But should we consider as base rate information that, on average, beat-the-market funds, such as Pearl's index funds; lag index funds; and that past performance bears little or no relation to future performance? We should, but we usually don't.[10]

Promoters of investments often employ our tendency to focus on similarity to fool us. They draw us into losing investments by making us think that we are similar famous investors, such as Donald Trump. "What would Donald Trump do?" asked *Biotech Fortunes,* a brochure I received several years ago. Jack Burney, its editor, promoted Zynex Medical Holdings, Inc. (ZYNX). Burney discovered Zynex when he saw an article saying that stroke victims could benefit from Zynex's NeuroMove, a small device for at-home use. "I recognize a winner when I see one!" wrote Burney. . . . This business model could literally generate hundreds of millions of dollars for ZYNX and its shareholders!" The stock should go $2.65 to $60. "So, what would Donald Trump do?" asked Burney. "Would he invest in a stock like ZYNX? Naturally, I don't know what he would do. I can only make educated guesses. . . . Donald Trump wants you to THINK BIG. . . . Trump also recommends you should keep critics in perspective! . . .

Finally, Trump suggests that you should always maintain your momentum." It turned out that thinking small and listening to critics would have been wiser. A lawsuit against Zynex and its executives was filed after its stock price dropped to zero.

Finding Patterns

Our ability to find real patterns is a mark of our intelligence, but our intelligence often backfires, as when we identify illusory patterns as real. Imagine that we are facing machines with two levers marked S and B. The machines dispense nothing if we pull the wrong lever but they dispense $10 if we pull the right one. We'll get to pull levers many times. A pattern is programmed into the machine, but we don't know what it is. Perhaps it is a pattern in which the machines dispense $10 every time we pull the S lever and nothing when we pull the B one. Or perhaps it is a pattern in which the machines dispense $10 every second pull, regardless of the lever we pull. How would we go about our task if we want to get the most money out of the machines?

We look for patterns by trial and error. We pull the S lever and see if $10 is dispensed. Next we pull the B lever, or perhaps we pull the S lever again, until we find the pattern that will dispense the most money. It turns out that the pattern programmed into the machines is one where S is the generous lever and B is the stingy one. Both lever S and B dispense $10 randomly, but lever S dispenses $10 in four out of five pulls on average while lever B dispenses it on average in only one of five pulls. The winning strategy is to pull the S lever every time because this strategy is likely to dispense the most money. Pigeons rewarded by food find the winning strategy after a few trials and stick to it. But humans rarely stick to that strategy.[11] Instead, we continue to try many strategies, switching between S and B until the game ends.

Now think of S as stocks and B as bonds. Stocks are the generous lever and bonds are the stingy one. Pulling the S lever every time is not sure to yield the most money, but it is likely to yield the most money. Similarly, stocks are not sure to yield higher returns than bonds even during periods extending into many decades, but stocks are likely to yield higher returns than bonds during long horizons. Smart investors with longtime horizons who want to maximize returns without regard to risk invest only in stocks, the equivalent to pulling the S lever every time. Smart investors who want to maximize returns but are also concerned about risk invest in both stocks and bonds in proportions corresponding to their desire for returns and aversion to risk. But we, normal investors, are often stupid. We regularly try to time the market, jumping from stocks to bonds and back again, accumulating less money on average than investors who buy and hold portfolios that combine stocks and bonds.

The world of investments is unnerving because it includes patterns, even if weak, which enable some investors to beat the market. And the promise of patterns sustains the hope of other investors.

Tactical asset allocation is one form of market timing, where investors find patterns in investment returns and switch between stocks, bonds, and other investments to profit from these patterns. Tactical asset allocators employ statistical tools and computer power in their search for patterns, and sometimes they succeed. In the late 1980s and early 1990s I worked with a group of investment professionals engaged in tactical asset allocation. We switched away from stocks before the crash of 1987, even if a bit too early, and clients were delighted when they were spared the crash. But we stayed away from stocks for a period after the crash, as stocks recovered, and clients were angry.

Successful market timing is difficult even in the hands of investment professionals who search for patterns systematically and rely on knowledge of finance, economics, and statistics. Wall Street strategists make recommendations to increase the allocation to stocks in portfolios or decrease them based on their beliefs that stocks would do well or poorly in the near future. But their recommendations mislead investors more often than they lead them right. Stock returns tend to be relatively low following recommendations to increase the allocation to stocks in portfolios, and they tend to be relatively high following recommendations to decrease their allocation.[12]

While successful market timing is difficult in the hands of investment professionals, it is virtually impossible in the hands of ordinary investors who rely on their intuition to uncover patterns. Such investors are forever trying to find winning patterns as they jump into stocks and out again, finding losing patterns instead. Gallup surveys and surveys of the American

Association of Individual Investors reveal that individual investors predict high future stock returns following months of high past stock returns. But more often than not, predictions of high future returns are followed by low actual returns.[13]

Encounters with puzzles bolster our desire to solve them and sharpen our ability to find patterns in data, whether true or illusory. In one experiment, some students read Kafka's *A Country Doctor,* a bizarre, surreal story that seems designed to disorient its readers. Other students read a conventional story. Subsequently, all students were asked to find patterns in strings of letters. Students who read the Kafka story found more patterns, both true and illusory, than students who read the conventional story.[14]

The search for patterns is exemplified in *The Bible Code,* originally published in 1997 by mathematician Michael Drosnin. Drosnin found many patterns in the letters of the Bible when arranged horizontally or vertically.[15] The words "economic collapse" and "depression" appear together in the Bible with the word "stocks" and the year 1929.[16] It turns out that *The Bible Code* is better at prophesying the past than the future. The book prophesied the stock market crash of 1929 but said nothing about the stock market bubble that was inflating in 1997, as the book was published, or its subsequent deflation.

The Bible Code predicated that Yitzhak Rabin, Israel's prime minister, would be assassinated. Rabin was indeed assassinated in 1996, before the publication of *The Bible Code,* proving yet again that the book is good at prophesying the past. Other mathematicians urged caution, noting that patterns are easy to find even when they are illusory. "When my critics find a message about the assassination of a prime minister encrypted in *Moby Dick,* I'll believe them," said Drosnin."[17] Brendan McKay, a mathematician, promptly identified a slew of assassinations encoded in *Moby Dick,* including those of Rabin, Kennedy, Martin Luther King, Jr., Trotsky, and even Drosnin himself.[18, 19]

Technical analysis of stocks and other investments involves a search for patterns in past prices that predict future prices. One such pattern is a "channel," where the price of a stock fluctuates up and down between a low price and a high price. The Web site of ChannelingStocks.com offers its subscribers stocks that trade within channels.[20] Increases in the prices of such stocks are likely to be followed by decreases, as prices encounter "resistance" at the top of the channel. Decreases in prices are likely to be followed by increases, as prices find "support" at the bottom of the channel. We know that many investors rely on price channels in their trading decisions, especially on the channel where the bottom is the lowest price during the preceding 52 weeks and the top is the highest price during that period. When investors are asked what a stock price close to its 52-week high indicates, most say that it is overvalued, likely to decline. And when they are asked what a price close to its 52-week low indicates, most say that it is undervalued, likely to increase.[21] The number of shares traded is especially high when stock prices breach their highest levels during the preceding 52 weeks or when they breach their lowest levels.[22] Moreover, reliance on price channels affects stock returns.

Consider news disclosed after the stock market closed for the day that an oil company just discovered a giant oil field. The discovery adds 20 percent to the value of the stock of the company and so we would expect its stock price to jump by 20 percent as the stock exchange opens the following day. Now imagine that the price of the stock is already at the top of its 52-week channel. As the price of the stock begins to ascend toward its extra 20 percent, it breaches the top of the channel. Investors who trade by the rules of channels sell the stock, delaying its ascent. In the end, a 20 percent ascent, which should have been completed within minutes after the stock market opens, is spread out over many weeks.[23]

The search for patterns in stock prices goes beyond price channels. Indeed, it goes beyond our planet.[24] Jeanne Long offered investors tools for predicting the future prices of stocks and commodities by studying the motion of the sun and planets in our solar system. These Astro-Tools have been automated in *Galactic Trader,* described as the first Real Time Planetary software.[25] Armed with *A Trader's Astrological Almanac,* investors can tune into the natural cycles of planets and prices.[26] A straightforward conjunction of Mercury and the sun is suitable for soybeans. Crude oil follows the relationship between the sun and Pluto. The chart for silver prices is paired with Venus and Jupiter. The British pound and the Dow Jones Industrial Average are amenable to the more intricate movements of Saturn.[27]

We know that some couples consult astrological charts when planning to have children. According to Vietnamese astrology, dates of birth determine success, luck, character, and good matches between people. More children are born in auspicious years than in other years. Moreover, children born in auspicious years enjoy better health and education, indicating that they are more likely to have been planned by their parents, enjoying better financial, psychological, and emotional support.[28]

We also know that some investors consult astrological charts in their investment decisions. Robert Citron, the Orange County, California, treasurer, used them while managing the county's money. "They were very accurate," he said.[29] Reliance on astrological charts and other dubious market-beating methods brought substantial losses to Orange County and earned Citron a one-year work-release jail sentence. The attraction of astrological charts seems to increase in times of market maelstrom, such as the 2008 financial and market crisis, when all other charts fail to point toward a safe direction. An e-mail from a Wall Street trader in late October 2008 said, "I got this from the most bearish man in Western civilization. It's legit. Panic lows occurred on day 27/28 of the 7th lunar cycle, which are this Sunday and Monday. The panics of 1857/1907/1929/1997 all marked their lows on these days in October!"[30]

Eclipses are perceived as bad omens by some in both Asian and Western societies, and these superstitions affect stock prices. Eclipses are associated with declines in stock prices and diminished trading as superstitious investors refrain from buying stocks. Declines in stock prices are especially pronounced when eclipses draw wide media coverage and public attention. But stock prices bounce back when eclipses end.[31]

Sometimes the search for patterns pays off, encouraging believers to keep the faith. The search for patterns paid off for a lottery winner. His favorite pattern consisted of the numbers on the uniforms of favorite sports heroes. "This is how our winner of $10.7 million did it," said a lottery advertisement.[32] The search paid off for Linda Welburn, a winner at a 25-cent Wheel of Fortune slot machine. Welburn was playing the middle machine in a bank of three when a woman on her left who was getting nothing but lemons abandoned it. Welburn noticed this pattern and took over the abandoned machine. The resulting $943,568 jackpot will help buy a house for her mother and put her son through college. The search for patterns also brought profits to Chris G. of Burlington, North Carolina, a satisfied customer of ChannelingStocks.com who wrote: "Your weekly stock ideas are excellent and your suggested support and resistance levels are accurate. . . . Also, many of the past weeks' stocks continue to channel and remain stocks to watch for future entries long and short . . . great job and thanks. . . . "

AVAILABILITY ERRORS

Availability errors compound representativeness errors, misleading us further into the belief that beating the market is easy. Casinos exploit availability errors. Slot machines are quiet when players lose, but they jingle cascading coins when players win. We exaggerate the likelihood of winning because the loud voice of winning is available to our minds more readily than the quiet voice of losing. Casinos magnify the effects of availability errors by clever programming of slot machines to pay lots of small winnings. This makes winnings available to our minds, leading us to exaggerate the odds of winning. "You want to give the newbie lots of positive reinforcement—to keep 'em playing," said Anthony Baerlocher, a programmer of slot machines. Other slot machines are programmed to generate high proportions of near misses. "You can see it on their faces every time," said Baerlocher, "They feel they have come *soooo* close. They're ready to try it again, because next time they're going to get it."[33] Scans of the brains of gamblers who experience near-misses show activation of a reward-related brain circuitry, suggesting that near-misses increase the transmission of dopamine. This makes gambling addiction similar to drug addiction.[34]

Promoters of trading software, like promoters of casinos, employ availability errors to persuade traders that beating the market is easy. The announcer in an eSignal commercial says: "It's no secret, successful traders have discovered the many benefits of eSignal's data and software." The first customer says: "I made $22,000 in a five-day period. . . . " The second says: "Well, my first seven trades were all winners with net returns in excess of 250 percent." Find out what eSignal can do for you, concludes the announcer. "Call for your risk-free 30-day trial and free software training CD. . . . " It might be that all eSignal traders are winners, like the two traders in the commercial. But it is more likely that many of eSignal traders are losers, but eSignal chose to make only winners available to our minds, enticing us to believe that the odds of winning are higher than they truly are.

Mutual fund companies employ availability errors to persuade us to buy their funds. Morningstar, a company that rates mutual funds, assigns to each fund a number of stars that indicate its relative performance, one star for the bottom group, three stars for the average group, and five stars for the top group. Have you ever seen an advertisement for a fund with one or two stars? But we've all seen advertisements for four- and five-star funds. Availability errors lead us to judge the likelihood of finding winning funds by the proportion of four- and five-star funds available to our minds.

An advertisement by the Strong group of mutual funds in mid-2000 extolled the performance of two growth and income funds, the Strong Blue Chip 100 Fund and the Strong Growth and Income Fund. The first earned a 37 percent return for the year ending on March 31, 2000, while the second earned almost 34 percent. Looking at Strong's Web site, I found that the two growth-and-income funds promoted by Strong were the ones with the highest returns among the nine growth-and-income funds listed on the site. In late 2002, when the stock market was near its low, Strong advertised the U.S. Government Securities Fund with close to a 10 percent return for the year ending the September 2002 and noted that the fund has five stars, "Morningstar's highest rating." Again, this advertised fund was the winning fund among the eight funds in its category. Subsequently, in October 2003, after the stock market recovered somewhat, Strong advertised its Large Company Growth Fund. "Thinking about the stock market? Chose a fund that's number 1." The fund was number 1 of the period ending September 2003, but it was no longer number 1 in October 2003 when the advertisement appeared.

Availability errors induce mutual fund managers to play the equivalent of a tennis tournament where only the top-ranked players appear on the list, making them available to our minds. Middle-ranked mutual funds are like middle-ranked tennis players and bottom-ranked mutual funds are like bottom-ranked tennis players: they get no notice. Imagine you have been playing in a tennis tournament, and now, midway through the tournament, you are in the middle of the pack. You have played conservatively until now and you are likely to end up without a prize if you continue to play that way. Doesn't it make sense to take some risks and adopt some aggressive moves? After all, what is there for you to lose? If the moves don't work, you'll end up at the bottom, as prizeless as the players in the middle. But if the moves work, you might win a major prize as one of the top players. Tennis players who lag behind take risks in their quest for prizes, and so do fund managers. Fund managers, who find themselves in the middle of the pack by mid-year, gamble by increasing the risk of their funds in the second half of the year.[35] If the gamble works, they are rewarded by bonuses and investors' money flowing into their funds. If the gamble does not work, their funds trail the average fund by an even greater amount than they would have trailed without the added risk. This gamble is evidently worthwhile in the eyes of fund managers. But what about the investors, asks the naïve observer; aren't they better off when their fund is in the middle of the pack than at the bottom? Aren't investors the losers in the gamble? Well, the gamble works for fund managers, the gamble works for fund companies, and, as the saying goes, two out of three ain't bad.

CONFIRMATION ERRORS

Confirmation errors contribute their share to the perception that winning the beat-the-market game is easy. We commit the confirmation error when we look for evidence that confirms our intuition, beliefs, claims, and hypotheses, but overlook evidence that disconfirms them. We hear the confirmation error in the voices of money managers who crow victory when they beat the market during a quarter while they dismiss their lagging performance over longer periods as aberrations. "You are comparing me to the wrong benchmark," they say. "Judge me over a full business cycle," they say. "I'm right and the market is wrong," they say. They'll accept anything but evidence disconfirming their cherished belief that they can beat the market. The remedy for confirmation errors is a structure that forces us to consider all the evidence, confirming and disconfirming alike, and guides us to tests that tell us whether our intuition, beliefs, claims, or hypotheses are confirmed by the evidence or disconfirmed by it.

One manifestation of confirmation errors is the tendency to trim disconfirming evidence from stories, as if it is no more than unappetizing fat trimmed off delicious steaks. The fact that a forecast of an imminent stock market crash was made years before its coming is unappetizing, so we tend to trim it off our stock market stories. And so it is with earthquake stories.

Geologists have been trying to forecast earthquakes for almost as long as investors have been trying to forecast the stock market. An earthquake killed more than 300 people in L'Aquila, Italy, on April 6, 2009, as houses collapsed on people as they slept. Wouldn't it be good if they have had a forecast of the coming earthquake? Well, Giampaolo Giuliani, an Italian laboratory technician, predicted a major earthquake on Italian television a month before it struck, relying on increased emissions of radon from the ground. But Guiliani's prediction brought him rebuke, not gratitude. Italy's Civil Protection Agency accused him of inciting panic.

Guiliani's L' Aquila story has been presented as one of many illustrations of the stupidity of public officials, but the story is likely an illustration of the ubiquity of confirmation errors bedeviling earthquake forecasters, stock market forecasters, and the rest of us. It turns out that Giuliani predicted that the quake would shake the ground a week earlier that it actually did, and that it would shake it in a town 30 miles away. Evacuating the wrong town at the wrong time would have saved no one. More important, there is as much evidence disconfirming the claim that radon levels forecast earthquakes as evidence confirming it. While radon levels were high in Kobe, Japan, before its 1995 earthquake, radon levels decreased in California in 1979, before three earthquakes hit.[36]

We see the power of the confirmation error in end-of-the-world forecasts that keep their hold on people's thinking during millennia despite mountains of disconfirming evidence and zero confirming evidence. Greatdreams.com tells us that "The Mayan calendar comes to an end on Sunday, December 23, 2012." It prophesies that "[o]nly a few people will survive the catastrophe that ensues." The year 2012 will likely come and go without an end-of-the-world catastrophe, but disconfirming evidence is not likely to sway believers. Instead, an error would be found in the calendar and a new end-of-the-world date would be set.

Investors who believe that they can pick winning stocks are regularly oblivious to their losing record, recording wins as evidence confirming their stock-picking skills but neglecting to record losses as disconfirming evidence. As physicist Robert Park said about the belief that high-voltage lines cause cancer despite strong evidence to the contrary, "It's often not deliberate fraud. People are awfully good at fooling themselves. They're so sure they know the answer that they don't want to confuse people with ugly-looking data."[37] I've recently encountered an investor who went a bit further. He realized gains on his stocks but never realized losses. He considered realized gain as confirming evidence of his stock-picking ability and never had to confront losses since, by his accounting, unrealized losses are no losses at all.

HINDSIGHT ERRORS

Hindsight errors persuade us further that winning the beat-the-market game is easy. "Don't gamble," said Will Rogers, "take all your savings and buy some good stock and hold it till it goes up, then sell it. If it don't go up, don't buy it."[38] Hindsight error is the belief that whatever happened was bound to happen, as if uncertainty and chance were banished from the world. So, if an introverted man marries a shy woman, it must be because, as we have known all along, "birds of a feather flock together" and if he marries an outgoing woman, it must be because, as we have known all along, "opposites attract." Similarly, if stock prices decline after a prolonged rise, it must be, as we have known all along, that "trees don't grow to the sky" and if stock prices continue to rise, it must be, as we have equally known all along, that "the trend is your friend." Hindsight errors are a serious problem for all historians, including stock market historians. Once an event is part of history, there is a tendency to see the sequence that led to it as inevitable. In hindsight, poor choices with happy endings are described as brilliant choices, and unhappy endings of well-considered choices are attributed to horrendous choices.

A physician came to ask for my advice in December 1994. He had worked hard and saved his money for many years and now, in his late forties, he could no longer continue at such a fast pace. All of his savings, $1.5 million, were in Treasury bills, and he was considering shifting some to stocks. But he was apprehensive. "The stock market is so high," he said. "It's bound to crash."

I told the physician that I had not the slightest idea where the stock market was going over the next three, five, or even ten years. But I rely on good evidence when I say that stocks are likely to do better than Treasury bills over many decades. And a man in his late forties still has many decades in front of him. I was feeling very smart in 1995 and kept feeling so through 1999, as if I could have seen with perfect foresight in December 1994 that the fabulous exuberance of the market was about to be born. But I kept reminding myself that I, like you and the rest of us, am subject to hindsight error.

Warren Buffett understands well the distinction between hindsight and foresight and the temptation of hindsight. Roger Lowenstein mentioned in his biography of Buffett the events surrounding the increase in the Dow

Jones Industrial Index beyond 1,000 in early 1966 and its subsequent decline by spring. Some of Buffett's partners called to warn him that the market might decline further. Such calls, said Buffett, raised two questions:

1. If they knew in February that the Dow was going to 865 in May,
   why didn't they let me in on it then; and
2. If they didn't know what was going to happen during the ensuing
   three months back in February, how do they know in May?[39]

Having Foresight

How much is clear foresight worth? Imagine that we are transported back
to October 31, 1976, investing $1,000 in shares of Warren Buffet's Berkshire
Hathaway and another $1,000 in the S&P 500 Index. Our $1,000 investment
in Berkshire Hathaway would have grown to $1,044,000 by December 31,
2000, while our $1,000 investment in the S&P 500 Index would have grown
to only $30,000.[40] Berkshire Hathaway shares continued their winning
streak in the first decade of our century. A $1,000 investment in the S&P
500 Index at the end of 2000 would have grown to $1,070 by the end of
April, 2010, but the same $1,000 investment in Berkshire Hathaway stocks
would have grown to $1,624. Why would investors invest $1,000 in the S&P
500 Index in 1976 or 2000 when they could have invested it in Berkshire
Hathaway shares? The answer is in the difference between foresight and
hindsight. Evidently investors, as a group, did not see Berkshire Hathaway's
performance in foresight in 1976 as clearly as they saw it in hindsight in
2000, and they did not see Berkshire Hathaway's performance in foresight
in 2000 as clearly as they saw it in hindsight in 2010.

Still, some investors did foresee Berkshire Hathaway's happy returns
years ago and recognized Buffett's great abilities. Carol Loomis extolled
Buffett's record of high returns back in 1970: "Buffett's record has been ex-
traordinarily good. In his thirteen years of operation . . . he compounded
his investors' money at a 24 percent annual rate."[41] By 1983 Buffett was
famous, and Mary Greenbaum wrote about "Warren Buffett, who has an
almost legendary reputation as a successful investor. . . . "[42]

Investors who foresaw Buffett's performance in the 1970s, 1980s, or more
recently are likely to resist a claim that their foresight is not as accurate as

their hindsight. After all, they did foresee Buffett's performance and might have even bought one or more Berkshire Hathaway shares. Investors who sold all their stocks in late 2007, before the great tumble of the stock market in 2008, are equally likely to resist that claim. But we should be careful before designating ourselves or others as foreseers of the future. Are we victims of the belief in the law of small numbers, having made a few forecasts that turned out well, or does our record show a high proportion of forecasts that turned out well among many forecast we have made? We might have forecasted in 1976 that $1,000 invested in Berkshire Hathaway shares would grow to more than a million dollars by 2000, but did we know that $1,000 invested at the time in shares of Mylan Laboratories would grow to more than a million and a half? Did we, by any chance, also predict that Enron or Webvan would be the next Berkshire Hathaway? A financial advisor shared with me a method she uses to disabuse clients of hindsight error. At the first meeting of each year she presents clients with a list of questions about the future and asks them to make forecasts. The questions would be along the lines of these:

- Will shares of Berkshire Hathaway perform better than the S&P 500 Index?
- Will American stocks do better than French stocks?
- Will there be a magnitude 7.0 or higher earthquake in California?
- Will Donald Trump get divorced?
- Will Martha Stewart get married?

At the end-of-the-year meeting clients might be tempted by hindsight to remember forecasts that came true. Why did you invest my money in stocks when it was obvious that they are destined for a collapse? Now the advisor takes out the list and educates her clients about the pitfalls of hindsight.

Overcoming Cognitive Errors

Warren Buffett has learned to overcome hindsight errors and confirmation errors by asking himself whether he has seen the fortunes of the stock market as clearly in foresight as in hindsight. He also looks for disconfirming evidence, reminding himself and others that partners who seem to be making good forecasts now made bad forecasts in the past. Institutional investors, including Buffett, are better at resisting cognitive errors because they are aware of them and because they have devised systems to overcome them. Investment companies use procedures which force them to consider all evidence, confirming as well as disconfirming. For instance, investment committees structure their meetings such that members are required to list both the advantages and disadvantages of selecting particular investments. We see the difference between individual investors and institutional investors in their selections of initial public offerings (IPOs). Individual investors in Taiwan are regularly misled by their belief in the law of small numbers. High profits on a handful of past IPOs entice individual investors into participation in additional IPOs. But these additional IPOs are more likely to bring them losses than gains. Institutional investors, in contrast, avoid participation in future losing IPOs even when participation in past IPOs brought profits.

We will always be normal, never rational, but we can increase the ratio of smart normal behavior to stupid normal behavior by recognizing our cognitive errors and devising methods to overcome them. Still, emotions face us even if we overcome cognitive biases, and some of these emotions mislead us. We will encounter these emotions in the following chapter.

CHAPTER 3

We Have Emotions, Some Misleading

When I was a teenager, I had a beautiful neighbor. It was her car, though—a beautiful red MGB roadster—that I coveted. An MGB was way beyond my teenage budget but the feeling stayed with me. I got one many years later, as a cure for the midlife crisis. Psychologists describe my feeling toward the MGB as positive affect, which is something investors know a lot about.

Investors speak about affect in the language of sentiment. We speak of the bullish sentiment that buoyed us in the dot-com boom of 1999 and the bearish sentiment that submerges us in the 2008 financial crisis. We might convince ourselves that we choose cars by weighing their utilitarian advantages, such as good safety records, against their utilitarian disadvantages, such as poor reliability. But we regularly choose cars for their expressive and emotional benefits and justify our choices by the cars' utilitarian benefits.

Reason instructs us to expect high returns only when we take high risks and warns us against investments promising returns higher than risks. But sentiment instructs us otherwise. We expect our investments to bring returns higher than risks when our sentiment is positive, as when we are in love, even when the object of love is nothing more than an investment. But when sentiment is negative we expect our investments to bring returns lower than risk. Sunshine conveys positive sentiment and short daylight carries negative sentiment. Stock returns tend to be higher on days when the sun shines and lower when daylight is short.[1, 2, 3]

HOW SENTIMENT AFFECTS INVESTORS

My MGB was exhilarating for a while before it brought trouble. The car with the most beautiful skin turned out to have a very sick body just beneath it. I never drove my MGB when I had to arrive on time, and I would always check my wallet for the AAA card with the number for the tow truck. I finally sold my MGB to a man as enamored by its skin as I was. It is wise to look under the skins of cars before we buy them. It is also wise to look under the skins of investments. I paid a few thousand dollars for my car lesson; investment lessons often cost much more.

We choose investments as we choose cars, and this is also the way we borrow and lend. Borrowers in South Africa are willing to pay higher rates when loans advertised by banks display attractive female loan officers.[4] Loan applicants on Internet sites post the rate of interest they are willing to pay, their credit scores, employment history, homeownership, and other financial information. They also post photographs. Lenders read posted loan applications and decide whether to grant loans.

Beauty matters in life and loans alike. Beautiful applicants are more likely to get loans and pay lower interest rates than less attractive applicants with the same financial information. Moreover, loans to beautiful loan applicants are bad investments because beautiful borrowers are much less likely to repay their loans than less attractive borrowers. Lenders to beautiful borrowers give up the utilitarian benefits of high interest rates and high likelihoods of being paid because they are fooled by the positive sentiment exuded by beautiful applicants. Or perhaps they are not fooled at all. Perhaps they willingly give up the utilitarian benefits of high interest rates and steady loan repayments for the expressive and emotional benefits of associating themselves with beautiful people.[5]

People are also willing to sacrifice substantial utilitarian benefits for the expressive and emotional benefits of picking lucky numbers and avoiding unlucky ones. Lucky numbers convey positive sentiment while unlucky numbers convey negative sentiment. Between $800 million and $900 million in business are lost in the United States on each Friday the 13th because people who consider the day unlucky stay away from work or business.[6] The number 18 is lucky by Jewish tradition because its digits correspond to the word "live." People often give gifts of money to family, friends, and charity in multiples of 18. One Jewish investor wrote to me: "I have this habit when buying or selling stocks . . . to get the cents at some multiple of 18 cents."

The number 8 is lucky to many in China; a man in Guangzhou bid an amount almost as large as seven times the average annual income of people in China for license plate APY888. The numbers 7 and 5 are neutral, but the number 4 is unlucky. Taiwanese consumers were more willing to buy portable radios priced at the lucky but expensive TW$888 than at the neutral but inexpensive TW$777. They were also more willing to pay TW$6,555.55 for a digital camera than TW$6,444,44.[7] Investments acquire positive or negative sentiment in the minds of investors as radios and cameras do. Stocks offered for sale in initial public offerings by Chinese companies are six times more likely to be assigned prices that end with the lucky number 8, conveying positive sentiment, than with the unlucky number 4, burdened by negative sentiment.[8]

The letter A evokes more positive sentiment than the letter B. We prefer an A on our exam to a B, and we would rather have an A rating on our bond than a B. Not all investors know that bonds rated A are actually third-rate bonds, lagging behind AAA and AA bonds, and few investors know that Class A shares are inferior to Class B shares. Class B shares are superior because they have all the benefits of Class A shares in addition to greater voting rights. Each Class A share has one vote, whereas each Class B share has five or ten votes. Yet investors are willing to pay more for Class A shares than for Class B shares although the returns of Class A shares are lower than the returns of Class B shares.[9]

Company Names Elicit Sentiments

Investors who sold stocks at a loss retain negative sentiment toward these stocks and are less likely to buy them again. In contrast, investors retain positive sentiment toward stocks they have sold at a gain and are more likely to buy them again.[10] German investors are more likely to buy stocks in initial public offerings and overpay for them when their sentiment is buoyed by the success of earlier public offerings, and Finnish investors are more likely to buy stocks in initial public offerings when their own purchases of stocks in earlier initial public offerings have turned out well.[11, 12]

Some company names, such as Barnings Incorporated, convey more positive sentiment than other names, such as Aegeadux Incorporated, because they are easier to pronounce. People expect higher returns from the stocks of companies whose names are easy to pronounce than from stocks of companies whose names are difficult to pronounce.[13] Stocks of admired companies are like beautiful loan applicants with easy-to-pronounce names, basking in the glow of positive sentiment. Stocks of spurned companies are like unattractive loan applicants, wilting in the dark of negative sentiment. We embrace stocks of admired companies, expecting returns higher than risks, while we shun stocks of spurned companies, keeping our distance from returns lower than risks.

Fortune magazine has been publishing the results of annual surveys of companies, admired and spurned, for almost three decades. *Fortune* asks senior executives, members of boards of directors, and securities analysts to rate the ten largest companies in their own industries on eight attributes of admiration, including quality of management, quality of products or services, and long-term investment value. The *Fortune* surveys encapsulate company histories and the ups and downs of their admiration and stock returns, as illustrated by IBM.

"No one was ever fired for buying IBM" rang true in the early 1980s, and IBM was the most admired company in the *Fortune* 1983 survey. But the early 1980s were a period of great transition as mainframe computing was fading and the outlines of personal computing were increasingly visible. At first, IBM seemed to master the transition well, introducing the IBM PC in 1981, but as the 1980s were giving way to the 1990s, it was becoming clear that technology and business leadership were shifting toward companies such as Microsoft and Intel. In January 1993, IBM announced a loss of almost $5 billion, the largest single-year loss in preceding U.S. corporate history.[14] IBM was ranked 218th in the 1993 Fortune survey, and slipped to 367th in 1994. Louis Gerstner, who joined IBM in 1993, turned it around, reintegrating major divisions and placing services ahead of products. IBM's *Fortune* rank rose to 36th in the 1999 survey to 15th in the 2010 survey.

IBM was admired during some periods and spurned during others, but the returns of IBM's stock failed to mirror its reputation more often than not. Although IBM ranked first in the 1986 survey, the return of its stock lagged the S&P 500 Index by almost 20 percentage points during the following 12 months. And even though IBM's 1994 ranking was its lowest,

367th, its stock beat the S&P 500 Index by more than 40 percentage points during the following 12 months.

Consider an experiment where one group of individual investors receives the names of companies, such as Google, Apple, Citicorp, and Bank of America, and those investors are asked to rate the future returns of these stocks. Another group of individual investors receives the names of the same companies and is asked to rate the risks of these stocks. If investors were guided by reason, where high returns come with high risks, we would have found that stocks rated high on returns are also rated high on risk, but this is not what we have found. Instead, we have found that investors are misled by the sentiment elicited by company names, as if Google and Apple are easier to pronounce than Citicorp and Bank of America. Investors admire some companies, rating their stock returns high and their risk low. They spurn other companies, rating their stock returns low and their risks high. Investments in stocks of admired companies are too good to be true, yet investors believe that they are good. Investments in stocks of spurned companies are too bad to be true, yet investors believe that they are bad. Evidence, however, indicates that sentiment misleads us into foregoing utilitarian benefits in stocks as in loans. On average, stocks of admired companies delivered lower returns than stocks of spurned companies.[15] Professional investors are swayed by sentiment no less than individual investors. The same experiment with professional investors at a major investment company yielded results identical to the results of the experiment with individual investors.

The Blindfold of Bankers

Bankers granted many mortgage loans in the years leading to the 2008 crisis, often to people with no assets and no income. They packaged these mortgages into securities whose returns were tempting and whose risks seemed low. Bankers who should have known that investments that look too good to be true are not good at all averted their eyes, and when the housing market crashed, so did banks. Subprime mortgages were especially tempting since their returns seemed especially high relative to their risks. One group of bankers noticed in 2006 that their bank's risk-management system treated securities backed by subprime loans as if they were no riskier than government securities, even though their promised returns were much higher than those of government securities. The bankers increased their holdings of such securities from $5 billion in February 2006 to $50 billion in September 2007, and collapse followed.[16]

The blindfold of bankers was partly woven of incentives. Bankers' bonuses increased as they accumulated more securities, whether they added to the banks' profits or brought their demise. But the blindfold was also woven of bullish sentiment, which led bankers to believe that their securities are sure to deliver returns higher than risks. That belief is starkly evident in an earlier crisis, the 1998 crisis that brought the demise of hedge fund Long Term Capital Management (LTCM). Many of LTCM's investments consisted of pairs of similar investments, one bought and one sold, such as the Royal Dutch and Shell pair.

Royal Dutch Petroleum was based in the Netherlands and Shell Transport and Trading was based in Great Britain but the two merged their interests in a fixed ratio until 2005, when they merged into one company. Yet the prices of the shares of Royal Dutch and Shell did not always conform to their fixed ratio. LTCM's traders bought Royal Dutch shares when their prices were relatively low and simultaneously sold Shell shares whose prices were relatively high. The extra profit came when the gap between the prices narrowed. But what if the gap widens rather than narrows during the subsequent months or years? The LTCM story illustrates the observation that markets can be crazy longer than investors can stay solvent.

The wealth of LTCM's partners in 1998 was tied to LTCM's fortunes much more closely than the wealth of typical bankers was tied to the fortunes of their banks in 2008. LTCM's partners had every incentive to consider risks along with returns, and they had every incentive to refuse to believe that investments offered returns higher than risks. Yet that belief was so strong that several partners leveraged their LTCM investments with many millions of personal loans. What looked to be too good to be true turned out to be just that when LTCM was dismembered.

Sentiment Surrounding Innovation

Technological innovations are imbued with positive sentiment, greeted as heralds of abundant new eras of returns higher than risks. Automobiles were in the vanguard of technological innovation in 1916, when an investor wrote to the *World's Work*: "Certainly, the opportunities for rivaling such successes as that of the Ford Company, for example, cannot all have gone by. And if it were not for participating in such enterprises in their early days, how would all the millionaires get their money?"[17]

The *World's Work* was clear in warning investors against the idea that technological innovations combine high returns with low risk, sure to bring riches to investors. "Perhaps the worst mistake that an investor can make is to become possessed of the idea that he should back a new invention. Just at the moment it is airships. A little while ago it was talking machines. Thousands of people in all the civilized countries of the world lost much money trying to reap fortunes from the much-heralded field of wireless telegraphy. It would be quite impossible to estimate the amount of money that has been thrown away by usually sane and sensible people during the past ten years in an effort to make a substitute for the cable and the telegraph and the telephone."[18]

Jason Zweig echoed the warning of the *World's Work* in a 1999 *Money* magazine column about Internet stocks. "I've been asked to answer the question 'Can you get rich by buying an Internet stock fund?' and the answer is no. . . . Many people investing in the Internet are basing their decision on a complete misunderstanding of how industries grow and investors prosper. The notion that a long-term investor can become rich simply by 'buying early' into a revolutionary new industry—like the Internet—is flat-out wrong."[19]

UNREALISTIC OPTIMISM AND OVERCONFIDENCE

We gain returns higher than risks when we win the beat-the-market game. Some investors play the beat-the-market game because they frame it incorrectly as tennis played against a practice wall but others frame it correctly as tennis played against possibly better players. Investors in that second group might be realistic about their good chances at winning the game with special information, skill, or powerful computers. Hilary Kramer, chief investment officer of A&G Capital Research, considers herself one of them. She has been a client of Goldman Sachs for many years and frames the game correctly. "They're not saints. They're not angels. It's

Wall Street," she said of Goldman. "There's a reason why Goldman Sachs made $12.8 billion in net revenue in the first quarter. This is the game. This is the way it's played. When you make a trade there's someone on the other side. Buyer Beware."[20] Kramer might be realistic about her chances at the beat-the-market game but other investors are unrealistically optimistic. Unrealistically optimistic investors are overconfident, believing that they are the better players when, realistically, they are not.

Individual investors are often unrealistically optimistic, but they are regularly joined by professional investors who are flattered as sophisticated players just before they are fleeced. Lloyd Blankfein, the chief of Goldman Sachs, described investors who lost to Goldman at the mortgage-securities game as sophisticated investors. But Phil Angelides, who questioned Blankfein at the Financial Crisis Inquiry Commission, said: "Well, I'm just going to be blunt with you. It sounds to me a little bit like selling a car with faulty brakes, and then buying an insurance policy on the buyer of those cars, the pension funds who have the life savings of police officers, teachers." Jeff Macke, an investment advisor, elaborated: "Of course [Goldman Sachs traders] know more than the other guys," he said to Paul Solman of PBS's *Newshour*. And, if they're selling it, well, you probably don't want to be a buyer." Macke failed to persuade Solman. "But pension funds don't bring in the math whizzes, the quants, the people that Goldman Sachs has," said Solman, "They're no match for Goldman Sachs' salespeople or traders." Macke was ready when Solman was done. "Generally speaking, they aren't," said Macke. "So, what is a pension fund doing involved in these securities?" Unrealistic optimism is a likely answer. Pension fund managers believed that they had a realistic chance to win their game when, in truth, they were unrealistically optimistic.

Unrealistically optimistic investors expect, on average, to be above average. At the height of the stock market in February 2000, individual investors surveyed by Gallup expected, on average, that the stock market would deliver a 13.3 percent return during the following 12 months. But, on average, they expected their own portfolios to deliver 15.5 percent. Unrealistic optimism diminished as the stock market crashed afterward, but that optimism was not gone. In February 2002, individual investors expected, on average, that the stock market would deliver an 8.9 percent return during the following 12 months. But, on average, they expected their own portfolios to deliver 9.7 percent.

Investors overestimate the future returns of their investments relative to the returns of the average investor. Investors even overestimate their past returns relative to the returns of the average investor.[21] Members of the American Association of Individual Investors overestimated their own investment returns by an average of 3.4 percentage points relative to their actual returns, and they overestimated their own returns relative to those of the average investor by 5.1 percentage points.[22] The unrealistic optimism we display in the investment arena is similar to the unrealistic optimism we display in other arenas. We expect higher-than-average satisfaction in our first job, higher-than-average salaries, and higher-than-average likelihood of having gifted children.[23]

Optimism, even if unrealistic, is mostly a blessing. Optimists are happier than realists; they recover faster from surgery and adjust more smoothly to major life transitions, such as leaving home for college, looking for a job, or healing after a divorce. Optimists respond to negative feedback with a positive sense that they are good, skillful, and effective, whereas realists perceive the same negative feedback accurately and integrate it into their sense of themselves.[24] Optimism bolsters self control necessary to overcome temptations on our way to our goals. Optimists gird themselves to exert greater efforts when they anticipate greater temptations, whether tempted by spending when they save for a house or watching television when they study for an exam.[25]

The proportion of unrealistic optimists among the self-employed is higher than the proportion among employees. Unrealistic optimists, whether self-employed or employees, have a more positive attitude toward work than realists; they work longer hours, anticipate longer careers, and are more likely to think that they would never retire.[26] But unrealistic optimism also encourages us to play the beat-the-market game when realistic assessment of our chances would have us refrain from playing. Unrealistic optimists tend to concentrate their portfolios in handfuls of stocks they pick rather than in the many stocks of diversified portfolios.

How Investors' Optimism Is Exploited

We tend to be unrealistically optimistic by nature but, just in case we are not, lottery promoters stoke our unrealistic optimism. A Swiss lottery

advertisement inadvertently speaks the truth, saying: "Lotto, Totto, Lose."
It turns out that in German "Lose" is just another lottery game, pronounced
differently than in English but giving players no better odds. More typical
is a television commercial where an older man in is fishing in a lovely
mountain lake. He says:

> When I was younger, I suppose I could have done more to plan
>   my future.
> But I didn't.
> Or I could've have made some smart investments.
> But I didn't.
> Heck, I could have bought a one-dollar Connecticut Lotto ticket, won a
>   jackpot worth millions and gotten a nice, big check every year for
>   20 years.
> And I did![27]

Promoters of stock trading brokers also stoke our unrealistic optimism.
A television commercial by an online broker showed a sequence of people
who say:

> We don't keep ourselves at a safe distance.
> We don't have blind faith.
> We read.
> We listen.
> We learn.
> We plan to retire rich.

The narrator concludes:

> Suretrade.com
> The smart tool for smart investors.

Stockbrokers and stock exchanges have good reasons to promote unrealistic optimism because unrealistically optimistic investors trade more often
than realistic ones, adding more to the revenues and profits of brokers and exchanges. High stock returns boost the optimism of investors, prompting them
to trade, while losses dampen optimism and the desire to trade. Stock trad-

ing increases following stock market gains, as optimism inflates, and stock trading decreases following stock market losses, as optimism deflates. This is true in the United States and in 45 other countries where it has been studied, ranging from Australia to Venezuela.[28, 29] This was also true a century ago. In 1912, the *World's Work* told the story of an investor who has profited from his bond investment. "When he was told that his bond is now worth about $975 against the $860 he paid for it four years ago, he thought there must be some mistake. . . . When he got that fact in mind he wrote again asking for the name of another bond that would do as well for [him] as this one."[30]

Trading on the New York Stock Exchange plunged after the crash of 1987, employees were laid off, and concern about the optimism of investors, reflected in their confidence, was palpable. The title of the panel convened by the exchange after the crash was Market Volatility and Investor Confidence. The panel recommended means to "decrease market volatility and/or increase investor confidence. . . ."[31] A brokerage company placed a full-page advertisement in the *Wall Street Journal* expressing its concerns under the heading "Investor Confidence Must Come First."

Investors' optimism inflated again in the late 1990s, following stock price inflation, and computer technology made it easy for individual investors to switch from day jobs to day trading, jumping into stocks and out of them in minutes. But optimism deflated as stock prices plunged afterward, and a plunge in trading followed. "In the old days it was, 'Buy whatever you can afford and go home happy,'" said Joseph Cammarata, president of Sonic Trading, a day-trading firm in New York.[32] Charles Schwab, a brokerage company, announced a new round of layoffs just before Labor Day, 2001. "Clients are bringing in a lot of money, but a lot of that money is staying in cash," said Christopher Dodds, its chief financial officer. "Schwab's customers have indicated that they do not intend to start trading more frequently any time soon."[33]

Optimism: Where Insiders and Muggers Roam

Some realistic outside investors trade despite lack of inside information because they have special skills that help them overcome the advantage of insiders. Yet other outside investors trade because they mistakenly believe that government regulations prevent insider trading. There are great advantages in effective policing of insider trading. Companies find it easier to obtain the money they need for expansion of their businesses in countries where the government is effective at preventing insider trading.[34] But a false belief that the government is effective at preventing insider trading is costly to outsiders. The good news about the work of regulators in the United States is that they are largely effective at preventing insider trading. The bad news is that they leave the impression that they are more effective than they truly are, promoting unrealistic optimism among outside investors who are persuaded that the playing field is level when, in truth, it is tilted toward insiders.

Russell Baker, a *New York Times* columnist many years ago, helped us understand the good and bad news about insider trading regulations in a letter he supposedly received from John, the New York mugger:[35]

> Dear Old Friend: As you have doubtless observed, it has been many a week now since I last stepped out of the shadows, put the barrel to your ribs and divested you of cash, trousers, and credit cards. You have probably asked yourself, 'Where is my faithful old stickup man, John? Doesn't he like me anymore?' The truth is, sir, that I'm terrified you'll take it amiss and move out of New York if I overwork my welcome.

John and his fellow muggers are the insiders in the mugging game and Russell Baker and his fellow citizens are the outsiders. Citizens who are aware that streets teem with muggers restrain their optimism, venturing into the streets as little as possible. And outside investors who are aware that stock markets teem with insiders restrain their optimism, venturing into stock markets as little as possible. The worst of all worlds for citizens is one where they venture into the streets frequently because they falsely believe that streets are free of muggers, and the worst of all worlds for outside investors in one where they venture into stock markets frequently because they falsely believe that stock markets are free of insiders. Unrealistically optimistic citizens are frequently mugged in such a world and so are unrealistically optimistic outside investors.

Insider trading is likely more common in China than in the United States, but Chinese investors restrain their optimism because they are under no illusion that their markets are free of insider trading. One Chinese official said that "insider trading is not only extensive, but also ingrained. . . . " Another asked, "Wouldn't you conduct insider trading if you had inside information? It is the reality of human nature. If you refuse, you will be side-lined and eliminated by the fierce competition simply because other people will take the chance when they have it." A third echoed this view, saying that "insider trading is not a taboo subject. It is very hard to outperform in the market and survive if you do not engage in something illegal such as insider trading. Many people do not trade shares unless they have inside information. We simply have no choice in such an environment. . . . " The challenge facing regulators in the United States and other countries that are relatively free of insider trading is the challenge of freeing markets of insider trading while keeping outside investors aware that markets are not entirely free of insider trading.[36]

To be sure, insiders delight in a market, such as in the United States, where they can trade on their inside information while regulators assure outsiders that the market is free of insiders. It is as if the mayor of a city assured its citizens that its streets are free of muggers, encouraging them to venture into the streets, only to be mugged. We know that the returns of insiders exceed average returns, implying that the returns of outsiders fall short of average returns. Citizens who are divested of cash, trousers, and credit cards by muggers who put barrels of guns to their ribs know that they have been mugged. They take precautions before they venture out into the streets again. Outsiders mugged by insiders do not always know that that they have been mugged and rarely take precautions.

THE ILLUSION OF CONTROL

Optimism, whether realistic or not, is associated with control, whether real or illusory. A sense of control is largely beneficial, and its absence is accompanied by pessimism, depression, and reluctance to face challenges. People who believe that they can control the future are usually wealthy and educated people, members of high socioeconomic groups. They are optimistic people with high self-esteem, ready to take action in pursuit of their goals. People who lack control try to compensate for it by imbuing their environment with order and structure. This includes finding patterns when none exist and adhering to superstitions and conspiracies.[37] First-year MBA students who lack the sense of control gained by second-year students are more likely to believe in conspiracies. Baseball pitchers whose success is more precarious than that of other baseball players are more likely to create rituals such as ones that link particular shirts to success. Superstition generally increases in times of economic uncertainty and precariousness.

A sense of control gained through lucky charms or rituals can be useful. In a golfing experiment, some people were told they were receiving a lucky ball; others received the same ball and were told nothing. Everyone was instructed to take ten putts. Players who were told that their ball was lucky made 6.42 putts on average while those with the ordinary ball made only 4.75. People in another experiment were asked to bring a personal lucky charm to a memory test. Half of them kept the charm with them, but the charms of the other half were kept in another room. People who had the charms with them reported that they had greater confidence that they would do well on the test than the people whose charms were kept away, and people who had the charms with them indeed did better on the memory test.[38]

The outcomes of golf and memory tasks are not random; they are tasks that can be improved by concentration and effort. A sense of control brought about by lucky charms or lucky balls can help improve performance if a sense of control brings real control. But no concentration or effort can improve performance when outcomes are random, not susceptible to control, as is often true in much of investing and trading.

One experiment in the world of trading involved 107 traders from the City of London investment banks. The traders were told that they would see a chart of an index whose value would change up or down. They were also told that even though changes in the index are partly random, three keys, Z, X, and C, have special effect. The task was to raise the index as much as possible at the end of each of four rounds of the game. Traders rated their success at raising the index at the end of each round and were compensated by the total value of the index at the end of the four rounds. In truth, movements in the index were random and the three keys had no effect on outcomes. Any sense of control was illusory. Still, some traders believed that they had much control while others believed that they had little. It turned out that traders with the highest sense of control displayed the lowest level of performance.[39]

FEAR AND ANGER

Anger is an emotion quite different from optimism but its effects on investment behavior mimic those of optimism. Anger induces us to underestimate our susceptibility to losses and other bad outcomes. Angry people have a higher than average likelihood to divorce, suffer cardiovascular disease, and face problems at work, whereas angry people rate themselves less likely to experience these problems. Fearful people and pessimistic ones assess risk as relatively high, while angry people and optimistic ones assess the same risk as relatively low. Fearful people and pessimistic ones were unwilling to take much risk, while angry people and optimistic ones often actively seek it.[40]

Anger can induce risky behavior and undesirable aggression, but anger is not all bad. Anger can speed up decisions and prod us to take risk when appropriate. The Balloon Analog Risk task is a computer-based measure of willingness to take risk. People click on pumps that inflate balloons on a computer screen. Each pump of the balloon without an explosion adds money into an account. But the money in the account associated with that balloon is lost if the balloon explodes. The objective is to get the most money while avoiding balloon explosions. People tend to be to be overly cautious in the balloon task, avoiding explosions but collecting relatively little money. Angry people, however, inflate balloons further, bearing the risk of balloon explosions but accumulating more money overall.[41]

We are sad when we face natural disasters, we feel guilty when we cause disasters, we are afraid when we don't know the causes of disasters, but we are angry when we know the causes of disasters. Anger at the investment establishment animates some beat-the-market investors, and online trading is their weapon. A late 1990s commercial by an online broker showed a crowd of people rushing toward the trading floor of a stock exchange where they are blocked by heavy doors and a glass wall. The traders on the ornate trading floor are all men in dark suits, content insiders in the investment establishment, while the people in crowd pressing to get in are the angry out-siders. "Until now, there has been a wall between you and serious trading," says the narrator, "That wall is coming down." We see the bursting doors and shattered glass wall as the crowd rushes in, and the horrified looks on the faces of the establishment traders, cowering in a rain of glass shards.

Anger against the investment and business establishment was on dis-play more recently. A day-trading company offered seminars in 2010 at a $3,995 fee, tapping into the anger of investors. "People put their trust in stockbrokerages that are now out of business, and have seen their 401(k) drop by 40 percent or more," said Michael Hutchison of that day-trading company. "I get e-mails from people saying, 'I worked for XYZ company for 20 years and I just got laid off,'" said Brian Shannon of another day-trading company. "They've got a severance package or a nest egg that they want to invest themselves."[42]

Angry drivers drive fast, change lanes aggressively, and cut in front of other drivers. They might enjoy the expressive and emotional benefits of their driving, but they are less likely to enjoy the utilitarian benefits of arriving safely at their destinations. The same is true for angry day trad-ers. Investors who switched from phone-based trading to Internet trad-ing traded more often and more aggressively. They might have enjoyed the expressive and emotional benefits of fast trading, but they sacrificed the utilitarian benefits for returns. Twice as many day traders lost money as made money and only one in five was marginally profitable.[43]

Fear and Exuberance

Bullish sentiment is accompanied by exuberance, bearish sentiment is accompanied by fear, and both exuberance and fear distract us on the way to the utilitarian benefits of investments. A stroke, tumor, or accident that causes ventromedial prefrontal brain damage dampens emotional reactions, including fear.[44] Dampened fear is not all bad. It helps brain-damaged drivers cross icy patches calmly, avoiding a tailspin, and driving ahead safely. Dampened fear helps cross icy patches on investment roads as well.

Here is an investment game: I'll toss a coin right before your eyes. If it comes out heads, I'll pay you $1.50. If it comes out tails, you'll pay me $1.

We'll play 20 rounds of this game. Before each round you can choose to participate or sit it out. Ready? Suppose that you have lost three dollars in the first three rounds because all three tosses came out tails. Do you choose to participate in the fourth round or do you choose to sit out?

Three losses in a row would arouse fear in normal investors. Many choose to sit out the fourth round. But there is no good reason to be afraid because the game is stacked in favor of those who play all 20 rounds. In each round we have a 50/50 chance to lose $1 or gain $1.50. Our maximum loss is $20 while our maximum gain is $30. And even if we lose, a $20 loss is hardly catastrophic. Yet brain-damaged players were more reasoned at the game than normal players. Undeterred by fear, brain-damaged players played more rounds of the game than normal players and won more money.[45] Still, dampened fear places brain-damaged people at a disadvantage when reason calls for sitting out rather than playing. Many people with ventromedial prefrontal brain damage went bankrupt because fear did not deter them from reckless investments with catastrophic losses.

We are less willing to take risk when we are frightened than when we are calm. In an experiment, a group of students were offered money to stand before the class the following week and tell a joke. A flat joke can be embarrassing, so it is not surprising that some students who agreed to tell a joke withdrew in fear when the time came to stand and tell a joke. But students who were frightened were more likely to withdraw than students who were not. Half the students in the experiment were shown a fear-inducing film-clip from *The Shining*, Stanley Kubrick's classic horror film, before deciding whether to tell a joke or withdraw. It turned out that a greater proportion of them withdrew.[46]

Few accidents are more horrifying than airplane crashes, and the fear elicited by aviation disasters depresses stock returns. Aviation disasters cause actual losses lower than $1 billion on average, but the loss in the value of stocks following an aviation disaster averages more than $60 billion.[47]

Investors are advised to rebalance their portfolios, buying stocks after their prices have fallen and selling bonds after their prices have risen. But investors are as afraid after stock prices crash as they are after a plane crash, and resist buying more. Financial advisors have all but given up on attempts to persuade investors to rebalance their portfolios in late 2008 and early 2009, buying stocks after their prices have plunged. Instead, advisors directed their efforts to calming investors' fear.

Emotions, like cognitive errors, can mislead us into costly beat-the-market games. Perhaps we would stop playing these games after we are educated. Then we would avoid the pitfalls of cognitive errors and emotions and focus on the utilitarian benefits of investments. Yet most investors continue to play beat-the-market games despite much education. Even financially literate investors prefer beat-the-market funds over index funds.[48] It is time to accept the fact that we engage in beat-the-market games not only because we are financially illiterate but also because we are willing to sacrifice some of the utilitarian benefits of our investment for expressive and emotional ones. We want the fun of playing beat-the-market games and the pride of winning them. Why we want to play and win is the topic of the next chapter.

CHAPTER 4

We Want to Play, and Win

J H.B. is the anonymous author of a 1930 book, *Watch Your Margin: An Insider Looks at Wall Street*. He is also "one of the most successful stock operators of the last twenty years." W. E. Woodward, J.H.B.'s friend, wrote the introduction to the book. "When a man writes an introduction to an anonymous book," wrote Woodward, "the idea pops into everybody's head that the rascal wrote the book himself and, for some reason or other, wants to deny his authorship."[1] Woodward assures us that our suspicions are unfounded. "Like everybody else, I am enormously fascinated by the art of money making," he wrote, "but I am quite incapable of making money myself, in any impressive quantity, and I haven't the faintest notion of how one goes about writing a book about stock speculation."[2]

"Do you know why people go into stock speculation?" asked J.H.B.

"To make money," answered Woodward.

"Not at all," said J.H.B., "They go in for the pleasure of getting something for nothing. . . . What they want is a thrill. That is why we . . . drink bootleg whisky, and kiss the girls, and take new jobs. We want thrills. It's perfectly human, but Wall Street is a poor place to look for thrills, for the simple reason that thrills in Wall Street are very expensive."[3]

J.H.B. was speaking in 1930, when Prohibition was the law, and whisky was bootlegged. The world has changed greatly since then, but our wants remain the same. Woodward is not entirely wrong. We do want to make money from investing and speculating. But J.H.B. is surely right. We want pleasure from investing and speculating, and we want thrills from playing the beat-the-market game and winning it. Wall Street is still a poor place to look for thrills and Wall Street thrills remain expensive, but we are willing to pay the price.

Congressman Spencer Bachus wanted to profit from his investments many decades after J.H.B. wrote his book, yet he wanted more than profits. Bachus, a ranking member of the House Financial Services committee, said: "My No. 1 goal is to profit from my investments and a secondary goal is an enjoyment of investing and to better understand the markets."[4] Bachus made a bit more than $30,000 profit from trading stocks and options in 2008. "Given the high trading volume, that isn't much," said Gary Gastineau, a man with decades of Wall Street experience. "[Bachus] traded more [options] contracts in a single year than I've traded for my own account in my entire lifetime."

Bachus is different from almost all of us by his position, but his goals are common. Profits are the utilitarian benefits of winning the beat-the-market game, and cognitive errors and emotions mislead us into thinking that winning is easy. But we are also drawn into the game by the promise of expressive and emotional benefits. Indeed, we are willing to forego the utilitarian benefits of profits for the expressive and emotional benefits of playing the beat-the-market game and hoping to win that game.

MORE THAN MONEY

Dutch investors care about the expressive and emotional benefits of investing more than they care about its utilitarian benefits. They tend to agree with the statement "I invest because I like to analyze problems, look for new constructions, and learn" and the statement "I invest because it is a nice free-time activity" more than they agreed with the statement "I invest because I want to safeguard my retirement."[5] German investors who find investing enjoyable trade twice as much as other investors.[6] And a quarter of American investors buy stocks as a hobby or because it is something they enjoy.[7]

Mutual Funds magazine interviewed Charles Schwab, the founder of the investment company bearing his name. Schwab said: "If you get . . . an S&P Index return, 11% or 12% probably compounded for 10, 15, 20 years, you'll be in the 85th percentile of performance. Why would you screw it up?"

The interviewer went on to ask Schwab why he thought people invested in actively managed funds at all. "It's fun to play around," answered Schwab. "People love doing that, they love to find winners . . . it's human nature to try to select the right horse. It's fun. There's much more sport to it than just buying an index fund."[8]

Like sprinters, swimmers, jockeys, and all other athletes, we want to win. Gold-medal winners are paid millions for endorsements of shoes, watches, and cereals, while silver- and bronze-medal winners are paid little, and fourth-place athletes are paid nothing. Gold medals also bring the emotional benefits of pride and the expressive benefits of a winner's image, perhaps printed on a box of Wheaties. It is no wonder that an Internet broker made the connection between investment competitions and sport competitions in an advertisement displaying a sprinter in starting blocks above a caption:

> If you're waiting for just the right time to start investing online,
> We have one thing to say.
> Bang.

Index funds encountered great resistance when they were introduced in the mid-1970s, expressed in the language of victory and defeat. If you settle for simply matching the S&P 500 Index, you're conceding defeat, wrote one commentator in 1976.[9] That resistance has never abated.

John McLaughlin, a stock trader–consultant–coach, responded to an article I wrote in the *Wall Street Journal* in 2009. I had noted some benefits of index funds and buy-and-hold investing, but McLaughlin disagreed. "The investment game is no longer a buy-and-hold game," he wrote, "It's a buy-and-sell game—it's called *Day-Trading*. . . . The winner's strategy is to get the other guy's money, now—not tomorrow, not next week, not next month—moment by moment, right now. And the winners do this to losers at will, with sophisticated software. . . . "[10] McLaughlin's Web site offered software along with testimonials. "My years of dreaming to be a winner are over," wrote MK. "Like you say, making money consistently like this makes me feel alive." And PD wrote that now he is "in the flow, in the groove. In control. And, finally, in the money."

In the Flow

MK and PD want the utilitarian benefits of money, but they also want the expressive benefits of a winner's image and the emotional benefits of feeling alive, in the groove, in control, and in the flow. This is the experience of athletes in the zone, car drivers going fast and changing lanes decisively, or day traders enthralled by the flickering colors of their monitors. Finnish investors who trade heavily tend to accumulate the most speeding tickets.[11] They feel the flow when they trade and when they drive.

Mihaly Csikszentmihalyi illustrated "flow experiences" with the example of a skier going down the slope: "[Y]our full attention is focused on the movements of your body, the position of your skis, the air whistling past your face, and the snow-shrouded trees running by. . . . The run is so perfect that all you want is for it to last forever, to immerse yourself completely in the experience."[12]

We challenge ourselves for the flow and the other expressive and emotional benefits of overcoming challenges. We express our tenacity and skills to ourselves and we express them to others. And we feel proud when we overcome our challenges and win. President John F. Kennedy set the challenge of going to the moon in a 1962 speech: "We choose to go to the moon in this decade and do the other things, not because they are easy, but because they are hard! Because that challenge is one we are willing to accept, one we are unwilling to postpone and one we intend to win!"[13] Marathon runners such as David Funderburke describe overcoming the marathon challenges: "Once I exceeded 19 miles, I wasn't all there mentally. . . . I knew my body hurt, I knew my body was exhausted—but I kept telling it to put one foot in front of the other. There was no option other than to keep going." Why did Funderburke run the marathon? "I'm not sure," he wrote, "but the reasons include a desire to challenge myself, to do something out of the ordinary, and to find out whether I had the courage and stamina (both physical and mental) to accomplish it."[14]

Flow comes when challenge meets skill. Skiers with intermediate skills lose themselves in intermediate-level ski slopes because their skills match their challenges. Beginner-level slopes cannot hold their attention because they are too slow and boring, while advanced-level slopes are too fast and scary, demanding skills they do not have. Ski lodges offer ski slopes with a range of challenges to match the range of skills among skiers. So do designers of gambles and investments. Gamble designers offer gambles with different prize structures and different levels of complexity. Lotteries offer games where players can pick their numbers or where they are assigned random numbers. And the broad choice of stocks, bonds, options, and funds enhances the play value of investments.

Attractive investments fit the interests and skills of investors. Companies that offer a very large number of mutual funds in their 401(k) plans draw fewer employees into them than companies that offer fewer funds. But this does not necessarily indicate that choice should be eliminated or that the number of funds be reduced. Rather, it indicates that employees are arrayed along a range from beginning investors who know little about investments and perhaps do not care to know more, to advanced investors who believe that they know much and are eager to apply their knowledge. Beginning investors feel overwhelmed by a broad choice of funds and procrastinate rather than enroll. They are helped by default programs that enroll them automatically into sensible investments. Advanced investors, however, are forever complaining that the array of offered investments is not sufficiently broad.[15]

Flow is exhilarating when skills equal challenges, but flow turns into anxiety when challenges exceed skills. John Nyquist was trading online in the late 1990s, and at first his skills seemed to match his challenges. Trading profits enabled Nyquist and his wife to quit working and buy a house on a golf course, where he traded in the morning and played golf in the afternoon. But the challenges facing Nyquist soon overwhelmed his skills and his profits turned into losses. In the end, Nyquist shoved his wife off the ten-foot balcony of their home in a desperate attempt to cover his losses with her life insurance. Then he rushed down to confess to her, "I lost all of our money." Sitting in prison, Nyquist described his situation as "complex" and "probably more suitable for a psychological journal than the financial press." His lawyer said that Nyquist "is not a bad person. He's someone who was under stress and strain, and he snapped."[16]

The Benefits of Playing and Winning

The expressive and emotional benefits we derive from work overlap the benefits we derive from leisure, hobbies, and play. The same is true for the benefits we derive from investing. We mention utilitarian money when we speak about the benefits of work, but we also mention the expressive and emotional benefits derived from mastery, accomplishment, responsibility, esteem, altruism, and learning. These are the benefits derived by open source programmers in projects such as Linux. One open source programmer wrote, "I pick and choose the work that's most interesting to me . . . It's great when you find a challenging problem to work on—either on your own or because someone needs it—you can spend hours on it. . . ."[17] These are also the expressive and emotional benefits derived by scam-baiters who turn the tables on Nigerian advance-fee scammers, inducing them to spend money on telephone and fax by pretending to be dupes ready to be scammed." It's a nice little hobby," wrote Brad Christensen. "It certainly beats stamp collecting."[18]

Open source programmers and scam-baiters sacrifice the utilitarian benefits of time and money for expressive and emotion benefits. So do many eBay bidders. Final bids in eBay auctions are typically higher than the fixed prices of the same products on the same Web pages.[19] Yet David Chess, a bidder, described the thrill of winning an eBay auction of the book *Codex Seraphinianus*.

"It occurs to me that I'm actually willing to pay a bit more than my initial maximum bid, and . . . I raise my bid. Reload the page a few more times. Decide I'm willing to pay even a bit more than that for the book, and raise my bid again. Reload the page some more. Tension mounts!"

"Five minutes to the end of the auction, and I'm still the high bidder, at my initial price (there haven't been any bids today except for my three). Three minutes. One minute. Forty-five seconds. Then suddenly . . . someone has swooped in and placed a last-minute bid that's higher than my initial maximum bid, but not higher than my third, for-sure-this-time, final bid. Hah!"

"Fifteen seconds left, no change. Five seconds left. Then the auction ends, and I win! I am ridiculously pleased by this. I send an e-mail off to the seller."

Many investors seek the challenge of the beat-the-market game and the thrill of winning it, and Stuart, the goofy boy of Ameritrade commercials, spoke to them. "I don't want to beat the market," says Stuart emphatically to his girlfriend's father. "I want to grab it, sock it in the gut a couple of times, turn it upside down, hold it by the pants. . . ." His girlfriend is enthralled. "I want to have his baby," she shrieks. "He's fun, he's different, he's a maverick," explained Ameritade's head of marketing, "That's the way people who are online traders think about themselves." Michael Marrona, who plays Stuart, was invited to perform a skit at options company Susquehanna Partners. Jeff Yass, a co-founder, said, "At Susquehanna, where the average guy is probably 25 or 26 years old, they all relate to Stuart."[20] Older guys seek the thrill of beating the market as well. A financial advisor told me about clients, a retired successful trader on the commodities exchange and his wife. The wife wanted a conservative well-diversified portfolio but her husband wanted to win the beat-the-market game by investing in Mongolian real estate. They did not stay clients long. "It was not a good fit," said the advisor.

DECIPHERING INVESTMENTS AND ASSESSING SKILLS

Individual investors overestimated their skills at deciphering investments a century ago. "Gamblers and nothing else" was the description of Americans who bought German marks in 1921, "hoping to reap a rich harvest upon the return of German money to the normal exchange value." German marks were sold in New York City for eight cents each in small stores and by door-to-door salesmen. "This traffic evidently was carefully planned to attract those unfamiliar with the purchase of foreign currency. . . ." The purchases by Americans "put thousands of good American dollars into Germany's till, and no doubt aided the country in amassing the first reparations payment of 1,000,000,000 marks in gold, recently discharged."[21] Individual investors continue to overestimate their skills at deciphering investments today. Bank-issued options, such as options on the German DAX Index, are popular among individual investors in Europe and Asia. Investors regularly face a choice between many options that differ only slightly from one another. That choice turns out to be confusing. Options on the German DAX Index with similar features vary greatly in price, and most individual investors fail to find the best ones.[22]

Many institutional investors, including those described as sophisticated by Lloyd Blankfein of Goldman Sachs, also overestimate their skills at deciphering investments. Mortgage-backed securities are prominent among investments that overwhelmed institutional investors recently. In April 2010, senators took turns asking Blankfein whether Goldman had an obligation to tell its clients that they were selling them shoddy securities. Blankfein responded that Goldman's sophisticated investors knew what they were buying. "People lost money in it," said Blankfein, "but the security itself delivered the specific exposure that the client wanted to have."

PERFORMANCE GAMES

Institutional investors are no less eager to play the beat-the-market game than individual investors, and they are not much better at it. Pension fund trustees compete with fellow fund trustees in market timing and selection of money managers. But, on average, pension funds would have earned higher utilitarian returns if they had stuck with index funds.[23] Yet pension funds and other institutional investors do not quit the beat-the-market game. Instead, they play performance games. "I did beat the market," they say, "if you measure my performance right."

There was a time when the 100-meter dash was measured in seconds, and crossing the ten-second barrier was the goal. Runners are not much faster now, but we have better stop-watches. Now we measure time by one-hundreds' of seconds, and running records continue to be broken. Investors are not running any faster in the beat-the-market race, so efforts go to inventing better performance measures. Many performance measures are vying for the role of the ultimate performance stopwatch, but the confidence that an accurate performance stopwatch exists is gone. It might be good if we would be granted a moratorium from performance games until we perfect a stopwatch. But that will never happen; the race is too tempting, and the desire to win is too strong. So individual investors continue to jump from mutual fund to mutual fund in search of winners, and institutional investors continue to hire and fire money managers. All players are exhausted, but the games go on.[24]

COMMUNITY MATTERS

Investing offers expressive and emotional benefits when practiced alone, but some investors find greater benefits when investing in communities. "I'd just moved to Chicago and was really missing my women friends," said one Beehive investment club member "The club replaced that."[25] Community matters to open source programmers and scam-baiters as well. Open resource programmers enjoy the joint effort and reciprocity of the community and the opportunity to gain esteem in the eyes of fellow programmers. "I do it for myself and for the people who are reading it," said Australian scam-baiter Lee Kennedy. He spends one to three hours each night at scam-baiting and describes his adventures to fellow member of the community on sweetchillisauce.com.[26]

Community breeds emotions. Ardent fans of sports teams enjoy higher levels of self-esteem and suffer fewer bouts of depression.[27] We give movies higher ratings when we watch them with other people and when our emotions are in sync with their emotions. We even synchronize our emotions, mimicking one another with no awareness that we are doing so.[28] Sam Walton, the founder of Wal-Mart, is one of many business leaders who have mastered the art of emotional contagion. "Don't be surprised if you hear our associates shouting this [Wal-Mart cheer] enthusiastically at your local Wal-Mart store," says the Wal-Mart Web site.[29]

Give me a W!
Give me an A!
Give me an L!
Give me a squiggly!
Give me an M!
Give me an A!
Give me an R!
Give me a T!

What's that spell?
Wal-Mart!
Whose Wal-Mart is it?
It's my Wal-Mart!
Who's number one?
The customer! Always!

Investment clubs are communities. Members of each club contribute at meetings and these contributions buy stocks chosen by the club. "We are all taking turns at researching a stock," said a club member. "You meet some good people and you have a lot of fun along the way."[30] Members of investment clubs often trade the utilitarian benefit of investments for the expressive and emotional benefits of learning, power, and fun. Sometimes members of investment clubs are aware of the trade-off, willingly foregoing investment returns for learning, power, and fun. At other times members are unaware of the trade-off. Yet a trade-off exists. The annual returns of investment clubs, on average, lagged the returns of the stock market by more than three percentage points. The average club even failed to match the average performance of individual investors.[31] Still, losses scare club members, especially older ones, as steep ski slopes scare beginning skiers. The value of the portfolio of the Satin Bags investment club declined in 2008, in the midst of the financial crisis. One member resigned and members were considering replacing their financial advisor. "Fifteen years ago, if stocks went down and investments went down, you could make it back," said one member. "Now we can't because of our age."[32]

The expressive and emotional benefits of learning, power, and fun are also at the center of Warren Buffett and Charles Munger's Woodstock of Capitalism, Berkshire Hathaway's annual meeting in Omaha. Berkshire Hathaway investors sacrifice the utilitarian benefits of time and money when they go to Omaha to hear Buffett and Munger in person since the media carry every word uttered by them. Some nonshareholders have been so eager to join the Woodstock of Capitalism that they offered Berkshire Hathaway shareholders as much as $250 for tickets at eBAY auctions. Buffett responded by offering tickets to nonshareholders for $2.50.

"If Warren Buffett is a religion, then I must be a disciple," wrote Peter Webb, an Englishman, after his "pilgrimage" to Omaha. Waiting for a shuttle bus, Webb watched Charles Munger, Buffett's partner and friend, walking past him on the way to his car. "I have to do a double take as I cannot believe I would see such a scene in the UK," he wrote. "Someone of celebrity status and very wealthy walking down the sidewalk to his car which is parked amongst where all the other cars were in the main parking lot. . . . I found out later that Buffett is in the telephone book as well. Again I can't imagine looking up a famous footballer and finding his name and number and address in the local directory."[33]

There is friendship and camaraderie in the investment community beyond Berkshire Hathaway. James Gorman, the chief executive of

Morgan Stanley, recalled in 2010 the advice of David Komansky, the chief executive of Merrill Lynch when he recruited Gorman a decade before. "Don't underestimate the importance of personal relationships inside and outside the firm."[34] But personal relations and friendships can turn into insider trading in a business centered on information. This is allegedly the case of two insider-trading rings centering on Raj Rajaratnam, founder of the hedge fund Galleon, and Zvi Goffer, who founded Incremental Capital after leaving Galleon. In the end, members of these rings turned on each other, some carrying wires supplied by the FBI to record incriminating conversations.

Friendship also rules in trading rooms where day traders congregate, trading side by side, cheering one another, even lending money to one another. But the trading room is not always cheerful, and tension often brings testiness. The testiness of the day-trading room was manifested tragically when trader Mark Barton, suffering losses and taunts, snapped, and killed nine of his fellow day traders.[35]

Investment clubs, trading rooms, and the Woodstock of Capitalism are face-to-face communities, but online investment communities are growing fastest in membership and variety. Some of today's investment clubs have moved beyond living rooms into the Internet. Brittany Crist formed the Dart Throwin' Monkeys investment club on the Internet, recruiting a soldier, a lawyer, a software engineer, a fireman, and several others fellow members at the Motley Fool Internet chat room. Crist enlisted the help of Bivio, an Internet company whose motto is "Invest with your friends," to build a site for her club where members can communicate with one another and track their investments. "People are craving ways to bring other people into their investment experience," said Ion Yadigaroglu of Bivio.[36] The benefits of investment clubs, says Bivio's site, are in learning, power, and fun.

Internet sites such as Yahoo! offer message boards where investors can gather, share rumors, information, and misinformation about companies and their stocks, debate companies' business prospects, and predict future stock returns. On September 16, 2008, when Yahoo!'s stock was at $19.26, an investor wrote: "OMG!! GOOG Buys YHOO for $36!!!" Rumors about a Google offer to buy Yahoo! abounded at the time as hopes of a Microsoft offer faded. The investor was not entirely serious. "Just kidding," he wrote. But he had hopes: "Any day now." There was a flurry of messages debating the prospects of Yahoo! that day and the following one, and then all was quiet until April 30, 2010, when Yahoo!'s stock was at $16.53 and another investor resurrected the 2008 message. "I have to bump it . . . too funny . . . having a heart stroke over a Google buyout. . . . Maybe this weekend?" Another wrote on the following day, "First, the government wouldn't allow . . . second, Google doesn't want a . . . sinking company like Yahoo!."

Our investment behavior brings us utilitarian, expressive, and emotional benefits. We like to trade, and we hope to win. But what is the sum of our behaviors? What happens as we rush into investments as a herd of bulls or a sloth of bears? This is the topic of the next chapter.

CHAPTER 5

We Join Herds and Inflate Bubbles

M any investors were bullish in December 1999 as Amazon's stock
neared its peak, and some posted their bullishness on the Yahoo.
com message board dedicated to Amazon.[1] "If you look at the chart and
pattern of [Amazon]," marveled one, "it will make at least 50–100% increase
once it breaks its previous high."[2] Another gushed about Amazon's gigantic
warehouses and "how huge the company is about to get," bolstering his
opinion with personal experience. "Any shipment I've received from
[Amazon] has been fast and often [at] a better price than the brick and
mortar stores."[3] But by late 2001 the price of Amazon's stock was one-
twentieth of its 1999 peak price.

Amazon's bubble resembles other bubbles at the time and throughout all
centuries.[4] We herd into investments because we want the utilitarian benefits of returns higher than risks, and we herd out because we want to avoid
returns lower than risks. But we also herd because herds are communities,
providing expressive and emotional benefits to their members.

Herds inflate bubbles and, in the end, bubbles disappoint as most
investors end up with returns lower than risks. Stock prices inflate as
unrealistically optimistic investors stampede into stocks of hot companies. Executives of hot companies rush to issue stocks to eager investors and entice them with wildly optimistic forecasts about fantastic
prospects. In time, investors see the truth and stock prices deflate as
investors stampede out.

HERDS OF BULLS AND SLOTHS OF BEARS

Investors stampede in herds and bubbles inflate and deflate, but the story of herds and bubbles is far from complete, and its details matter more than its outline. Investors form two herds rather than one, a herd of bulls and a sloth of bears, and each splinters into smaller herds. Not all investors were in Amazon's bullish herd in 1999 and not all stampeded into its stock. One bearish investor expressed his pessimism about Amazon and its stock in December 1999 on its message board, as bullish investors expressed their optimism: "[Amazon] is like tulips in Holland. It will wilt, just like they did. People will get hurt. . . . This is 1929 times ten. . . . Watch out."[5]

Yahoo! bulls and bears stampeded in opposite directions as Amazon bulls and bears did. In December 1999 when Yahoo!'s stock price was also close to its peak, a bullish investor responded to the doubts of a bearish one: "You have no imagination. Do you really think Yahoo! and [its] business model in 2015 will be anything like it is now? . . . What people see is that Yahoo! is becoming the Internet brand and whatever the Internet becomes, Yahoo! will be at the center of it. . . . The sky is the limit."[6] Another investor was more succinct in his bullishness on General Electric in August 2000, when its stock was nearing its peak: "GE is a BEAST. Put this stock in a drawer and wake up rich. God Bless Jack Welch!"[7] But in December 1999, as Home Depot's stock was nearing its peak, a bearish investor wrote: "There is more to investing than buying, it is called selling. Heard the saying, bulls make money, bears make money, pigs . . . get slaughtered."[8]

Some investors were in nervous bull herds, anticipating the pop of a bubble but hoping to ride it a little longer. "A needed correction will occur," wrote an investor on Amazon's board in December 1999. "Still long . . . until signs of true financial collapse emerge."[9] Other investors decided it was time to dismount a bubble. One wrote on Amazon's board at the time: "First time I shorted a stock was yesterday. . . . I believe in the Internet sector and believe in their potential. . . . However, I think that a big correction is coming."[10] Yet other investors were wary of manipulation and suspicious of the media. One wrote in August 2000: "CNBC leading you to the slaughter. Parading out the bulls and sucking in the individual investor for what promises to be a slaughter by the end of the year. . . ."[11] And some investors were baffled, unsure about which herd to join. One wrote at the end of 1999 on Home Depot's board: "I bought in at 71 and then again in the low 90s.

Should I still be buying in or are we nearing the top? What is the long-term prospect? Any opinions would be appreciated."[12]

The bullish herd was smaller in 2002, following stock market losses, than in late 1999 and early 2000, following gains, but many investors remained bullish. Some bulls berated short-selling bears. Short sellers don't "care if their attempts harm America, they are only after a buck," wrote one. "Greedy bastards."[13] Short sellers sell borrowed shares, pushing stock prices down and profiting when stock prices go down. A short-selling bear taunted bulls who berated them with an ode to short sellers: "Shorts are the avatars of divine perfection. Gardens of flowers spring in their footsteps. The soft glow of their halos brings comfort in the darkest night. When they breathe, gentle perfumed zephyrs fill the air."[14]

The 2002 period is also marked by hope, hindsight, regret, and sober lessons for the future. One investor wrote: "Jeez. My 1,000 shares haven't done too damn well recently. My broker advised me to sell in 2000, and I resisted. I'm an idiot."[15] This investor would have benefited from the advice of a 1908 investor who said: "I have always made money by becoming . . . reckless when the rest of the world was scared, and I have kept it by getting scared when the rest of the world got reckless!"[16] Warren Buffett offered the same advice more recently in different words: "I will tell you how to become rich. Close the doors. Be fearful when others are greedy. Be greedy when others are fearful."[17] But one investor was skeptical of this advice, writing in July 2002 on GE's message board: "The world has changed and nobody believes those tired old broker/huckster mantras: 'Real men only buy when there's blood in the streets,' 'the market always bounces back,' and, my favorite, 'don't worry, you're in it for the long term.'" Fact is, even if you do believe all of that, only a fool isn't taking at least some of his money off the table right now. My advice, take your rent money out of the game. Later, when things have settled down, you can play again. Don't try to beat the market: you don't know where the bottom is."[18]

EVERYBODY HERDS

Investors everywhere run in herds, large or small, bullish or bearish. Chinese investors herd as they speak to one another about their investments and infect one another with their bullishness or bearishness.

Investment infection in China spreads most easily among neighbors who share brokerage branches because physical proximity facilitates investment infections as it facilitates virus infections.[19] German investors herd. Individual investors at a major German discount broker trade in tandem; they join the bullish herds of some stocks and the bearish sloths of others.[20] American investors herd. Americans draw one another into the stock market, and drawing power is especially strong in sociable communities.[21] Americans herding extends beyond stocks, to industries. Investors who are bullish on a stock of a company tend to be bullish on stocks of other companies in its industry.[22]

Taiwanese, South Korean, and Finnish investors herd.[23] Herding is widespread among individual investors in Taiwan. They might enjoy the expressive and emotional benefits of the herd community, but they sacrifice some of the utilitarian benefits of stock returns.[24] Finnish investors join the herd of stock market investors when their neighbors have gained in the stock market. Yet neighbors' stock market losses do not discourage stock market investing among Finnish investors, probably because neighbors tell neighbors about gains but keep quiet about losses.[25] Herding extends into choices beyond investments, such as choices of cars. Finns are likely to buy cars bought by their neighbors.[26] Swedish investors bond to one another while in college and share its common imprint. They form long-term friendships and interact in like-minded communities, many years after graduating. Swedish investors choose stocks chosen by their former classmates and tilt their portfolios toward growth stocks or value stocks if their former classmates do the same.[27]

Employees herd. Librarians in 11 libraries of a large university faced a choice whether to participate in a retirement savings plan sponsored by the university. Rates of participation varied greatly among libraries, ranging from 14 percent of librarians in one library to 73 percent in another. Recommendations of some librarians in each library influenced other librarians, and participation levels varied among libraries by the extent of these influences.[28]

Institutional investors herd even more than individual ones. Investments chosen by one institution predict investment choices of other institutions in the following months.[29] From 1997 to March 2000, as the prices of stocks of technology stocks multiplied more than fivefold, institutional investors bought approximately two-thirds of new technology stocks while individual investors bought the other third directly or through mutual funds. Hedge funds were the most aggressive buyers of technology stocks, but they were equally aggressive in selling technology stocks in early 2000, as stock prices began to plummet. Individual investors were buyers when hedge funds were selling, and buying was especially intense among individual investors trading online.[30]

Managers of mutual funds herd and their herding upsets stock markets. Mutual fund managers charge as herds into stocks as they are upgraded by analysts and they stampede out when stocks are downgraded. The prices of downgraded stocks fall at first, as the herd of mutual fund managers sells them, and then bounce back. The prices of upgraded stocks rise at first, as the herd of mutual fund managers buys them, and then slump back. Mutual fund managers who are concerned about their professional reputations and employment prospects are especially prone to herding, afraid that running in a direction different from the herd might cost them their jobs.[31] "Momentum" investors are likely to buy stocks whose prices increased rather than stocks whose prices decreased.[32] Foreign investors who reside outside Korea are more likely to join the momentum herd than foreign investors in branches and subsidiaries located in Korea or foreign individuals living in Korea.[33]

AFFINITY FRAUD

Investors in herds give little credence to their own information and much credence to the information conveyed by the herd. Investors do that even if, in truth, the herd's information is useless or worse. The herding instinct and the desire for community open the door to "affinity fraud," where con men win the trust of members of their communities and proceed to fleece them. Bernard Madoff's community was the Jewish community; his clients infected one another with tales of high returns with low risk. Madoff's Ponzi scheme victims included Hadassah, the Women's Zionist Organization of America, director Steven Spielberg's Wunderkinder Foundation, and Yeshiva University. "How could someone who is held in such high esteem in the Jewish community knowingly rip off what were supposed to be his friends, the organizations he admired and supported?" asked Kenneth Bandler of the American Jewish Committee.[34]

The desire for community and the herds it inspires is hardly limited to the Jewish community. Hezbollah's version of Bernie Madoff is Salah Ezzedine, a Lebanese Shi'ite businessman. Ezzedine is suspected in a Ponzi scheme that ensnared the head of Hezbollah's faction in the Lebanese parliament and many others with promises of 25 to 55 percent returns. "Everyone invested with him, everyone," said Muhammed Shur, the owner of a grocery store. "He was supposed to be a religious man and gave a lot of money to charity." Shur placed $45,000, his family's entire savings, in Ezzedine's hands. "You can go through this village one by one," he added. "Some of the people even mortgaged their homes to invest with him."[35]

Christians are no more immune to affinity fraud than Muslims or Jews. The fraud perpetrated on members of El Camino Church in New York City was small by Madoff's standards, but many members of the Christian Evangelical Church have lost their savings.[36] Federal prosecutors alleged that Bryant Rodriguez defrauded his fellow churchgoers of about $600,000. The pastor, the Reverend Miguel Amadis, said: "When I met this guy, he convinced me he was a true original Christian. Man, this guy could talk. He could convince anybody." "We're going through a very hard time," he said to his congregation. "We have to stay united."

Marcia Sladich's community was part of the religious network headed by the Reverend Sun Myung Moon. She defrauded her investors of $15 million with promises of risk-free real estate investments that would double their money. The investment contract is incomprehensible, brimming with misspellings. The contract said, in part: "[T]he agreement of booths parties convenants and agrees that the Shares will be to engage in a fund for of business this can generate fkom the investment."[37]

Smart and Stupid Herd Behavior

Herd behavior has acquired a bad reputation for good reason. But herd behavior is often useful. Animals in herds do well by imitating one another. When gazelles in a herd see one of them gallop suddenly and fast, they act as a herd, imitating the galloping gazelle even if they do not see the lion crouching in the grass. Herd behavior saves gazelles the mental effort of processing the odds that lions are ready to pounce, and herd behavior usually saves their lives. Herd behavior in investments can be beneficial as well. Investors are smart sometimes as they join herds, assigning little credence to their own information and judgment and much credence to the information and judgment of the herd. Yet at other times they are stupid as they join herds. But how can investors tell the difference between smart and stupid, distinguishing herds charging in the right direction from herds charging in the wrong one? How can prospective investors in affinity frauds find out, before it is too late, that the herd they are about to join is charging in the wrong direction?

Good judgment of information is one part of the answer. Good assessment of the consequences of a wrong choice is another. The consequences of choosing the wrong restaurant by joining the herd at its entrance are small, while the consequences of choosing the wrong investment are large.

But how could have Madoff's investors obtain information about Madoff's operations when Madoff guarded his information so closely and distorted it? In truth, Madoff's investors had the information they needed to avoid his scheme but failed to apply good judgment to it. One part of their information was in the maxim "If it sounds too good to be true, it probably is." The complementing part was Madoff's reported returns, combining high returns with low risk. My mother would tell the fable of a village woman who borrowed a spoon from a neighbor, returning it the following morning along with a teaspoon. "The spoon gave birth to the teaspoon last night," she explained. Next she borrowed a cart, only to announce the following morning that the cart had died. People who are gullible enough to believe that spoons give birth should not be surprised when carts die. Madoff's returns were too good to be true. Investors who follow the too-good-to-be true maxim might regret it from time to time. After all, opportunities to invest in fabulous hedge funds that promise great returns and deliver them are not as impossible as spoons giving birth to teaspoons. But investors who follow the maxim are not likely to fall for Madoff-like schemes.

Next, Madoff's investors could have reflected on the credence of the information in the hands of members of the herd. Compare Madoff's investors to shoppers of washing machines consulting a *Consumer Reports* survey. *Consumer Reports*' information is the information of the washing-machine herd, based on *Consumer Reports*' own laboratory analysis of many machines and questionnaires completed by thousands of users. We are smart to set aside our information and follow the *Consumer Reports'* herd, not only because its tests are rigorous, but also because its reports are unbiased. *Consumer Reports* is not tempted to skew its reports toward companies that advertise in it because it accepts no advertisements. Moreover, *Consumer Reports* has the incentives to provide unbiased reports; its revenues depend entirely on subscriptions and donations of readers who expect unbiased reports. It surely does not follow the practice of Wall Street–rating agencies that accept payments from companies whose securities they rate.

Compare Madoff's prospective investors to *Consumer Reports* readers. Madoff's prospective investors had little information of their own about Madoff's investments, but they should have known that the reliability of the information in the hands of current Madoff's investors was far from that of current readers of *Consumer Reports*. Moreover, incentives were not set in favor of Madoff's prospective investors. It turned out, too late for Madoff's investors, that some prospective investors did investigate Madoff's investments and concluded that his reported returns could not possibly be true. These prospective investors chose not to invest, but there was no feasible way for them to profit from their analysis by selling Madoff's shares, since Madoff's company was a private company whose shares were not traded on the stock exchange. There was also no feasible way for them to profit by selling their information to current Madoff's investors who could have benefited from it. Harry Markopolos, one of these prospective investors, tried to convey his Madoff information to the Securities and Exchange Commission. The Commission did have an incentive to uncover Madoff's fraud but was overwhelmed and perhaps incompetent.

Madoff's prospective investors would have been wise not to follow the herd into Madoff investments. But what is the difference between an investment with Madoff and an investment in a stock, whether Google or Enron? After all, typical investors knew little more about Enron before it collapsed than they knew about Madoff before he confessed. Yet the difference between Enron and Madoff is in the incentives to uncover information and communicate it. Enron, unlike Madoff's company, was a public company whose stock was traded on the stock exchange.

James Chanos specializes in uncovering information about companies whose stock prices are too high. Chanos is bearish when most investors are bullish, a prominent example of contrarian investors who counter the conventional investors of the bullish herd.[38] Chanos started accumulating his Enron information in October 2000 and concluded that the bullish herd was wrong, ignorant of Enron's questionable accounting practices, and confused by its cryptic disclosures. Chanos had the incentive to sell Enron's stock since he could profit as its price fell. And he could sell Enron's stock since it was traded on the stock exchange. Investors considering joining Enron's herd by buying shares did not have Chanos's information, but they benefited from it since the sale of shares by Chanos drove the shares' price lower, such that later buyers were spared the full brunt of Enron's collapse.

BUBBLES IN EFFICIENT MARKETS

Herds inflate bubbles and deflate them, but investors and financial economists are still debating the meaning of bubbles and their existence. Charles Kindleberger defined a bubble in his book *Manias, Panics and Crashes* as "an upward price movement over an extended range that then implodes." That definition is neutral. It does not tell us whether the prices of stocks, houses, or mortgage-backed securities exceed their true values as bubbles inflate, or whether prices merely track values as values increased. But the word *bubble* has come to be associated with overvalued investments, where prices exceed values. Bubbles are contentious because their existence implies that markets are not efficient. The efficient market hypothesis, in its extreme form, claims that prices never deviate from value, so bubbles are evidence that markets are not efficient.

Typical institutional investors believe that not all markets are efficient and that even markets that are efficient most of the time are not efficient all the time. Indeed, typical institutional investors attempt to beat the market by identifying deviations of prices from values, buying investments whose prices fall short of values and selling investments whose prices exceed values. In this way institutional investors deflate bubbles. Institutional investors buying investments whose prices fall short of values drive prices up, closer to values, and institutional investors selling investments whose prices exceed their values push prices down, closer to values. At times, however, institutional investors attempt to beat the market by riding bubbles, inflating them at first and dismounting before they deflate. This is what hedge funds did successfully at the time of the technology bubble. Hedge funds bought overvalued technology stocks in the late 1990s, inflating the bubble, but dismounted before it began deflating, selling these stocks.[39] This "greater fool" plan in which investors buy overvalued stocks, planning to sell them later at even higher prices, worked for hedge funds but it does not work when fools are unable to find greater fools. Indeed, it is mostly individual investors who bought technology stocks from hedge funds when the bubble was fully inflated.

More than a dozen options trading in China were virtually certain to have no value when they expired. Nevertheless, the options were heavily traded at grossly inflated prices. Investors who overpaid for these options were disappointed when they could not find greater fools who would buy them at even higher prices.[40] The Shanghai Composite Index of Chinese stocks multiplied more than fivefold in the two years from October 2005 to October 2007, but it was decimated by October 2008, losing more than two-thirds of its peak value. "The market was going wild," said an investor in April 2008 after the market lost almost half of its value. "Everybody was talking about how much they had earned, how much more they would invest, and which stocks had jumped 20 times, or even 30 times."

"These days my family quarrels a lot," said another investor. "My husband asked me to sell; I wanted to hold for a while. Now my husband condemns me as so stupid that we lost our family's savings."[41]

The Michigan Surveys of Consumer Attitudes and Behavior reveal that individual investors are bullish when they expect the economy to expand, believing that stocks would provide the best of all worlds, combining high returns with low risk. And individual investors are bearish when they expect the economy to contract, believing that low returns with high risk are forthcoming. Moreover, individual investors adjust their portfolios to fit their beliefs, moving money into stocks when they expect the economy to expand, and shifting money out of stocks when they expect the economy to contract. Yet individual investors are misled by bullishness and bearishness more often than they are led right. Stock returns tend to be low in months following high readings of consumer confidence.[42]

Extreme bullish sentiment is often accompanied by proclamations of "new eras," with returns higher than their risks. In the late 1990s some stock market seers prophesied that the Dow Jones Industrial Average would reach 36,000 soon, as investors learned that stocks are no riskier than bonds yet yield much higher returns. And in 1930, after the crash of 1929, George Frederick wrote: "By far the most significant thing that the October–November 1929 stock panic did was to put the acid test to the so-called new era [which] was all rainbows and sunshine, and was bomb-proof. . . . Wiseacres now recall that prophets of a new era usually appear just before a panic deluge."

The soberness of Frederick following 1929 resembles the soberness following the late 1990s. New eras do come, but returns higher than risks are rare. "There had been recognition by sound, conservative economists that there really was a new era," wrote Frederick. "What then happened was that the unrestrained optimists, the opportunist bankers, the greedy stock promoters, and the unthinking public began, pell-mell, to discount this new era for years ahead, and over-reached themselves. The new era set up new standards, but the unthinking seized upon them as license to indulge in unrestrained imagination and unlimited standards of valuation."[43]

Individual Investors in Bubbles

High stock returns draw investors into the stock market, making them think that now is a good time to invest in the financial markets. *The Literary Digest* wrote in 1918: "All kinds of people buying stocks." A clerk bought one share of the preferred stock of a northwestern utilities corporation, a logger bought ten shares, a rancher bought five, and a widow bought six. The *Digest* went on to note: "Slightly more than half the [buyers] had not previously owned any stocks in this company. . . . A reasonably safe assumption would be that most of the new buyers had not previously owned any kind of stock whatsoever."[44]

Many individual investors thought the stock market was overvalued in the last six months of 1999, following immense stock returns, yet many of them thought that buying stocks was a good idea. Fewer individual investors thought that the stock market was overvalued in the six months ending in July 2002, following precipitous declines in stock prices, yet few thought buying stocks was a good idea. Almost half of the individual investors surveyed by Gallup thought that the stock market was "overvalued," as in a bubble, in the last six months of 1999, while less than one in twenty thought that the stock market was "undervalued." The proportion of individual investors who thought that the stock market was overvalued declined to approximately one in four in the six months ending in July 2002, and the proportion of investors who thought that the stock market is undervalued increased to almost one in five. Gallup went on to ask if investors think that now is a good time to invest in the financial markets. We might have presumed, by logic, that investors were more likely to answer "yes" in 2002, when they tilted toward the conclusion that the stock market is undervalued, than in 1999, when they tilted toward the conclusion that the stock market is overvalued. Yet these were not their answers. In 1999, investors judged the market overvalued yet believed that it was a good time to invest. Fewer investors judged the market overvalued in 2002 than in 1999, yet fewer investors thought in 2002 than in 1999 that it was a good time to invest. Only one-quarter of investors in both periods believed that the stock market was "valued about right," a belief consistent with market efficiency, implying that individual investors who believe that the market is not efficient outnumber those who believe that it is efficient by a ratio of three to one.[45]

When Bubbles Are Made to Order

Hedge funds inflated the dot-com bubble and rode it, but they did not create it. No hedge fund founded a dot-com company or helped found one. But Magnetar, a hedge fund, and Paulson & Company, another hedge fund, had a hand in creating securities that let them profit from the bubble that crested in the financial crisis of 2008. Bankers made many mortgage loans for houses in the period leading to the crisis, often to people with no assets and no income. They packaged these mortgages into securities whose returns were tempting and whose risks seemed low. Subprime mortgages were especially tempting since their promised returns were especially high.

Magnetar, named for the super-magnetic field created by the last moments of a dying star, persuaded banks to create mortgage securities. Next, it pressed banks to include in them the mortgages most likely to default and bet that the mortgages would indeed default by selling short the mortgage securities it helped create.[46] John Paulson of Paulson & Company had a role in the selection of mortgages for securities created by Goldman

Sachs, and sold them short. Many investors, including large American and European banks, pension funds, and insurance companies, bought mortgage securities, underestimating their risks. These buyers lost, and Magnetar, Paulson & Company, and Goldman Sachs gained.[47]

R.B.S., the Royal Bank of Scotland, bought $840.1 million of Abacus 2007-AC1 created by Goldman Sachs. The money paid by R.B.S. to Goldman went to Paulson & Company, which advised Goldman on Abacus and bet against it. R.B.S. earned what seemed to be an easy $7 million fee when it invested in Abacus, but, in the end, lost its entire investment. Bankers who should have known that investments that look too good to be true are not good at all averted their eyes. And when the housing market crashed, so did the banks. R.B.S. is now owned mostly by the British government.[48]

The Flash Crash

We tend to focus on bubbles lasting years, but bubbles lasting days, hours, or minutes qualify as well, and so do "negative bubbles," in which prices deflate rather than inflate. The "flash crash" of May 6, 2010, is a recent example, where the Dow Jones Industrials Average plunged almost 10 percent within five minutes, erasing a billion dollars of market value. Stocks that sold for $40 a few minutes before were suddenly selling for a penny. The flash crash likely originated when an investment company sold a substantial quantity of futures contracts on a stock index, causing a decline in its price. The decline in price triggered a computerized herd, which proceeded to sell stocks, as programmed, until humans stopped it. Months earlier some investors set "stop-loss" orders on stocks they owned. Investors who own a stock selling at $40 today can set a stop-loss order such that the stock is sold automatically when its price falls to $30, perhaps in a month or a year. This way, investors plan to stop losses beyond the $10 that separates $40 from $30. Yet not all investors who placed stop-loss orders understood that a stop-loss order does not guarantee that the stock would be sold at $30. If the price of the stock falls in one swoop from $40 to $20, never pausing at $30, it would be sold for $20. Investors with stop-loss orders might have been on vacation on May 6, 2010, or at the office, but computers traded for them as if they had joined a herd. The selling of stocks pushed their prices down, triggering additional stop-loss sales. In the end, some prices spiraled all the way down to one penny.

The price of Vanguard's Total Stock Market Exchange-Traded Fund (VTI) did not drop to a penny on May 6, 2010, but its decline was large enough to inflict substantial losses on Gary Pinder. Pinder bought the fund in March 2009 and set a stop-loss order on it, which he revised from time to time. On May 5 he set the stop-loss price at $49.17. Yet VTI's stock never paused at $49.17 on May 6. Instead, it paused at $41.15 long enough to let a computer program sell Pinder's stock. Then VTI rebounded to $57.71, leaving Pinder behind. Ironically, Pinder set his stop-loss "to take the emotion out of selling," fearing that he might join a human herd, only to join a computer one. "When I first started working, I hoped to have the option to retire by age 50," said Pinder. "The bursting of the dot-com bubble probably put us back to 55. The 2008–2009 crash put us back to age 60 or so. And now we'll maybe have to work an extra year, or just live with less money whenever we do retire."[49]

A selling wave of futures followed by a selling wave of stocks also marked the crash of 1987. That crash, like the flash crash, renewed debates about the need for "circuit breakers" to halt herds when prices move outside bounds. Following the crash of 1987, the Market Volatility and Investor Confidence Panel recommended that circuit breakers be installed to interrupt trading when prices move outside bounds. The panel's reasons for circuit breakers were grounded in the need to protect us from our cognitive errors and emotions. Circuit breakers provide a time-out to investors, amid frenetic trading, to pause, evaluate, inhibit panic, and restore confidence. And circuit breakers counter the illusion of liquidity by making it clear to investors that markets cannot be relied upon to always absorb waves of buying or selling by herds of humans or computers with little change in prices.[50] It turned out that a lesson taught in 1987 had to be learned again in 2010.

Savings precede investments, providing the money needed for investments. Yet it is hard to save what we are tempted to spend. Mental accounts and self-control help us save, and this is the topic of the next chapter.

We Want Self-Control and Mental Accounts

I s a $500,000 "legacy" different from a $500,000 "inheritance"? A high school teacher received $500,000 from the estate of his aunt and placed it in the hands of a financial advisor who invested it in stocks. The timing of the stock investment turned out to be unfortunate, just before a stock market crash. The frightened teacher called his advisor and demanded that the stocks be sold. The advisor tried to persuade the teacher that selling stocks at the time would be unwise, but the teacher insisted and the advisor complied. Soon after, the teacher consulted a lawyer and sued the advisor, claiming that an investment in stocks was never suitable for him. At trial, the teacher called the $500,000 a legacy while the advisor called the same money an inheritance. The label, legacy or inheritance, had no effect on the amount of money invested or the amount of money lost, but both teacher and advisor had good reasons to insist on their labels because labels are likely to sway jurors and the rest of us. The legacy label makes the money almost sacred, to be kept intact for children, grandchildren, and the generations that follow. The teacher argued that the advisor should not have placed legacy money in stocks that could lose some of their value. The inheritance label makes the money almost profane, to be invested in stocks that might zoom or crash, or be spent on anything from mundane groceries to luxurious cruises. I was retained as an expert witness by lawyers representing the advisor. The jury sided with the advisor, and I imagine that labels played a part in their decision.

MENTAL ACCOUNTING

Does it matter to you whether your aunt labeled money she left to you as inheritance or legacy? Do you spend hard-earned dollars as easily as you spend dollars you win in a lottery? Do you distinguish the "income" dollars paid as dividends on your stocks from the "capital" dollars of the stock itself? We often place monies in distinctly labeled "mental accounts" and treat them accordingly. Mental accounts resemble checking accounts, and money in our mental accounts resembles money in our checking accounts. Mental accounts help us keep track of our money and direct it to where we want it to go. We make sure that there are sufficient balances in each of our mental accounts just as we make sure that we have sufficient balances in each of our checking accounts, so checks we sign at grocery stores or send to electrical companies do not bounce.

The simplicity of mental accounting helps us face two major life challenges. One is the challenge of dividing our spending, saving, and investing between the present and the future. How much shall we spend, save, and invest during our working years and how much in retirement? The other is the challenge of dividing today's spending among all we want today. How much shall we spend on groceries and how much on movies? How much on rent and how much on travel?

Methods of Mental Accounting

Mental accounting is common to all, from lottery buyers in Florida, to prostitutes in Oslo, and even members of gangs in Philadelphia. Some of the Oslo prostitutes placed wages, welfare money, and health benefits in straight-life mental accounts, allocating it carefully for straight-life expenses such as rent. But they placed prostitution money in fast-life mental accounts. Fast-life money was burning holes in the women's pockets, and they spent it quickly on drugs, alcohol, and clothes. One prostitute said: "Trick money is worthless. I'm a lot more careful with the [money] I get every two weeks on my job then with the money I've earned on the street."[1]

Marty, a Philadelphia gang member, placed "honest money" in a mental account distinct from "bad money." Marty liked going to church and often made little offerings from money he received from his mother, but he would not put in the money he stole. "Oh no," he said, "that is bad money; that is not honest money."[2]

We can buy our lottery tickets with any money, whether from earnings, such as wages or dividends, or from transfers, such as social security benefits and unemployment compensation. Yet we are more likely to buy lottery tickets with money from transfers than with money from earnings. Transfer payments make up substantial portions of the money in the hands of older individuals and those with lower incomes. Individuals in both groups are among the most avid lottery players.[3]

Middle-class men and women practice mental accounting. One elderly couple maintained a joint account and two sets of checking and savings accounts, one for daily expenses, such as groceries, and the other for larger expenses, such as taxes. The wife was responsible for paying daily expenses from one account and the husband was responsible for paying larger expenses from the other.[4]

Working-class men and women practice mental accounting as well. "I have a silly little system," said one woman in the 1950s, describing her tin-can mental accounting. "Whenever my husband gets paid I take away so much for my grocery money and put it in my kitchen drawer. Then I take all the rest and I put it into a tin can. . . . If my husband doesn't have enough money for gas out of his allowance, or if we go out for some entertainment, we just take the money out of the tin can. . . . I've tried to budget with envelopes, labeling them for this and that, but we always took money out of the wrong envelope whenever we ran low. . . . Now I've found the checking account together with the tin can the best system."[5]

Mental accounting has migrated from the tin cans of the 1950s to today's spreadsheets, cell phones, and the Internet. "We seemed to be spiraling into debt with one income," said Kelly Conrad about the time that her husband left his job to care for their children. "We had a lot of arguments about where the money went, and we couldn't answer that because we were living our lives and not giving a lot of attention to our budget." This is when she started tracking their spending on an Excel spreadsheet and found that groceries and restaurants were weighing them down. "Getting it on paper, we both saw what we were dealing with," she says. "Finances are not a big deal anymore."[6] Mint.com and similar Web sites are a step beyond spreadsheets, making it easy to track our expenses on shopping, entertainment, restaurants, gas, and groceries. We can split ATM withdrawals into spending categories and even tweet our purchases as we make them.

The Cost of Mental Accounting

Mental accounting can be costly even when it is useful, as when it assures cash for emergencies.[7] We sacrifice wealth when we simultaneously pay high interest rates on credit card balances while keeping cash in bank accounts at much lower interest rates. In the documentary *The Secret History of the Credit Card*, the interviewer asked a group of credit card holders:

> *Interviewer:* By the way, while you were running up balances on your credit cards or currently have balances on your cards, do you have cash in the bank?

(All four card holders nod their heads.)

> *First woman:* Oh yeah.
> *Second woman:* Yeah.
> *First man:* I can wipe my debt out.
> *Interviewer:* So why don't you do it?
> *Second woman:* I feel that it's a nest egg. You never know what's going to happen tomorrow. You might need that money for something else.
> *Interviewer:* So, even though you're paying double-digit interest and you could get rid of the balance or most of it, you're still going to make those payments and keep the cash in your bank account.
> *Second woman (nods her head):* Right.
> *First woman:* If you lose your job or, you, you know, something bad happens, you have to have money and you don't want to live off of a credit card, so you need to have that money saved somewhere in case something happens.[8]

The tendency to keep money in separate mental accounts despite its cost is evident in large-scale study, beyond the stories of the four credit card holders. People who borrow from payday lenders at interest rates amounting to several hundred percent often also have credit cards with large balances available at much lower interest rates, yet they fail to use the cheaper sources for their loans.[9] Mexican borrowers practice credit card mental accounting as Americans do, and they too pay its price. Mexican cardholders forego a 16 percent saving in their financing costs as they borrow on cards with high interest rates while cards with lower interest rates reside in their wallets. One-third of them said that they used different cards for different purposes, a hallmark of mental accounting.[10]

SELF-CONTROL

Simplified accounting is one benefit of mental accounting. There is a smaller danger of a bounced check when small bills are paid from one bank account and major purchases from another. But the benefits of mental accounting as a tool of self-control are even greater. Self-control stops us from buying a shiny new car today when we need the money for today's rent. And self-control stops us from going on a vacation today so we might enter a nursing home in old age.

Imagine yourself as a four-year-old at a nursery school. A teacher escorts you into a room and together you play with some toys. Then the teacher says that you would play again with these toys some more later but asks you to sit for now at a table on which there is a bell. The teacher shows you two marshmallows and says that he or she must leave for a while. If you wait until the teacher comes back, you can have the two marshmallows. You can ring the bell at any time you want to call the teacher back, but if you ring the bell you'll get only one marshmallow, not two. Would you be able to resist the urge to ring the bell before 15 minutes are up?

Children who resist the temptation to ring the bell have better self-control than children who ring the bell, and differences in self-control have profound consequences in life, including financial life. Children who exercised sufficient self-control to resist the temptation of the marshmallow grew up to be more academically and socially competent, verbally fluent, smart, attentive, able to plan, and able to deal with frustration and stress. They also scored higher on the SAT.[11]

Do you prefer $1,000 right now or would you rather wait a month for $1,100? Money uncovers in adults what marshmallows uncover in children. The difference between the two sums amounts to 10 percent over a single month, yet deficient self-control leads some adults to the impatient choice of the immediate $1,000, as deficient self-control leads some children to the immediate marshmallow.

Impatient adults have substantially higher revolving credit balances than patient adults in identical circumstances.[12] American military servicemen were offered choices such as between an immediate payment of $22,283 or an annuity paying $3,714 every year for 18 years. The annuity offered a better deal in that it implied an annual interest rate more than double the interest rate commonly available at the time. Yet more than half the military officers chose the immediate payment, and so did more than nine out of ten enlisted personnel.[13]

Mastering Self-Control

Each of us is born with a capacity to acquire self-control, just as we are born with a capacity to learn a language. Some master self-control and are able to exercise it even in the face of substantial lottery prizes. John Gonsalves won a $5.1 million Megabucks jackpot in 1994, yet was still owed more than $1 million when he died in 2008. "He didn't change his life at all," said his son. "I think he went on one vacation. He really didn't want to live high off the hog, so to speak."[14] But not all lottery winners master self-control. One study followed Florida lottery players who won substantial prizes ranging from $50,000 to $150,000, comparing them to winners of small prizes of less than $10,000. Winners of substantial prizes were less likely to file for bankruptcy during the two years following their wins than winners of the small prizes, but winners of substantial prizes were as likely to file for bankruptcy as winners of small prizes three to five years later. This suggests that insufficient self-control leads many winners of substantial lottery prizes to splurge rather than save.[15] Indeed, a study at a large Mexican retail chain shows that customers who are most likely to default on their credit are those who spend large portions of their purchases on luxuries. Luxury spenders are also likely to be the ones with the least self-control, able to whittle away large lottery prizes into nothing, and proceed into default and bankruptcy.[16]

Temptations are all around us today, from plasma television sets to iPads and luxury automobiles. iPads could hardly be imagined a century ago but temptations abounded then as now. Early in the twentieth century, consumers were tempted by furniture displayed in the catalogs of Sears Roebuck and Montgomery Ward. Spiegel's catalog added the temptation of easy credit.[17]

Incentives help in the task of self-control, whether the task of ceasing smoking or the task of increasing savings. One study divided smokers who wanted to quit into two groups. Money was deposited in accounts for the people of the first group, money that they could have six months later if urine tests showed that they were free of nicotine. Otherwise, the money would go to charity. People who were offered that incentive were more likely to quit smoking during the six months than people in the second group who received no incentive. Moreover, people in the first group were also likely to stay off smoking after twelve months.[18] Nature, reflected in our genes, affects our mastery of self-control. The MAOA gene encodes monoamine oxidase A, an enzyme that affects neurotransmitters such as serotonin, dopamine, and epinephrine in parts of the brain that regulate impulsiveness and cognitive ability. Some forms of the MAOA gene are associated with impulsive and addictive behavior as well as lack of conscientiousness. These forms of the gene are also associated with the accumulation of credit card debt, reflecting deficient self-control.[19]

The battle of self-control waged in the brain is illuminated in functional magnetic resonance imaging. Parts of the limbic system associated with the midbrain dopamine system light up when we are offered immediate rewards, while regions of the lateral prefrontal cortex and posterior parietal cortex are turned on when we must choose between smaller immediate rewards, such as one marshmallow, and larger delayed rewards, such as two marshmallows. Our choices to exert self-control or succumb to temptation are determined in the battle between the two brain systems. We choose to wait when the frontal-parietal system wins.[20]

Heroin addicts are more likely to lose the self-control battle than those not addicted. People in both groups were offered a choice between immediate but smaller money awards and larger awards to be paid with a delay ranging from a one week to six months. Heroin addicts were much more likely than nonaddicts to choose the immediate smaller award and their degree of impatience corresponded to a measure of impulsiveness.[21]

Resisting Temptation

Conscientiousness is a personality trait at the other end of impulsiveness. Conscientious people have a high propensity to plan. They tend to agree with the statement "Before going on a vacation, I spend a great deal of time examining where I would most like to go and what I would like to do." Those of us who agree with this statement are more likely to accumulate substantial wealth than those who disagree with it.[22]

Foods that enhance levels of serotonin improve self-control and reduce impulsive choice. Thanksgiving dinner provides a good setting for a study of the effect of food on self-control because the traditional Thanksgiving meal combines foods rich in tryptophan, such as turkey, with foods rich in carbohydrates, such as mashed potatoes. Tryptophan is the amino acid that synthesizes serotonin, and carbohydrates have the capacity to enhance the relative concentration of tryptophan by lowering the concentration of competing amino acids. The effects of Thanksgiving meals are evident on Black Friday, the Friday after Thanksgiving, when buyers stand in lines at stores, waiting for doors to open. People who had the traditional Thanksgiving dinner exhibited lower impulsiveness, reflected in a lower willingness to buy a Dell Home Inspiron personal computer on Black Friday, than people who had pizza, quesadilla, lasagna, pasta, burritos, salmon, or noodles.[23]

We are regularly advised not to shop for food when we are hungry. This is good advice because hunger diminishes our self-control as it diminishes our blood sugar. Blood sugar is brain fuel, making it easier to think. The decline in self-control when our blood sugar is low is evident not only in choices of food but also in choices of money. People who drank a sugary soft drink before being asked to choose between a small but immediate amount of money and a larger but delayed amount of money were more inclined to wait for the larger amount than people who drank a soft drink that contained an artificial sweetener.[24]

It is easier to resist the temptation of a chocolate cake when we do not face it, and it is easier for men to resist the temptation of a woman's pretty face when they do not see it. Men who saw photographs of attractive women were impatient, likely to choose the small immediate amount of money rather than wait for the larger but delayed amount. But photographs of less-attractive women had no such effect on men. Women were no more likely to choose the small immediate amount after seeing photographs of men, whether attractive or not. But they were more likely to be impatient after seeing photographs of attractive cars, choosing the small immediate amount rather than wait for the delayed larger one.[25]

We resist the temptation of chocolate by buying it in small quantities, and we resist the temptation of chocolate cake by pushing it away. This is what I do when a waiter places a cake in front of me before I have a chance to say, "No, thank you." Pushing temptation away is effective in bolstering self-control and so is pulling a goal closer. This push-and-pull is evident in an experiment where people faced temptation-related activities, such as partying, and goal-related activities, such as studying. The people in the experiment were asked to push a lever away from them or pull it toward them when presented with a temptation or a goal. People were quicker to push the lever away from them when faced with a temptation and quicker to pull the lever toward them when faced with a goal.[26]

Pride, Guilt, and Anger

Success at self-control and failure are both motivated by emotions and are accompanied by them. We experience guilty pleasures when guilt accompanies the pleasure of surrendering to temptation. And pride bolsters self-control and accompanies it. This was the pride felt by John Shedd, celebrated as a prodigious saver in the pages of the *World's Work* magazine a century ago.[27] Shedd was 22 years old when first employed by Marshall Field. He worked for ten dollars a week for a few months and then for 12. At the end of the first year Field came around and asked him how much he had saved. Shedd replied, "Five dollars a week. . . ." Field complimented Shedd on this achievement and turned to ask a high-salaried man in the same department how much he has saved. "Nothing," said the man. "You will not receive another cent increase from me until you have demonstrated your ability to save," said Field.

More recently, *Money* magazine celebrated Cathy and Brian Lindberg who accumulated a six-figure portfolio from a $44,000 annual income. How do a career serviceman and a former $10-an-hour silk-screen printer do that? "We pay ourselves first," said Cathy. "We have money automatically taken from our bank account and invested every month," said Brian. "Most people wait to save until the end of the month when they've paid all their bills. But by then, there's usually nothing left to pay yourself."[28]

Exercising self-control and resisting temptation brings pride, but it also provokes anger, as illustrated by New York City's Mayor Michael Bloomberg, a man obsessed with his weight yet cranky when he forces himself to diet.[29] It is as if our temptation self who is hungry is angry at our virtuous self who wants to diet. In one experiment, people could choose one of two thank-you gifts, a virtuous apple or a tempting chocolate candy bar. Later in the experiment they had to choose one of two movies, an anger-themed one, such as *Anger Management,* and a non-anger-themed one, such as *Billy Madison.* People who chose the virtuous apple were more likely to choose the anger-themed movie than people who chose the tempting chocolate candy bar.[30]

The "Voice of Should" and the "Voice of Want"

The voice of virtue is the "voice of should." We should choose an apple and we should choose exercise at the health club. The "voice of want" is the voice of temptation. We want the chocolate candy bar and we want to sit on our sofa, watching a movie, rather than running on a treadmill at the health club. We tend to be unrealistically optimistic about our ability to listen to the voice of should and muster the self-control necessary to withstand temptation. Managers of health clubs exploit that unrealistic optimism, promoting contracts that provide unlimited visits for a monthly fee. It turns out that the monthly contracts work better for health clubs than for their members. Club members who chose the monthly contracts visited their clubs less than five times each month on average, in effect paying a fee exceeding $17 per visit. They would have saved money by paying the $10 per-visit fee.[31]

Managers of credit card companies, like managers of health clubs, design their offerings with knowledge that we are unrealistically optimistic about our ability to listen to the voice of should and silence the voice of want. A documentary about credit card practices included an interview with Shailesh Mehta, the former head of the Providian credit card company. One practice called for inducing cardholders to believe their credit cards are free by eliminating the annual fee. "We made it look like it's a giveaway," said Mehta, "and took it back in the form of . . . penalty pricing or stealth pricing." Mehta understood very well that we are better at self-control before we face temptation. "When people make the buying decision, they don't look at the penalty fees because they never believe they'll be late. They never believe they'll be over-limit, right?"

Elizabeth Blascruz received her credit card from a company that emulated Providian's practices. "I got an offer for a credit card with a credit line of $500," she said. "I remember when the balance was about $480 or so, and I was late on a payment, they added on a late fee and increased my interest rate. Well, that, of course, took it above the $500 credit line. And with that, they charged me an over-the-limit fee. That bill had maybe $60, $70 dollars of fees. And every month, it was the same thing. Unless I paid all that and more, which of course, at the time, I couldn't afford to do, there was no way I could ever get ahead."[32]

Excessive Self-Control and Frugality

Insufficient self-control might be more common than excessive self-control, but excessive self-control does exist. Indeed, one survey found that excessive self-control is as prevalent as insufficient self-control. In particular, excessive self-control is reflected in the tendency to spend less today than what we describe as our ideal level of spending, whereas insufficient self-control is reflected in the tendency to spend more today than what we describe as our ideal level of spending.[33]

People who accumulate considerable savings are people who have mastered the skills of self-control, by nature, nurture, or their combination. They tend to be frugal people, spending conservatively and agreeing with statements such as "Making better use of my resources makes me feel good." Some of them are "millionaires next door," whom you would never know were wealthy. "We live well below our means,"[34] says the typical next-door millionaire. "We are fastidious investors. On average, we invest nearly 20 percent of our household realized income each year." The millionaires not only exercise self-control but also teach it to their children. The first in the list of rules is "Never tell children that their parents are wealthy." The second is "No matter how wealthy you are, teach your children discipline and frugality."[35]

We are driven to spend or refrain from spending by the balance between the anticipated pleasure of spending and the anticipated pain. That balance varies from person to person and levels of frugality vary along with that balance. Tightwads go much further than mere frugality. The prospect of spending money pains tightwads. Spendthrifts, in contrast, are not pained much by that prospect.[36] The interplay in the brain is revealed in functional MRI of people who see a product followed by its price and then are asked to decide whether to buy it or not. Seeing the price caused greater activation in the insula among people who decided not to buy the product than among people whose choice was to buy.[37] The insula is a brain region associated with painful sensations such as social exclusion and disgusting odors.

A 1930 book tells a story about Russell Sage, a wealthy man and well-known tightwad. "Mr. Sage was parsimonious, close-fisted, and . . . his personality was not particularly pleasing. . . . Mr. Sage simply wanted the money." Sage left home to pick up some shoes he left to be patched by the cobbler. "He didn't send the butler because Mr. Sage believed in carrying all money transactions personally. In his hand he held fifty cents to pay the cobbler. The sidewalk was icy, and Mr. Sage slipped, fell, and the fifty-cent piece rolled away. He spent some time pawing around in the dark looking for it. In the end he found not only the fifty cents, but also thirty-five cents more that somebody else had lost in the same place."[38]

People with excessive self-control are reluctant to indulge. They often benefit from devices that counter their excessive self-control. These relax self-control by inducing people to anticipate their future regrets at not indulging, reminding them of their own regrets about refraining from indulging in the past, and the regrets of others.[39] Other devices include commitment to future indulgence. Women in one experiment were given a choice between a spa package valued at $80 or $85 in cash. Most chose the spa package, explaining that they were afraid that they would spend the cash on utilitarian products such as groceries if they did not commit themselves to the luxury of the spa package.[40]

There are great benefits to an effective combination of mental accounting and self-control everywhere in life, beyond financial life. Yet its greatest benefit in our financial life is in helping us balance our spending and saving over our lifetimes, so we do not live like kings when we are young only to live as paupers when we are old, and so we do not live like paupers when we are young only to leave a king's fortune when we are gone. We will examine the balance between spending and saving in the next chapter.

C H A P T E R   7

We Want to Save for Tomorrow and Spend It Today

T wo men stand at an elevator with large orange signs under their arms in a television commercial by a large investment company. The man whose sign says $1,989,203 is glancing furtively at the other man, trying to read his number. The commercial is part of the company's "Number" marketing campaign, aimed at simplifying our saving plans by calculating the Number, the amount of money we need to have by the time we retire.

WHAT IS YOUR NUMBER?

The survey underlying this marketing campaign reveals what we are anxious about our retirement numbers. Two-thirds of us say that we think about the Number at least sometimes. Yet almost half of us say that calculating the Number is difficult and we don't know where to start. When I clicked on the Number Web site, it asked for my age, whether I'm married, my income, the age at which I plan to retire, the income I'll need in retirement, and when I plan to die. Actually, the company was circumspect about the last item, asking about the age through which I'll need income. I got my Number, precise to the last dollar.

The surprising fact in the survey is not that almost half of us think that calculating the Number is difficult, but that more than half of us think that it is easy. In fact, calculating the Number is almost hopelessly difficult, as

evident in the debate among economists about whether we are well prepared for comfortable retirements or doomed to exhaust our savings before we exhaust our lives. Christian Weller of the Economic Policy Institute
stated that "the average American household has virtually no chance to
reach an adequate retirement savings in the next 50 years."[1] And one economic report proclaimed that almost half of us are at risk of substantial declines in income during retirement.[2] Yet other economists have concluded
that the state of retirement savings is not bad at all. They found that those
of us who approach retirement age are saving more than our parents, and
they argue that our financial burden would likely lighten once our children
become financially independent. Moreover, we can rely on government
programs that pay most of our medical expenses and at least minimal living expenses.[3]

Calculating the Number is exceedingly difficult, not only because it requires much information, but also because much of that information is
uncertain. We need to know the future rate of return on our savings and
the future rate of inflation. Neither is certain. We need to know our medical
and nursing care expenses since the number of private-sector employers
who offer retiree health benefits is declining and there is great uncertainty
about medical care that is now provided by the government. Moreover,
we must set the consequences of saving too little, spending too much, and
running out of money in retirement, against the consequences of saving
too much, scrimping too much, and leaving much more money behind
when we are gone. Some recommend that we use the "4 Percent Rule" as
our "glide path," spending 4 percent of our savings each year until we spend
our last dollar just before we take our last breath. But this rule is far from
perfect, likely to lead us to accumulate too much savings when financial
markets are up and spend too little when they are down.[4]

Some are still looking for the Number. Others are trying to identify the
glide path. But most of us just muddle our way through the years in an uncertain world, trying to strike a balance between saving too little and saving
too much. Our capacities for mental accounting and self-control help us
along our way at some times and stand in our way at other times. Mental
accounting helps us distinguish what we are permitted to spend from what
we must save. Self-control helps us manage our conflicting desires to spend
and save.

MENTAL ACCOUNTS FOR CAPITAL AND INCOME

Money is fungible in the eyes of rational investors. A dollar labeled dividends is as green as a dollar labeled capital, so rational investors are indifferent between the two. But money is not always fungible in the eyes of normal investors, and distinctions between monies affect our behavior, whether spending, saving, or investing. We give ourselves permission to spend income dollars from dividends; interest; and wages on rent, groceries, and movies. But we are reluctant to give ourselves permission to dip into capital by selling stocks or bonds and spending that money on the same rent, groceries, and movies. A gift card might seem fungible with cash, especially when it is for a store where we regularly shop, but we distinguish gift cards from cash. We typically spend more than the amounts on the gift cards we receive, but we typically save some of the cash we receive as gifts. Moreover, we tend to buy luxury products we really enjoy with gift cards, while we buy practical ho-hum products with gifts of cash.[5]

Don't Dip into Capital

More than 4,000 shareholders of Con Edison, New York's supplier of gas and electricity, overflowed New York's Commodore Hotel in May 1974. Many shareholders were left outside, including Sydell Pflaum, a 76-year-old widow who relied on the $90 quarterly dividend for precious financial support. The meeting followed Con Ed's announcement that it was suspending its dividend because its cash was depleted by soaring fuel prices in the wake of the Arab oil embargo. But Con Ed's reasoning did not sway Pflaum, who flew in from Miami Beach, fuming with anger. "Where is Luce?" she asked, referring to Charles F. Luce, Con Ed's chairman. "Since I can't get in, maybe he'll at least pay my way back home."

Con Ed's shareholders at the meeting described poignantly the hardship of life without dividends. A woman said: "Who is going to pay my rent? I had a husband. Now Con Ed has to be my husband." A man said: "A lady came over to me a minute ago and she said to me, 'Please say a word for the senior citizens.' And she had tears in her eyes. And I really know what she means by that. She simply means that now she will get only one check a month, and that will be her Social Security, and she's not going to make it, because you have denied her that dividend."

I remember reading the Con Ed news at the time and wondering about the contrast between financial theory describing the behavior of rational investors and the actual behavior of normal investors. When rational investors do not receive their company-paid dividend check, they create "homemade dividends" by selling stocks and spending the proceeds as if they were company-paid dividends. But normal investors consider selling stocks for homemade dividends as an egregious violation of the don't-dip-into-capital rule, a saving and spending rule combining mental accounting and self-control.[6]

We apply the rule by placing dividends from stocks and interest from bonds in "income" mental accounts and distinguish them from "capital" mental accounts that contain the stocks and bonds themselves. Clear boundaries between mental accounts containing income and mental accounts containing capital, coupled with rules that prohibit violating the boundaries of these mental accounts, help us when we are tempted by weak self-control to dip into capital. We feel free to spend income, but we prohibit ourselves from ever dipping into capital by selling stocks or bonds and spending the proceeds.

It is no wonder that Con Ed shareholders refused to sell stocks. Indeed, comments by shareholders at the Con Ed meeting tell us that they considered dividends as the equivalent of salaries. One shareholder said, "Until we get the dividends, the officers should get no salaries." Another demanded that Luce take a 50 percent cut in his pay. "We took a 100 percent cut," he said. Luce himself knew why his investors wanted dividends. Speaking with a heavy heart he said: "Investors buy Con Edison stock for assured income. . . . Most of our stockholders are women, many widowed. . . . When the dividend check doesn't come, there is a real hardship for many people."

Dipping into Capital: Then and Now

The distinction between capital in the form of stocks and income in the form of dividends is not a relic of the 1970s. Pain in 2008, the time of the financial crisis, was inflicted by banks rather than by utilities. Jo-Ann

Cooper, a 60-year-old marketing consultant, owned 2,900 shares of Bank of America, and the cut in its dividend reduced her quarterly income by more than $900. Yet Cooper refused to sell her Bank of America shares as Con Ed shareholder refused to sell theirs decades before.[7]

Jonathan Clements, who wrote a personal finance column in the *Wall Street Journal,* tried to persuade a reader to substitute homemade dividends for company-paid dividends. He had no success. The reader wrote in 2007:

"I'm 72 years old, married, and retired with a part-time job. We are going to file an income of $63,800 for 2006, which includes both salaries (my part-time jobs) and our Social Security checks. We have $150,000 in American Funds stock, which has been frustrating. Are there products that you recommend where the fund money can be used for some sort of income (dividends)?"

"Beyond the lack of dividends," asked Clements, "are you happy with how American Funds have performed? If so, you could simply create your own dividend each year, by selling a part of your holdings."

"Thank you for your response," answered the reader. "Yes, I am happy with the American Funds, but dipping into capital does hurt a little at my age; must be anxiety."[8] What is true for Jo-Ann Cooper in 2008, Clements' reader in 2007, and Con Ed's shareholders in 1974 is generally true, evident in a large-scale study; we are more willing to spend dividend dollars than capital dollars. Investors who received dividends spent almost all of them, as if they were salaries. Moreover, investors who received much in dividends spent more overall than investors who received little in dividends, even when the two groups had similar overall incomes.[9]

Invisible Dips into Capital

In truth, cash dividends paid by companies are dips into capital since stock prices decline when cash dividends are paid. There is $1,000 of capital in shares of stocks worth $1,000, but that $1,000 declines to $900 when a company pays a $100 cash dividend. We dip into capital when we spend the dividend because we are now left with stocks worth only $900. This is why, rationally, a $100 dividend check received from a company is no different from a $100 homemade dividend created by selling $100 worth of stock. Yet the change of label from capital to dividends facilitates dips into capital by making such dips invisible.

Stock dividends, unlike cash dividends, require no company cash. And stock dividends illustrate further the power of the labels of mental accounts. A company pays stock dividends when it sends each shareholder an extra share for each number of shares she already owns. But the company sends shareholders no cash. A shareholder who had four shares before a stock dividend might now have five. Stock dividends make no sense to rational investors because they do the equivalent of cutting a pizza into five slices rather than four without increasing the size of the pizza. Yet many normal shareholders who are deprived of their usual cash dividend are happier when their companies pay stock dividends rather than no dividend at all. One shareholder at the Con Ed meeting asked why a stock dividend was not paid "so at least the blow which was given to stockholders by the omission of the [cash] dividend would have been much less." Luce, Con Ed's chairman, answered that a stock dividend would not make shareholders better off, echoing the rational pizza logic. But a stock dividend would have made many Con Ed shareholders happier because stock dividends, like cash dividends, are labeled as income and therefore can be sold without a visible violation of the don't-dip-into-capital rule. Normal investors have not changed much since 1974. First Horizon, a bank squeezed by the financial crisis of 2008, replaced its cash dividend with a stock dividend. The bank acknowledged that its stock dividend places no money into the pockets of shareholders but said that some shareholders find the additional shares useful.[10]

SAVING AND SPENDING OVER A LIFETIME

The task of planning the sequence of spending and saving over our lifetimes is daunting, made more complicated by uncertainty and conflicting desires to spend and save. Insufficient self-control might leave us destitute in old age, while excessive self-control might lead us to live as if we are destitute. It is difficult to find the right balance between spending and saving, and it is even more difficult to enforce that balance.

We want some experiences now and other experiences later. This is true for our experience in colonoscopies and visiting abrasive aunts as much as it is true about our experience in saving, investing, and spending. Patients undergoing colonoscopies were prompted every sixty seconds to report their level of pain on a scale from "no pain at all" to "intolerable pain." Later they were asked to assess the entire experience. The two features of a colonoscopy most closely associated with the assessment of the entire experience were the most painful minute during the colonoscopy and the level of pain at the end of the colonoscopy. In particular, people judged the colonoscopy experience worse when the most painful minute was relatively painful, but they judged the experience better when the end of the colonos-copy was relatively painless.[11] People prefer improving sequences, whether colonoscopies that end on a painless note, sequences where the every year's salary is higher than the year before, or weekend visits that end with good friends rather than with irritating aunts. Imagine that you were asked to schedule two visits to a city where you once lived, one this weekend and one on the following weekend. You'll spend one weekend with former work associates you like a lot, and one with an irritating, abrasive aunt who is a terrible cook. Who would you prefer to visit first and who would you post-pone to last? Nine in ten people preferred the improving sequence in which they keep the best for last.[12] The clash between the impatient desire for a reward now and the desire for an improving sequence sometimes ends in a compromise, as when we prefer job offers that include a bonus now and a salary sequence that increases in future years.[13]

Self-Control and Outside Control

Reminders to save bolster self-control and enhance savings but they are rarely sufficient.[14] Low- and moderate-income people bolster self-control and diminish the temptation to spend by paying more taxes than they owe during the year so they might receive substantial tax refunds at the end of the year. Yet temptation is only postponed till tax-refund time. Programs that make it easy to deposit portions of tax refunds into saving accounts help resist temptation.[15] Payroll deductions to 401(k) saving accounts bolster self-control during our working years. We need not fight the temptation to spend 401(k) money since it never passes through our hands. Later on, the prospect of penalties bolsters our self-control when we are tempted to withdraw money from our 401(k) accounts before the age of 59½. Payroll deductions to Social Security bolster our self-control with outside control;

no 30-year-old can touch his Social Security money even for the shiniest of new cars. Moreover, while we might deplete our 401(k) in retirement or even earlier, we cannot deplete our Social Security money since it is paid monthly, allowing no advance payments. Pensions resemble Social Security in their lifetime guarantee and restrictions on advance payments. In retirement, my father would tell about the time, decades before, when he asked to tap his pension fund for an extra room to our home for our growing family. He was sad when the managers of the fund turned him down, but he was grateful to them in retirement.

Football players find self-control difficult when they are young and earning millions, and the self-control of many does not improve in retirement, when the stream of income dries. Football players suffer repeated and brutal injuries in the game, and early-onset dementia is unfortunately common among them. Retired football players have a pressing need for lifetime care, yet nine in ten players are willing to give up that lifetime care for immediate cash. "We're all creatures of the immediate, and, if someone has an immediate need, they figure they'll just have to take their chances," said Ron Mix, a former football player who now negotiates compensation for fellow players along with Mel Owens, another former player. "What I think is wise versus what he thinks is wise is irrelevant," said Owens, "because he thinks he's making a good decision. Might be."[16]

Spouses bolster self-control. Men across many countries view women as better budgeters, possessing greater self-control.[17, 18, 19] The majority of men in the Philippines reported in a survey that they would be profligate in spending if their wives did not control their incomes. Men in the Philippines often keep some of their incomes from their wives surreptitiously, a practice so common it has a name, Kupit, which literally means to pilfer, filch, or steal in small quantities. Female empowerment is not only a worthy goal on its own but also the road to the goal of increased saving. A study in the Philippines found that savings accounts that commit their holders to save enhance both savings and the power of women in decisions within families.[20]

Rotating savings and credit associations harness the power of the community to supplement self-control with outside control to facilitate saving through commitment, social rewards, and social sanctions. The associations are especially popular among women in South America, Asia, and Africa. Members of each association meet regularly, and each contributes an amount to a common pot. The pot goes to one member, commonly chosen by lottery, who might use it to invest in a business, buy a television set, or pay school fees. The role of associations in building social ties in communities is as important as its role in facilitating savings. Meetings are social occasions, and recipients of the common pots are often required to host meetings at their homes and provide food and drink. One woman said, "We were brought into a group to get more strength. We started to develop the ability to speak to each other, voicing ourselves, and then we went into savings and credit."[21]

In Peru, default rates of poor borrowers decline when they are responsible for the loans of one another. Borrowers who share one culture or live in one neighborhood form strong social connections to their fellow borrowers and are more likely to repay their loans than borrowers with weaker social connections. Moreover, relationships between those who pay and those who default deteriorate, indicating that paying members know the defaulting ones and punish them.[22] The threat of such punishment serves as outside control. Wesabe.com harnesses the power of the community through the Internet. It describes itself as part money management tool and part community. "We believe that one person's good financial decision can be leveraged to an entire community," it wrote. "Find solutions to your money problems . . . you're not alone in wanting a better financial life."

Investors did not have the self-control help of 401(k) and Social Security programs a century ago but they were not without help. The *World's Work* advocated a method to bolster self-control by limiting the temptation of cash. Here is its advice to a young man who has saved $1,000 out of his earnings: First, invest $1,000 in a first-class bond. Next, estimate of how much you can save next year. Next, borrow the amount you plan to save and invest it in another good bond. Last, arrange to repay the borrowed amount in equal monthly installments coming due on your monthly paydays.[23] The New York Stock Exchange designed a similar program in 1953. Keith Funston, the president of the Exchange said that they "make it easy for people to buy securities by small but regular cash payments." Payments could be as small as $40 every three months, or as much as $1,000 a month.[24]

Methods that bolster self-control are useful in accumulating savings or ceasing smoking, but purists insist that smokers quit "cold turkey" and purists insist that we employ no more than "sound moral discipline" to accumulate savings. Soon after the crash of 1929, the *Literary Digest* quoted Hastings Lyon, a lawyer and lecturer on finance at Columbia University, saying that sound moral discipline is one of the finest things about the responsibility of investing. Lyon was impatient with the argument that people should take out insurance in order to force themselves to invest money. "A man ought to achieve the moral dignity of being able to save without the pressure of [insurance] premium or other contract instatements."[25]

CONVERTING INCOME INTO CAPITAL AND CAPITAL INTO INCOME

The right dividend for us when we are young and saving for retirement is zero. Young investors who collect dividends might be tempted to spend them, and their self-control might not be strong enough to withstand temptation. The right dividend for us when we are older and retired is higher. We need this higher dividend to supplement income from pensions and Social Security. But we must calibrate that supplement in retirement so our money lasts our lifetimes. The necessary supplement is smaller for retirees with high incomes than for retirees with low incomes. Indeed, a study of many investors found that the preference for stocks that pay high dividends is especially strong among older investors, and particularly among those with low income from sources other than dividends.[26]

Dividends from stocks form a system that we use to regulate our spending and saving. Interest from bonds is another system. Retirees are at a difficult spot when interest rates on bonds drop close to zero. They can choose to live on diminished interest from their bonds or dip into the capital of their bonds, selling some to supplement their income. Neither choice is palatable. Inflation imposes great costs on bondholders, diminishing the value of their bonds' capital, but inflation brings bondholders one benefit, obscuring dips into the bonds' capital. A $1,000 bond that pays $40 of interest per year has a 4 percent "nominal" yield. But if the annual rate of inflation is 3 percent, the "real" yield is only 1 percent. In effect, holders of the bond receive $10 in real interest income, which takes into account the effects of inflation, and they dip $30 into their bond's capital. Dorothy O. Mulvey, an 82-year-old former bond trader, advised fellow retirees to dip into their bonds when interest rates dropped, but she would have much preferred to advise them otherwise. "That pains me," she said. "I'm a conservative person."[27] Retirees dip into capital, whether stocks or bonds, only after cutting on dinners at restaurants and trips to visit the grandchildren.

In retirement, most of us spend more than we earn, reducing our savings, while during our working years we spend less than we earn, accumulating savings. In retirement we need systems that convert capital into income, such as in the form of dividends and interest, while in our working years we need systems that convert income into capital. Piggybanks are good at converting income into capital, making it easy to put coins in and hard to take them out even when tempted. We tend to think about the piggybanks we give to children, but piggybanks are also useful for adults. "We used to buy a 3-liter bottle of Coke every day," said Socorro Machado, a Nicaraguan homemaker. The daily $1.75 burdened the family's budget. Then Catholic Relief Services, an aid organization, provided Machado and her neighbors padlocked wooden boxes into which they can put their money. "Now we buy a bottle of Coke just once a week, and we put the money in savings"[28]

Houses serve as big piggybanks. Monthly mortgage payments made out of income combine a portion that goes toward mortgage interest with another portion that adds to the equity capital in the house. Equity capital from mortgage payments is augmented by equity capital from appreciation in the value of houses to form the largest portion of the capital of most American families, even after the devastating blows of the recent financial crisis.

Piggybanks can be broken and their coins spent, but it was difficult to break the home equity piggybank decades ago, before the advent of mortgage refinancing. More recently, some homeowners refinanced their homes to obtain mortgages with lower interest rates, but others tapped their home equity, converted it into income, and spent it. Many of these were forced into foreclosure when the value of their homes fell below the amount they owed on their mortgages.

DIPPING INTO CAPITAL WITH HIGHER DIVIDEND INCOME

Alpine Dynamic Dividend Fund, one of several "dividend capture" mutual funds, aims to increase the flow of dividends beyond the usual four quarterly payments. The fund buys stocks of companies that pay generous dividends just before they pay their quarterly dividends and holds them long enough to collect their dividends. Afterward, the fund sells these stocks and buys other stocks just as they are about to pay their quarterly dividends. This way, the fund collects six dividend payments per year from its stocks rather than the usual four, boosting the amount it pays to shareholders as dividend income. The dividend capture strategy does not increase the total return of the fund since the prices of the stocks the fund buys drop when dividends are paid. In truth, shareholders dip into capital, losing in capital what they gain in income. But dips into capital are obscure rather than transparent.

"Split-capital" funds offer another method for opaque dips into capital. The Gartmore Monthly Income Fund, a split-capital fund, emphasized the attraction of high dividend income in its brochure. "In the current falling interest rate environment, the days of double-digit income returns appear to be long gone. However, the thirst for income remains undiminished."

The "income group" of split-capital funds receives all the dividends collected from the stocks in the fund, plus a fixed amount of capital at the end of the fund's life. The "capital group" receives no dividends, but it receives any capital appreciation beyond the fixed amount paid to the income group. This split increases the dividend income paid to the income group of shareholders beyond what they would have received without the split, but it deprives the income group of capital appreciation beyond a fixed amount, thereby dipping into capital.

"Covered calls," created when we sell call options on stocks we own, also obscure dips into capital. The Chicago Board of Options Exchange (CBOE) describes covered calls as a way to generate income. The CBOE notes on its Web site, "[T]he covered call generates income from the premium received from the call contract's sale that can supplement any dividend income paid to eligible underlying stockholders." Covered calls are not a money printing machine. What they add to the income pockets of investors they take it out of the capital pockets since they deprive stockholders of capital appreciation beyond a fixed stock price. Still, obscured dips into capital with covered calls make them useful for retirees. Arnold Feldman, a 82-year-old man, sold calls on his shares of Exxon Mobil Corp. "The returns on CDs and money markets and bonds are so low that I'm looking for a way to generate better returns and some income."[29]

Several Japanese mutual funds invented ingenious opaque methods to convert capital into income. One fund invests in stocks of utilities that pay high dividends. The fund sends its shareholders monthly checks it labels dividends. But the checks include both dividends received by the mutual fund from the stocks it holds and capital gains that come from increases in the prices of these stocks. In fact, the fund's shareholders dip into capital as they cash their checks, but such dipping is obscured by the dividend label on the checks.

Another Japanese fund goes a step further. The fund invests in bonds, but the monthly dividend checks it sends to shareholders include not only the interest it collects from the bonds and the capital appreciation of these bonds, but also the proceeds from the sale of bonds themselves. In time, the value of this mutual fund will dwindle to zero as more and more of its bonds are sold and the proceeds of these bonds, along with interest and capital gains, are converted into dividends.

American mutual fund companies, such as Vanguard and Fidelity, also offer funds that convert capital to income, although their conversion is transparent and violations of the don't-dip-into-capital rule are obvious. Vanguard's Managed Payout Funds offers three funds, the Growth Focus Fund, which pays 3 percent each year, the Growth and Distribution Fund, which pays 5 percent, and the Distribution Focus Fund, which pays 7 percent. Vanguard states that money for these payments will come from income, including interest and dividends, as well as from capital, including capital gains and capital itself. Yet Vanguard tries to avoid dipping into capital even in its 7 percent Distribution Focus Fund. It writes in its prospectus that "the Fund does seek to preserve the "nominal" (or original) value of invested capital over the long term."

We want to spread our saving and spending over our lifetimes so we do not live as if we are rich when we are young only to live as poor when we are old. Yet what we really want is to be rich throughout our lifetimes, free from any fear of poverty. Hope for riches and freedom from the fear of poverty are our twin desires and the focus of the next chapter.

CHAPTER 8

We Want Hope for Riches and Freedom from the Fear of Poverty

omeone is going to win the lottery," said an Internet broker's advertisement in the late 1990s, "Just not you." Stocks were the lottery tickets of the stock market boom, and Alteon WebSystem's shares were David Callisch's lottery tickets. Callisch hoped to be rich when he joined Alteon in 1997, and his lottery tickets seemed to have the winning number. By 2000, when Nortel Networks bought Alteon, Callisch's shares were worth $10 million. He planned to retire from his 7 a.m. to 11 p.m. workdays and spend more time with his children. "I should have stopped, sold it all, taken some time off and figured what to do," said a sad Callisch later. Instead, he held on to his shares, and when he finally sold them in 2002, they were worth a small fraction of their $10 million value.[1]

RICHES AND POVERTY

Callisch's aspirations to be rich enough to retire early and stay home with his children are shared by the many who gamble on stocks and lottery tickets. Most lose, but some win. Robert Harris, an ironworker, won $270 million in the Mega Millions lottery. He chose his lottery numbers by the birth dates of his grandchildren. Winning "is just great," said Harris. "To know I won't have to go ask for a job or work for somebody else, that I can finally stay home and enjoy my grandkids." Harris delighted in telling his incredulous boss that he was quitting. "When I told him that I did hit and I wasn't coming back, he realized that it's true. He asked me to give it back for a few weeks and finish what I was doing, but I told him, 'No, thank you.'"[2]

Concentrating portfolios in a single stock is unreasonable, perhaps irrational. So is buying lottery tickets. We can reasonably expect to lose half our money when we buy lottery tickets since lottery operators typically pay in prizes only half of the money they collect. Yet Harris and countless others buy lottery tickets. Callisch could have easily reduced his risk without reducing the return he could reasonably expect. He could have done so by diversifying his portfolio among many stocks rather than concentrating it in Alteon's. Indeed, Callisch was urged to diversify his portfolio by his relatives, his colleagues, and his broker. But he would not listen. Callisch is one of many investors who do not diversify their portfolios. The average number of stocks in portfolios of investors at a large brokerage company was four, about the same number reported decades ago.[3]

Callisch and Harris might not be rational, but they are perfectly normal. They share two desires with rest of us, hope for riches and freedom from the fear of poverty. Hope for riches urges us to invest our entire portfolio in stocks and lottery tickets. Fear of poverty urges us to invest our entire portfolio in government bonds and hold tight to Social Security. When President Franklin Roosevelt introduced Social Security he said: "We can never insure one hundred percent of the population against one hundred percent of the hazards and vicissitudes of life, but we have tried to frame a law which will give some measure of protection to the average citizen and to his family against the loss of a job and against poverty-ridden old age."[4]

We resolve our internal conflict by dividing our portfolios into mental accounts, some devoted to hope for riches and others devoted to freedom from the fear of poverty. Self-control and control by others help us when we are tempted to dip into the wrong mental account. Yet it is hard to resist temptation. Fred Schwed, Jr., the author of *Where Are the Customers' Yachts?*, told of a man, seven-and-a-half million dollars rich in 1929, who gave his wife a million and a half dollars in government bonds to be placed in the freedom-from-fear-of-poverty mental account. "My dearest," he said, "these securities are now yours; they are not mine. They represent quite as much income as we shall ever really need for the rest of our lives." The man, aware of his self-control problem, went beyond relinquishing to his wife control over the bonds. "But if by any incredible chance I should ever come to you and ask for these bonds back again," he said, "under no circumstance give them to me, for you will know I have gone crazy." He placed the other six million in the hope-for-riches mental account and kept control over it to "continue to speculate and make more money." Unfortunately for the man and his wife, his control rule was not strict enough. Six months later he needed money to recover the six million he had lost. "He went for the money to the wife of his bosom, who demurred. But he was a persuasive man: He got the bonds back. Temporarily."[5]

Layers of the Portfolio Pyramid

We know portfolios such as the one constructed by the man in Schwed's story as "behavioral portfolios," arranged as layered pyramids of mental accounts.[6] We place bonds in a mental accounting layer at the bottom of the pyramid, designed to free us from the fear of poverty, while we place stocks in a mental accounting layer closer to the top of the pyramid, intended to give us hope of riches. In practice, pyramid portfolios include many layers, each associated with a goal, retirement income at the bottom of the pyramid, college education in the middle, and at the top perhaps being rich enough to tell our boss we're quitting to spend our lives on cruise ships.

Layered portfolio pyramids have been with us for many years. A 1929 article recommended insurance for the bottom layer of the portfolio pyramid and a cash reserve in the savings bank in the layer above that. When these layers have been set, investors are in position to buy safe bonds and guaranteed mortgages on real estate. The next layer can be composed of preferred stocks that promise higher returns than guaranteed mortgages, and the top layer can consist of common stocks that promise returns exceeding those of preferred stocks.[7]

A 1952 manual of mutual funds listed the layers of portfolios from bottom to top as the income layer, balanced layer, growth layer, and aggressive growth mutual funds. Safe bonds, issued by governments and large corporations are suitable for the income layer; other bonds as well as stocks with generous dividends, such as utility stocks, are suitable for the balanced layer; stocks that pay modest dividends but promise steady increases in their prices are for the growth layer; and stocks that pay no dividends but promise terrific increases in their prices are for the aggressive growth layer.[8]

Gena and John Lovett, people in their late 50s, lost money in the bust following the late 1990s boom, but their layered portfolio provided freedom
from the fear of poverty. One of the layers in the Lovetts' portfolio layers
was devoted to bequests for the kids. Now that layer is empty. Another of
the Lovetts' portfolio layers consists of John Lovett's salary while working.
This layer is intact because John can postpone his retirement. "Our retirement [portfolio] is one-half of what it was a year ago," said Gena. "And
because John works for GE we have mostly GE stock. I suppose we should
have diversified, but GE stock was supposed to be wonderful. John's simply
not looking at retirement. We simply told our kids that we're spending their
inheritance."[9] Postponing retirement when we are in our 50s and spending
the kids' inheritance are sad but not disastrous consequences of a stock
market crash. The Lovetts are no longer rich, but neither are they poor.
Consequences would have turned disastrous, however, if the Lovetts had
no freedom-from-fear-of-poverty layers underlying the hope-for-riches
layers of their portfolio.

Lottery Mentality

Hope for riches is always animating us, sometimes driving us into mania.
In 1999, Alan Greenspan, then chairman of the Federal Reserve Bank,
warned that the dot-com stock mania is like a lottery mania.[10] "What lottery
managers have known for centuries," Greenspan said, "is that you could get
somebody to pay for a one-in-a-million shot more than the [financial] value
of that chance." Greenspan tried to mask the embarrassing link between
stocks and lotteries as best as he could. "That's good for our system," he
said. "With all of its hype and craziness, it's something that, at the end of
the day, probably is more plus than minus." Tony Auth dispensed with
Greenspan's mask in a cartoon linking stocks with lotteries, reminding us
that the government that provides some freedom from the fear of poverty
in the form of Social Security accounts also provides hope for riches in the
form of lotteries.

Government employee: "This is terrible! More and more of our citizens
are becoming addicted to day trading. They all think they'll get rich, but 70
percent of them lose money. As they go further into debt, they run up huge
credit card debt, always thinking they're one trade away from hitting the

jackpot. It's so stupid! They should cut out all this day-trading nonsense. And play the state lotteries."

Indeed, government taxes on gambling can be used to support government programs, including Social Security. Congress is considering a proposal to legalize online betting and collect $42 billion in the process. Congressman Brad Sherman tried to mask it: "We will not pass an Internet gaming bill," he said. "We will pass a bill to do something very important, funded by Internet gaming."[11]

Some who aspire to be rich can reasonably expect to reach their aspirations through steady savings invested in safe bonds. But risky investment in stocks, in small businesses, or even lottery tickets, offer many of us the only hope to reach our aspirations, whether millions in bank accounts, ample retirement incomes, or the means to help our children and grandchildren pay college tuition and buy homes of their own.

"I've dug so many holes for myself over the years," said a lottery player, "that, realistically, winning the lottery may be my only ticket out."[12] This lottery player's perceptions of life and its chances are common. When asked about the most practical way to accumulate several hundred thousand dollars, more than half of surveyed Americans said: Save something each month for many years. But more than one in five said: Win the lottery, and most of these were poor.[13] Wes Ball of the Ball Group, a research and advertising company, said: "We found something we called "lottery mentality." We encountered people who thought it was a complete waste of time to save money. They figured they didn't have enough money to do anything else, so why not spend the money on lottery tickets?"[14]

Lottery players sacrifice the utilitarian benefits of sure money for the emotional benefits of hope. So do football fans who bet on the success of their teams even when the odds favor their opponents.[15] Investors, like lottery players and football fans, often sacrifice money for hope.

Lottery-like stocks, like lottery tickets, offer hope of winning large prizes. Stocks of bankrupt companies are one example of lottery-like stocks. Such stocks usually cost only a few pennies yet carry hope of extraordinary returns if bankrupt companies come back to life. Individual investors are attracted to stocks of bankrupt companies, owning on average 90 percent of them. But stocks of bankrupt companies are losers on average, losing more than 28 percent of their value during the year.[16]

Lotteries and lottery-like stocks attract the same people. Regions of the country where lotteries are popular tend to be regions where investors seek lottery-like stocks.[17] Sometimes lotteries substitute for lottery-like stocks. When the Taiwanese lottery offers large jackpots, it draws investors who would otherwise trade lottery-like stocks.[18]

Internet stocks were the lottery-like stocks in the Internet boom, and investors were still seeking them when the boom peaked in early 2000. "What Internet mutual funds have the best records?" asked investor G.T. of Newport, Michigan, in March 2000.[19] Monument Internet Fund gained 208 percent in 1999, WWW Internet Fund gained 176 percent, and the Munder NetNet Fund gained 175 percent. The debacle of Internet stocks soon followed. The WWW Internet fund was down 57 percent in 2000 and down a further 52 percent in 2001. The Munder NetNet Fund that was down 54 percent in 2000 was down a further 48 percent in 2001. The Monument Internet Fund disappeared, changing its name to Monument Digital Technology.

It is hard to rebut the sensible scolding administered to gamblers and speculators and buyers of lottery tickets and lottery-like stocks. But George Frederick stood up for hope in 1930, rebutting the scolds. "Isn't speculation, to any degree, unsound and immoral?" he was asked. "Speculation is impossible to avoid by anybody," he answered. "Your wife speculates when she buys a hat. . . . She speculated when she married you. All hope is nothing else but speculation, and if you want to take hope out of the world you might as well blow it up."[20]

Hope was scarce in Albania in 1996 as it declined into desperate poverty following its transition from communist rule. Poverty deepened as income from smuggling was eliminated when the United Nations lifted sanctions against Yugoslavia. Albanians were ready to blow up their world, and lottery-like pyramid schemes provided the dynamite. Almost two-thirds of Albanians invested in pyramid schemes; the amount of money promised by the schemes' operators was huge, almost half the country's income. The collapse of the schemes threw Albania into chaos. Some 2,000 people were killed in the violence that followed.[21]

Hope drove Colombian investors into pyramid schemes more recently, and hope blinded them to fraud. David Murcia Guzmán is a villain in the eyes of Colombia's authorities, but he is a folk hero to Colombia's poor reaching for hope. "My only flaw was that I dared to dream," said Guzmán, owner of fleet of exotic cars, including a Ferrari, a Maserati, and a Lamborghini. "What is criminal about dreaming?" Guzmán's investors are still dreaming. "David Murcia was only trying to redistribute the wealth a little in Colombia," said one of his impoverished investors.[22]

AWAY FROM POVERTY AND TOWARD RICHES

Lottery authorities advertise them as entertainment. "The lottery is fun. Entertaining. Exciting." But we do not buy lottery tickets because we want to be entertained. Movies are entertaining and they cost no more than a handful of lottery tickets, yet poor people spend larger proportions of their incomes on lottery tickets than rich people, while they do not spend larger proportions of their incomes on movie tickets than rich people.[23] We seek hope when we buy lottery tickets, not entertainment.

We are driven to gamble, whether through lottery tickets or stocks, when we feel poor. David Gleitman, a podiatrist, was earning about $200,000 a year from his medical practice, but that was before insurance companies cut reimbursement for surgeries that once commanded handsome fees. By 2000, Gleitman was suffering patients who complained about $10 copayments for toenail clipping. Annual income from his medical practice had declined to less than a quarter of its former level; Gleitman was spending most of his time trading stocks, magnifying his risk by borrowing money from his broker. The 2000 plunge in the stock market cost him $1 million, almost 80 percent of his portfolio.[24]

We are driven to gamble when we are reminded that we are poor. Experimenters paid people waiting at a bus station $5 in single dollar bills to complete a questionnaire. One version of the questionnaire, given to half the people, was designed to make them feel adequate, with incomes in the middle of the income range. It asked whether their annual incomes were less than $10,000, between $10,000 and $20,000, and then, in increments, to the top category of more than $60,000. The other version of the questionnaire, given to the other half, was designed to make them feel poor. It asked whether their annual incomes were less than $100,000, between $100,000 and $250,000, and then in increments to the top category of more than $1 million. Next, the experimenters showed each person five $1 lottery tickets and asked how many they wished to buy. People who were made to feel poor bought more lottery tickets than people who were made to feel that their incomes were adequate.[25]

We are driven to dream of power when we feel powerless. Sharon and Russ Gornie, a young couple who own a carpet store, felt powerless. "We are trying to make some aggressive money very quickly," said Sharon. The couple live in a modest house, far below their aspirations. "This is our dream house," said Sharon, pointing to blueprints of a fancy house. "We look at it when we are off to work in the morning and when we come home tired. . . . Isn't it beautiful?" Experimenters asked one group of people to reflect on situations in which they felt powerless and asked another group to reflect on situations in which they felt powerful. They found that people who were made to feel powerless were more eager to buy high-status items such as silk ties than people who were made to feel powerful.[26]

Aspirations for a home of our own drive us even if we should be guided by utilitarian benefits to rent rather than own. Many are seduced by the expressive and emotional benefits of a beautiful dream house. We take pride in home ownership and feel powerful, knowing that no landlord can kick us out. We take pleasure in our freedom to drill holes in walls for hooks to hold our favorite paintings. We take comfort in our freedom to knock down walls if we wish. Aspirations for houses mark people everywhere, from the United States to China and France. The petit bourgeoisie in France are tempted by images of happy domestic life into large mortgages that become stones around their necks.[27]

We might think of American subprime borrowers as greedy gamblers, lured into fancier houses than they could afford and larger mortgages. But hope and aspirations animated homebuyers more than greed. Steve Sanders, a mortgage banker, wrote that home buyers rushing to fulfill their dreams were willing to sign anything placed in front of them. "After witnessing literally thousands of signings," he wrote, "I will tell you that most people are so focused on getting into their new home that they have no idea what it was they just signed." [28]

Democrats wanted to help people reach their dreams for homes and so did Republicans. Republican Senator Phil Gramm was persuaded to support subprime lending by his mother's story.[29] "Some people look at subprime lending and see evil. I look at subprime lending and I see the American dream in action. . . . My mother lived it as a result of a finance company making a mortgage loan that a bank would not make. . . . What incredible exploitation," he said sarcastically. "As a result of that loan, at a 50 percent premium, so far as I am aware, she was the first person in her family, from Adam and Eve, ever to own her own home."

Money Brings Benefits

Riches are good for us, improving our mental health, even if temporarily. The General Health Questionnaire (GHQ) score is a measure of mental well-being used internationally by medical researchers. The GHQ-12 score is based on answers to 12 questions such as:

- Lost much sleep over worry?
- Felt you could not overcome your difficulties?
- Been thinking of yourself as a worthless person?

A study of Britons who won medium-size lottery prizes ranging up to 120,000 British pounds concluded the prizes boosted mental well-being by 1.4 GHQ points.[30] Money helps us sleep well, knowing that we have what we need to fix the roof if it leaks. Money buys our way out difficulties, and money makes us feel worthy. Drivers of beaten-up Toyotas might scream obscenities when they are stuck in traffic jams, but drivers of Rolls Royces are not rattled.

Freedom from the fear of poverty improves our mental health as riches do. Retirees who have at least some of their income in the form of pensions or annuities have greater freedom from the fear of poverty than retirees who draw income from their savings, concerned that they might outlive their money. Retirees with pensions or annuities were more satisfied with their life in retirement than retirees with similar incomes from sources other than pensions or annuities. Retirees with pensions or annuities also had fewer symptoms of depression than retirees without such pensions or annuities.[31]

Lottery Bonds

Bonds attract us with freedom from the fear of poverty, but lottery bonds that also carry hope for riches are even more attractive. Premium bonds, the British version of lottery bonds, are popular, held by one-quarter of British households.[32] They come in denominations as low as a single British pound, making them available even to the very poor. The bonds offer freedom from the fear of poverty in a promise to pay back the invested amount, and they offer hope for riches in a monthly lottery with prizes ranging from fifty to one million British pounds. Lottery bonds are available in Kenya, Mexico, Venezuela, Colombia, Japan, and South Africa, where First National Bank introduced the Million-a-Month-Account (MaMA). The account pays almost no interest, but its prizes range from one thousand rands to one million.

Lottery bonds are not offered in the United States today because they might violate state laws prohibiting private lotteries, but they are likely to be popular in the United States when offered. Centra Credit Union of Clarksville, Indiana, launched a pilot program of savings accounts that awards prizes. These accounts were especially attractive to low-to-moderate income Americans who play the lottery and have little savings.[33]

While lottery bonds are largely absent in the United States, indexed annuities resembling lottery bonds are widely available. The lottery part usually comes in the form of an index, such as the S&P 500 Index of stocks. A $1,000 indexed annuity might promise investors a minimum $1,000 at maturity, seven years later. In addition, the annuity might promise to pay the full increase in the level of the S&P 500 Index during the seven years. Investors receive $1,500 if the S&P 500 Index is up 50 percent during the seven years, but they receive their $1,000 minimum even if the S&P 500 Index is down 50 percent at maturity.[34]

Variations of indexed annuities are popular in many countries as "structured products," offering prizes that catch investors' fancy. One Swiss structured product offered prizes linked to increases in the prices of metals and oil. Another linked prizes to Black Sea stocks. Its promotion noted that the Black Sea region is rich in energy sources, minerals, metals, and agriculture, that it is a prime corridor for transportation of energy sources and merchandise, and that it grows at double the rate of occidental Europe.

Balancing Hope and Fear

Hope for riches and fear of poverty have always gripped us, leading us to buy in hope and sell in fear. We frustrate ourselves and our financial advisors when we shift the balance between hope and fear. Our hope for riches grows when stock markets boom and our fear of poverty recedes. We berate ourselves and our financial advisors for investing so much of our money in bonds that give us much freedom from the fear of poverty but little hope for riches. Our fear of poverty grows when stock markets go bust and our hope for riches recedes. Now we berate ourselves and our advisors for investing so much of our money in stocks that gave us much hope for riches but little freedom from the fear of poverty. This back-and-forth lurch between our desire for hope for riches and our desire for freedom from the fear of poverty has always been with us, evident in the story of an investor caught in the Panic of 1907.

At first he said that he believed in the future of the stock and intended to keep it. But fear gripped him when he saw the value of his shares dip below the $600 he paid for them. Desperately he wrote to his broker, sending the stock for immediate sale for a total of $525. "He took that money and put in into the savings bank. It is still there."[35] Financial advisors tell investors to rebalance their portfolios, reducing their investment in stocks after their prices increase and reducing their investment in bonds after their prices increase. But investors are driven by hope and fear to do the opposite. They increase their investment in stocks after increases in stock prices and decrease their investment in stocks after falls in prices. Increases in the uncertainty of stocks magnify fear and lead investors to pull money out of stocks, while reductions in the uncertainty of stocks magnify hope and lead investors to put money in stocks.[36]

The voice of hope was loud during the stock market boom years of the 1990s and during the real-estate boom in the early years of our century, but the voice of fear grew louder in the bust years that followed. Concetta McGrath, a 76-year-old widow, sold her home in 2001 and invested the money in the stock market, hoping that it would supplement her monthly $800 Social Security check. McGrath despaired soon after, cashing out after she had lost a third of her money and investing most of what she had left in bank stocks. By 2004 she lost some more and coped by joking: "My friend and I were saying, 'Gee, you know, we won't live more than two years. . . . That's the only way you can look at it. I'm too old to look for a job." [37]

Fear of poverty diminished after 2004 when stock prices rose, and hope for riches expanded. But fear was back in the crisis of 2008. Carol J. Emerson, a 65-year-old woman whose income consisted almost entirely of dividends, was worried. "If I were guaranteed that the dividend would remain unchanged, I could ignore that the underlying value of my stocks has eroded," she said. "But that is not the way it works. If the value of the stocks doesn't go up again, there are not a lot of companies that can keep on paying a 16 percent dividend." Emerson was trying to keep hope alive. "I don't obsess about what is happening, but it is always in the back of my mind."

Corlette McShea, a 61-year-old divorced woman, was still working in 2008 but concerned about her retirement prospects. "What a terrible situation that you have a house that is paid for and you can't even afford to stay in it because the real estate taxes keep going up," she said. "In my neighborhood, there's houses up and down the street that are for sale and not even an offer. I'm stuck. I'm stuck with the house; I don't know what my investments are doing; and here's this annuity with A.I.G. that is in jeopardy. Every way I look, I'm feeling kind of scared and panicked."[38] Still, many investors are able to balance well their desires for hope for riches and freedom from the fear of poverty. Nearly half of the investors of a large broker owned speculative stocks, satisfying their hope for riches. Yet they were older, richer, more experienced, and more diversified than the investors who did not own speculative stocks. These investors have established substantial freedom from fear of poverty mental accounts, affording them a sober chance at riches without too great a chance of descent into poverty.[39]

The desires for hope for riches and freedom from fear of poverty are universal, but the relative strengths of these desires varies from person to person, influenced by personalities, life experiences, and cultures. This is the topic of the next chapter.

CHAPTER 9

We Have Similar Wants and Different Ones

Eric Stein, a scam artist, promised investors 20 to 25 percent in 90 days. Before he was caught, Stein defrauded almost 1,800 investors of $34 million. Sitting in prison, Stein said: "Truth is, 25 percent on a quarterly basis is impossible—can't happen. But you're not going to believe that it can't happen. Because you want to believe that it can happen. . . ." Entrepreneurs were eager to hand over their money, including owners of car dealerships, owners of golf courses, and restauranteurs. So were doctors, and especially dentists. "They're risk takers. [Some] guys—we call them "hard money" or a "mooch"—just like to play it really big," said Stein. "We know for a fact that he's going to tell his friends that he's in this huge deal. . . . We used to call it "golf course talk." So, you're playing the psychological aspect as well as the financial aspect."[1]

We all want hope for riches and freedom from fear of poverty, but some of us are passionate about hope for riches while others care more about freedom from the fear of poverty. Those of us who are passionate about hope for riches are willing to tolerate the risk of investments necessary to realize our hopes, knowing that investments that may bring us riches if we are lucky can plunge us into poverty if we are unlucky. Those of us who care mostly about freedom from the fear of poverty are not willing to tolerate as much risk. The balance each of us strikes between the desire for hope for riches and the desire for freedom from the fear of poverty is shaped by our circumstances, life experiences, gender and age, personalities, and cultures.

CIRCUMSTANCES MATTER

Some of us can buy both freedom from poverty and hope for riches. We can afford to lose the money we gamble in hope of riches, knowing that we need not fear poverty. But others feel compelled to gamble even what they can barely afford to lose. Not all who gamble succeed, and some failures are heartbreaking. Indian farmers with large plots of land can choose to grow food crops such as mangoes, grapes, and rice, or commercial crops such as cotton, turmeric, and tobacco. Food crops from large plots can sustain families, offering freedom from the fear of poverty. But commercial crops offer hope for riches, even if modest.

Farmers with large plots can choose to grow both commercial crops and food crops, combining hope for riches with freedom from the fear of poverty. But farmers with plots too small to sustain a family are in a terrible bind as their families cannot survive on the small quantities of food crops their small plots yield. Such farmers feel compelled to gamble by growing commercial crops, hoping that crops are bountiful and crop prices are high. Farmers who gamble on commercial crops and fail have little to fall back on, and many have been driven to suicide. "He was worried, but he never talked about suicide," said the widow of a farmer who committed suicide when his cotton crop failed. "If not cotton, what?" said another farmer. "It's a vicious circle."[2]

LIFE EXPERIENCES MATTER

The life experience of the "depression babies," the generation that experienced the Great Depression, taught them to shun financial risks. Decades later they invest little in stocks and are pessimistic about future stock returns. Investors who were young in the early 1980s soured on stocks following the disappointing stock market returns of the 1970s. Yet investors who were young in the late 1990s, during the stock market boom years, remained enthusiastic about stocks.[3]

Still, there is wide variation in the willingness to trade hope for riches for freedom from the fear of poverty among investors of the same generation. We see this variation in responses to an offer to replace current portfolios with new ones. Think about your own response to such an offer. There is a chance that the new portfolio would turn out well, satisfying your hope for riches by raising your standard of living during your entire lifetime. Yet there is an equal chance that the new portfolio would turn out badly, adding to your fear of poverty by reducing your standard of living during your entire lifetime.

Let's say, for instance, that you will find your fate, rich or poor, by a toss of a coin; heads would bring you a 50 percent increase in your standard of living while tails would bring you an X percent decrease in your standard of living. What is the maximum X percent reduction you are willing to commit to before I toss the coin? Would it be 10 percent? Would it be 20 percent? The first implies you value the freedom from the fear of a 10 percent descent into poverty as much as you value the hope for a 50 percent uplift into riches. Those willing to commit to no more than a 10 percent descent into poverty for an equal chance for a 50 percent uplift into riches crave riches less than those who are willing to commit to a 20 percent descent into poverty. Instead, they crave more freedom from the fear of poverty. Those willing to commit to no more than a 10 percent descent into poverty are less willing to tolerate risk than those willing to commit to a 20 percent descent.

GENDER AND AGE MATTER

A survey revealed that men crave hope for riches more than women, while women crave freedom from the fear of poverty more than men. On average, men are more willing to accept a chance of a greater descent into poverty in exchange for a chance for uplift into riches. This is true for men and women surveyed in 23 countries, ranging from China to Germany, India, Italy, and Turkey. Young people crave hope for riches more than older ones.[4] A further survey revealed links between risk tolerance and overconfidence, maximization, regret, and trust.[5]

Some people believe that they can pick stocks that would earn higher-than-average returns, while other people believe that they are unable to pick such stocks. What do you believe? One manifestation of investment confidence, or perhaps overconfidence, is a belief that we have the skill to pick winning stocks. Men are more confident than women about their skills at picking stocks, and the relatively young are more confident than the relatively old. Moreover, investors who are confident in their ability to pick winning stocks are also willing to take greater risks than investors who are less confident. Perhaps confident investors rely on facts when they believe that they control risk, or perhaps they are overconfident, deluded into thinking that they control risk as some think that they can control tigers by holding on to their tails.

Do you agree with the statement "I always want to have the best; second best is not good enough for me?" People who do not settle for second best have a high desire for "maximization." Investors with high desire for maximization set high goals for themselves, motivating them to take greater risks for a chance to reach their goals. Indeed, the survey revealed that people with high drive for maximization are willing to take greater risks. People with high drive for maximization also tend to be confident, perhaps overconfident, in their ability to pick winning stocks. On average, men have a higher desire for maximization than women, and the relatively young have a higher desire for maximization than the relatively old.

Do you agree with the statement "Whenever I make a choice, I try to get information about how the other alternatives turned out and feel bad if another alternative has done better than the alternative I have chosen?" People with high tendency for regret are always looking back with hindsight, wondering if they could have made better choices. Women tend to have higher tendency for regret than men, and the relatively young tend to have higher tendency for regret than the relatively old. Moreover, "maximizers" are always wondering if they could have made better choices, whereas easy going "satisficers" are satisfied with their choices even if they are not the best. Indeed, the survey revealed that maximizers have a higher tendency for regret than satisficers.

PERSONALITY MATTERS

In our desires for hope for riches and freedom from the fear of poverty, personality matters as much as gender or age. Personality affects thoughts, feelings, preferences, and behavior, and it is reflected in all parts of life, including schooling, employment, and investment. Personality combines nature with nurture. On the nature side, variants of two genes, 5-HTTLPR and DRD4, affect our willingness to take risk, including the risk of falling into poverty as we reach for riches. These two genes regulate dopamine and serotonin neurotransmission and are linked to emotional behavior, anxiety, and addiction.[6] Genetics account for 20 percent of differences between people in the willingness to take risk, assessed by comparing identical twins to fraternal twins. Genetics also account for between 35 and 54 percent of the likelihood of turning into pathological gamblers.[7]

Nurture affects personality as well. We know that some people are shy by nature and others are outgoing because even babies exhibit shy or outgoing behavior. But we also know that shy babies do not always grow into shy adults. Nurture can help shy children overcome their shy nature. Moreover, personality might change as people age. Sensation seeking, which urges us into skateboard stunts and fast driving, peaks in adolescence and diminishes with age.[8]

Conscientiousness is a personality trait in people we describe as organized, responsible, and thorough. Conscientious people desire freedom from the fear of poverty more than people who are not as conscientious, and they desire hope for riches relatively less. Conscientious people are less willing to take risk than less conscientious people. Extroversion is a personality trait in people we describe as enthusiastic, talkative, and outgoing. Extroverted people desire hope for riches more than introverted people, and they desire freedom from fear of poverty relatively less. Extroverted people are willing to take risk more than introverted people. Openness is a personality trait in people we describe as curious, imaginative, and original. Open people, like extroverted people and unlike conscientious people, desire hope for riches more than people who are not as open, and they desire freedom from fear of poverty less. Open people are also more willing to take risk than less open people. Agreeableness is a personality trait in people we describe as appreciative, generous, and kind. Agreeable people, like conscientious people, and unlike extroverted or open people, desire freedom from the fear of poverty more than people who are not as agreeable, and they desire hope for riches relatively less. Agreeable people are less willing to take risk than less-agreeable people. Extroverts tend to be the most confident in their ability to pick winning stocks, and agreeable people tend to be the least confident. Conscientious people tend to lean toward maximation, while open people lean away from it.

The Keirsey classification of personalities is similar to the more-familiar Myers-Briggs one. It classifies people into four major personalities, Guardians, Artisans, Idealists, and Rationals. Guardians are disciplined, frugal, and cautious. They handle money conservatively. Artisans are optimistic, daring, and impulsive. Their personalities dispose them toward taking high risk but away from the self-control and steadiness necessary for accumulating substantial savings. Idealists are trustful, imaginative, and compassionate. But Idealists have little interest in accumulating wealth or the details of money management. Rationals are logical, skeptical, and curious. They see financial markets and investments as systems, like computers, and they attempt to understand and control them.

Guardians are more likely than others to say that they respect tradition, and Rationals are least likely. Guardians are also most likely to say that they like self-discipline, whereas Artisans are least likely. So Guardians find it easy to save money whereas Artisans find it difficult. Idealists are most likely to say that they feel compassion for the needy and express interest in socially responsible investments, whereas Rationals are least likely. Rationals and Artisans are most willing to take risk, whereas Guardians and Idealists are least willing. Rationals are most confident, or overconfident, in their ability to pick winning stocks, whereas Guardians are the least confident.[9]

CULTURE MATTERS

Culture is the set of beliefs, values, and expected behaviors that people transmit from generation to generation. Would you say that, generally speaking, most people can be trusted or would you say that you have to be very careful in dealing with people? Trust is one aspect of culture. Levels of trust vary among countries; they are relatively high in China and they are especially high in Norway, Finland, and Sweden. They are relatively low in Brazil, Malaysia, and Portugal.

Parents are good at transmitting to their children both levels of trust and willingness to take risk.[10] Trusting people are more willing to take risk than less-trusting ones.[11]

Culture affects personality and is affected by it. Americans tend to be more extroverted than Hong Kong Chinese, but Irish tend to be more extroverted than Americans. The English tend to be more conscientious than Moroccans, but not as conscientious as Germans. Still, people vary even within one country. German Swiss tend to be more conscientious than French Swiss. French Swiss tend to be more conscientious than French, and German Swiss tend to be more conscientious than Germans.[12]

Immigrants are frequently amazed by the differences between the cultures of their old countries and new ones. I immigrated to the United States from Israel decades ago but still recall my astonishment at discovering some of these cultural differences. I was traveling by train from New York City to Philadelphia not long after arriving in the United States when I overheard a conversation between two men sitting in the row ahead of mine. One said to the other, "I told my daughter that I'm paying her college tuition but she is on her own after that!" I was astonished. The common practice for parents in Israel at the time was to support their children long after college. For instance, it was common for the parents of the bride and the groom to pay substantial portions of the down payment for a condominium for the new couple at a time when down payments amounted to more than half the price of a condominium.

Individualistic Cultures and Collectivistic Ones

Geert Hofstede studied the cultures of many countries and identified several cultural dimensions that distinguish each from others.[13] The place of a country along the span between individualism and collectivism is one of these cultural dimensions. Ties between individuals are loose in individualistic countries, where individuals are expected to look after themselves, their spouses, and their young children. In contrast, ties between individuals are strong in collectivistic countries where people are integrated into cohesive groups of extended family and friends who are always expected to support one another.[14] I would not have been astonished by the conversation between the two men on the train had I known that culture in the United States places it closest to the individualistic end of the span between individualism and collectivism. Culture in Israel places it closer to the collectivistic end of the span, and culture in China and Vietnam places them even closer to the collectivistic end.

Culture clash is poignant in the documentary *Daughter from Danang,* which followed Heidi, a young American woman coming to Vietnam. Heidi was born in Vietnam to an American soldier and Kim, a Vietnamese woman, and taken to the United States at the end of the Vietnam War. "There were so many rumors," said Kim years later as she was waiting to see the daughter she named Hiep when she was born. "I was so frightened. If I didn't send my child away both she and I would die." At the end of the visit, Heidi was sitting with her mother and siblings when Tinh, her brother, said, "For 22 years, we've had no news of you, so we, your siblings, have taken care of our mother. Now we hope you'll assume the filial responsibility a child has toward parent. Perhaps you could bring her to live near you."

Heidi was incredulous as she spoke to the translator. "He wants me to bring her to the U.S. to live me with me?" Tinh offers a compromise. "And while we're waiting for her to go to the States, maybe Hiep could, with the consent of her family, help support our mother with a monthly stipend." The family gathering ends with Heidi-Hiep in tears, telling the cameraman, "I can't do this anymore."[15]

Chinese are more willing to take risk than Americans. Chinese, on average, were willing to risk more than a 17 percent decline in their standard of living for an even chance at a 50 percent increase, whereas Americans were willing to risk less than a 13 percent decline for the same chance. It might be that Chinese are more willing to tolerate risk than Americans because the relatively collectivistic culture of China offers them a safety net of support from family and friends if they take risk and fail, whereas the relatively individualistic American culture offers less of a safety net. The story of Ashley Revell, a 32-year-old man, illustrates the importance of safety nets of family and friends in decisions to take risk or shun it. Revell sold all his possessions, including his clothes, and bet it all on red at a roulette table in Las Vegas. Revell hoped for riches, but he was also free from the fear of poverty because he had a safety net of family and friends. "But I'd still have my friends, my family, and they'd always be there for me. So they gave me the security to be able to do this," he said. As luck would have it Revell won, walking away from the casino with $270,600.[16]

The importance of the safety net of family and friends is evident in a study that compared the financial situations of people who have migrated relatively far from their places of birth to the financial situations of people who stayed near. People who migrate relatively far have weaker safety nets than people who stay close. People who migrated far were more likely to default on loans and go bankrupt than people who stayed close.[17] The relation between the willingness of people to take risk and the place of their country along the span between individualism and collectivism is evident in the study of 23 countries, beyond China and the United States. People in countries closer to the collectivistic end of the span are more willing to take risk than people closer to the individualistic end.[18]

Stronger safety nets of family and friends in collectivistic countries might be the reason for the higher willingness to take risk among people living there, but another relationship indicates that safety nets do not always quiet fear of risk. Some countries provide stronger public safety nets than other countries. France is almost as individualistic as the United States, providing relatively little private safety nets of family and friends. But France is very different from the United States in providing relatively substantial public safety nets in forms such as generous health and unemployment benefits. Public social spending in France amounted to one-third of its net national income while public social spending in the United States amounted to less than one-fifth of its net national income. If strong safety nets make people more willing to take risk, we should expect to find that the willingness to take risk is higher in countries with strong public safety nets than in countries with weak ones. Yet this is not what we find. If anything, people in countries with relatively strong public safety nets are *less* willing to take risk than people in countries with relatively weak safety nets. This raises the possibility that people in countries with strong public safety nets, such as France, are less willing to take risk than people in countries with relatively weak safety nets, such as the United States, because of nature or culture. Unwillingness to take risk might create demand for strong public safety nets, whereas higher willingness to take risk might induce lesser demand for strong public safety nets.[19]

Differences in average income offer another part of the answer to the question about the reasons for differences among countries in the willingness to take risk. People are more willing to take risk in countries where average incomes are low than in countries where average incomes are high. It might be that relatively low incomes induce people to take risk in the same way that low incomes induce the poor to spend larger proportions of their incomes on lottery tickets than the rich. As one of my Chinese-born students described the situation of many people in China, "What do they have to lose?

Uncertainty Avoidance, Egalitarianism, and Harmony

Uncertainty avoidance is another of Hofstede's cultural dimensions. People in countries where uncertainty avoidance is relatively high are uncomfortable in unstructured situations, such as in encounters with what is unknown or surprising. People in such cultures try to minimize unstructured situations by strict laws and regulations, by safety and security measures, and by insisting on an "absolute truth" rather than tolerating diversity of opinions. The United States ranks relatively low on uncertainty avoidance, along with China and Vietnam, but Portugal, Japan, and Poland rank relatively high. The description of uncertainty avoidance makes it likely that it is related to the willingness to take risk, and evidence across the 23 countries in the study indicates that it is indeed so. The willingness to take risk is relatively low in countries where uncertainly avoidance is relatively high.

Harmony and mastery are two poles of another cultural dimension, identified by Shalom Schwartz.[20] Values associated with mastery include ambition and daring. People of countries that value mastery strive to get ahead whereas people in relatively harmonious countries prefer to fit into their communities. Norway ranks high on harmony and so do Finland and France, but Israel, India, and the United States rank relatively low. Egalitarianism and hierarchy are the two poles of another cultural trait. Values associated with egalitarian cultures include equality and social justice, and people in egalitarian countries are socialized to feel concern for everyone's welfare. Countries where culture is harmonious tend to have egalitarian cultures. Norway, Finland, and France, which rank relatively high on harmony, also rank relatively high on egalitarianism. Israel, India, and the United States, which rank relatively low on harmony, also rank relatively low on egalitarianism. Evidence across the 23 countries in the study indicates that the willingness to take risk is relatively low in harmonious and egalitarian countries.

CHINESE, AMERICANS, AND CHINESE-AMERICANS

Each of us has several identities and the prominence of these identities affects our preferences and behavior. Our identities include that of a father or mother, that of a teacher or policeman, that of someone who loves to study mathematics or avoids mathematics as if it were a disease. Changes in settings and circumstances bring some identities to the fore while other identities recede. One study focused on Chinese-American adults born in China, Taiwan, and other East Asian countries who have lived in the United States for five years or longer. Chinese identity was brought to the fore in one group with questions such as "Where were you born?" and "Name one Chinese landmark that you've visited or would like to visit." American identity was brought to the fore in another group with questions such as "What town do you live in at the moment?" and "Name one U.S. landmark that you've visited or would like to visit." To enhance the influence of identities further, the first set of questions was presented in Chinese while the second was presented in English. American stereotypical preferences for uniqueness and noncooperation were more pronounced when American identities were made evident.[21]

American investors overload their portfolios with American stocks and Chinese investors overload theirs with Chinese stocks. We know this as "home bias," where the proportions of home-country stocks in investors' portfolios exceed their proportions in the world portfolio. Familiarity underlies a portion of home bias; American investors are more familiar with American stocks while Chinese are more familiar with Chinese stocks. Chinese-Americans have a lower tendency for home bias than Americans born in the United States of parents who were also born in the United States. Chinese-Americans are more likely to agree with the statement "It makes sense to invest half of my entire portfolio in stocks, bonds, and other investments outside the United States."[22]

Gold, like international stocks and bonds, is included in some portfolios because these investments diversify the portfolios.[23] But investments in gold vary greatly among countries. In developed countries such as the United States, investors commonly hold gold through stocks of gold-mining companies. But in developing countries such as China and India, investors prefer to own physical gold, as jewelry or coins. Gold serves as a store of savings in countries where the banking system is underdeveloped or restrictive. In rural India, gold serves as a credit card, enabling owners to get instant loans secured by gold deposited with the lender. But culture is an important driver of the demand for physical gold, displayed in part by the Indian and Chinese tradition of giving gold jewelry at weddings and holidays. Chinese-Americans express higher levels of agreement with the statement: "Gold is or should be part of my investment portfolio" than do Americans born in the United States to parents born in the United States.

Home ownership is an important goal among Chinese-Americans, even among those with limited means. Home ownership among Chinese-American households is higher than home ownership in most other groups, and homes are often purchased with the joint savings of entire families.[24] The preference for real estate, beyond one's primary residence, is reflected in levels of agreement with the statement "Real-estate properties, not including my primary residence, are or should be part of my investment portfolio." Levels of agreement among Chinese-Americans are higher than levels of agreement among Americans born in the United States to parents born in the United States.

Culture also affects gender roles in financial decisions. Chinese-Americans, both men and women, were more likely to agree with the statement "Wives, not husbands, should be responsible for daily household finances, such as daily expenses" than Americans born in the United States to parents born in the United States. The same is true for levels of agreement with the statement "Husbands, not wives, should be responsible for management of savings and investments." Still, unsurprisingly, men in both groups expressed greater agreement with this statement than women.

CULTURE DOES NOT EXPLAIN EVERYTHING

Sometimes culture is called upon to explain more than it can. The savings rate in China is high relative to the savings rate in the United States, but not all agree on the reasons underlying the difference. Some have attributed the high savings rate in China to the self-discipline embedded in Confucian culture. Yet Confucian culture has been marshaled to explain many contradictory things. For much of Chinese history, the Confucian culture was considered one that promotes laziness and spendthrift behavior rather than discipline and thrift. In the 1950s and early 1960s, Confucian culture explained Chinese poverty through its emphasis on family, morality, and prestige, which made it difficult to create wealth through enterprise and technological innovation. In particular, spending on expensive burial rites associated with ancestor worship prevented Chinese households from accumulating enough savings to fund capitalist enterprises. In the 1980s, when Japan and the "Asian tigers"—Hong Kong, Singapore, Taiwan, and South Korea—were prosperous, Confucian ideals of harmony, honesty, and responsibility were called upon to explain thriving business. Yet the harmony of Confucian culture was described as a mere cover for corruption during the 1998 Asian financial crisis.[25]

Economics, politics, and demographics likely underlie Chinese savings rates more than Confucian culture. These elements include an expansion of the working-age population at a faster rate than expansion of the population as a whole, as well as constraints on consumption imposed by the Chinese government. Moreover, constraints on borrowing in China make it necessary to save for expenditures that would have been facilitated by borrowing in countries such as the United States. Consider the statement "I find it easy to save money even though I am tempted by the many things I would like to buy." If Confucian culture makes it easier for people to exercise self-control in saving, we would have expected to find that Chinese-Americans would find it easier to save than Americans who were born in the United States to parents who were also born in the United States. Yet the survey revealed no significant differences in the ease of savings between the two groups.[26] Still, Chinese-Americans are more likely to agree with the statement "It makes sense to use credit cards, but only if you pay the balance in full every month" and with the statement "It makes sense to take out a loan to purchase a house, but it does not make sense to take a loan for the purchase of a television, refrigerator, or even a car."

We are similar in many ways. We are all subject to hindsight error and overconfidence, and we all know fear and exuberance. Yet we are different in many ways, each of us shaped by nature, nurture, personality, circumstances, life experiences, and cultures. This chapter focused on differences between us. The next chapter takes us back to similarities. In particular, it focuses on our reluctance to face our losses and our even greater reluctance to realize our losses.

CHAPTER 10

We Want to Face No Losses

My wife and I had little use for a car while we studied at Columbia University in Manhattan, but we needed two cars when we moved to Philadelphia. We bought a new car and a used one, a giant Dodge Polara. I was amused by my memory of a high government official being driven in a Dodge Polara. Quite an impressive car, I thought. Now I had one of my own for a few hundred dollars.

The Polara was trouble from the start. The engine would die in the middle of the road, and I had to open the hood and stick a screwdriver into the carburetor to revive it. The rear axle was bent, and I spent an entire day at the junkyard, looking for a replacement. The engine oil light came on often, going off after I have changed engine oil and coming on again soon afterward. The cost of repairs soon exceeded the purchase price of the Polara, and they kept mounting.

Reason prodded me to rid myself of the car, but I could not bring myself to do so. Instead, I kept throwing good money after bad, reluctant to cut my losses. Finally, I took my Polara to the Dodge dealership and its mechanics quickly diagnosed one of its many problems. The engine oil light kept coming on because the engine block was cracked, letting gasoline seep into the engine oil. All I needed, they said, was a new engine, which they would be pleased to install at a price not much lower than the price of a new car. This bad news was wonderful news. The mechanics made my decision for me. It was time to realize my loss. I drove my Polara to a dealership where it and several thousand additional dollars bought me a new car.

REALIZING LOSSES

I am reluctant to realize my losses and you are probably reluctant to realize yours. We share that reluctance with people as rich and famous as Martha Stewart. Stewart, the former chairman and chief executive officer of Martha Stewart Living Omnimedia, started a catering business out of her home, and, after decades of enterprise, her fortune amounted to hundreds of millions of dollars. On December 27, 2001, Stewart sold shares of ImClone Systems after being tipped off by Peter Bacanovic, her broker, that ImClone's chief executive Samuel Waksal and members of his family were dumping shares. Stewart and Bacanovic were convicted of obstructing justice and lying to the government, and on October 8, 2004, Stewart entered the Alderson Federal Prison Camp to serve a five-month sentence.[1]

Evidence presented at Martha Stewart's trial highlights her reluctance to realize "paper losses." "Just took lots of huge losses to offset some gains," Stewart wrote in an e-mail to Mark Goldstein, a friend, on December 22, 2001, "[M]ade my stomach turn." Stewart's reluctance to realize her losses is puzzling to rational investors. The price of a share of stock I've bought for $100 a month ago might have declined to $40 by now. I have a $60 paper loss. I can choose to realize my $60 paper loss by selling the stock at $40 or choose to keep a $60 paper loss by holding on to the stock. But I am $60 poorer today than a month ago whether I realize my loss or keep it as a paper loss.

Moreover, tax considerations give an edge to realized losses over paper losses because realized losses reduce taxes while paper losses do not. Tax considerations also give an edge to paper gains over realized gains since realized gains add to taxes while paper gains do not. If Martha Stewart were rational, she would have felt her stomach turn when the prices of her stocks declined and she incurred her paper losses. This is when her wealth decreased. But she would have rejoiced when she realized her losses since the tax benefits of realized losses added to her wealth.

Rational investors follow the maxim "Cut your losses and let you profits run." They are eager to realize losses quickly while they are slow to realize gains. Our parents prod us to cut our losses with sayings such as "Let bygones be bygones" and "Don't cry over spilled milk." I, along with fellow professors of finance, educate my students to recognize the tax benefits of realizing losses and to overcome their reluctance to realize them. Financial advisors regularly tell their investors to cut their losses and let their profits run. Why are normal investors such as Stewart and the rest of us disposed instead to sell winners too early and ride losers too long? The answer to the puzzle is in our cognitive errors of mental accounting and hindsight, our emotions of regret and pride, and our inner struggle for self-control.

Buying a stock marks a hopeful beginning. We place the stock into a mental account, record its $100 purchase price and hope to close the account at a gain, perhaps selling the stock at $150. As stock fate has it, the stock's price plummets to $40 during the following month rather than increases to $150. This is only a paper loss, we console ourselves. The stock's price would surely recover very soon and climb higher. We do not need to acknowledge our loss fully because it is only a paper loss. We do not realize the loss yet by selling the stock. The mental account containing the stock is still open, keeping alive the hope that losses will turn into gains.

REGRET AND PRIDE

We need not acknowledge our paper losses fully before we realize them, but we face them and they gnaw at us. We feel stupid. Hindsight error misleads us into thinking that what is clear in hindsight was equally clear in foresight. We bought the stock at $100 because, in foresight, it seemed destined to go to $150. But now, in hindsight, we remember all the warning signs displayed in plain sight on the day we bought our stock. Interest rates were about to increase. The CEO was about to resign. A competitor was ready to introduce a better product.

The cognitive error of hindsight is accompanied by the emotion of regret. We kick ourselves for being so stupid and contemplate how much happier we would have been if only we had kept our $100 in our savings account or invested it in another stock that zoomed as our stock plummeted. Regret is painful enough when we face our paper losses, but the pain of regret is searing when we realize our losses because this is when we give up hope of getting even by recovering our losses. It is no wonder that Martha Stewart felt her stomach turn when she realized her losses.

Pride is at the opposite end of the emotional spectrum from regret. Pride accompanies the realization of gains. We congratulate ourselves and feel proud for seeing in foresight that our $100 stock would soon zoom to $150. Realizing gains by selling our stocks seals our gains and amplifies our pride. Regret is painful while pride is pleasurable, but both are teachers, warning us against behavior likely to inflict regret and encouraging us to toward behavior likely to bring pride. But sometimes the lessons of regret are overly harsh and the lessons of pride too encouraging. Stocks go up and down for many reasons and no reason at all. We need not kick ourselves with regret every time stock prices go down, and we should not stroke ourselves with pride every time they go up.

Responsibility Amplifies Regret

Our pain of regret rarely rivals that of Emily Cikovsky. Cikovsky and an associate moonlighted for Google five years before its shares were offered to the public. The two prepared PowerPoint slides and speaking notes for cofounders Sergey Brin and Larry Page. Brin and Page were ready to pay Cikovsky in Google options but she chose to be paid $4,000 instead. Abbe Peterson, Cikovsky's associate, chose to receive 4,000 options on Google shares instead of her $5,000. Stock splits turned Peterson's 4,000 Google options into 16,000 and on the day following Google's public offering, Abbe Peterson was more than $1.7 million richer. Emily Cikovsky cannot remember how she spent her $4,000.[2]

Years ago I saw scribbled in our school's bathroom a song by Devo, a popular band at the time. The last lines said, "Freedom of choice is what you got. Freedom from choice is what you want." We want freedom from choice because responsibility for choice opens the gate to regret. I was never burdened by the responsibility for a choice between payment in cash or in Google stock options because I never worked for Google. You probably have not been burdened by that responsibility either. You and I might be disappointed not to have had Google stock options, but we do not feel regret for foregoing them. But Emily Cikovsky and Abbe Peterson had choices and bore responsibility for outcomes. Responsibility opens the gate to pride as it opens it to regret, but the pain of regret when our choices turn out poorly is greater than the joy of pride when our choices turn out well.

Hindsight error adds to the burden of responsibility since it makes it seem as if the outcomes of choices were clear in foresight, not only in hindsight. We blame ourselves for choosing the one that ended up poorly. We alleviate the pain of regret when we recognize the error of hindsight. This is what Emily Cikovsky did when she contemplated her unfortunate choice of cash over Google options. "Do I wish I'd had the shares? Yes," she said.

But "what's always in the back of my mind is that an IPO is never guaranteed. . . . And nine out of ten start-ups fail."

Following convention also reduces responsibility and alleviates the pain of subsequent regret, since it is easy to imagine doing the conventional thing and harder to imagine deviating from convention. Think of a woman who had a choice between two roads from home to work, each equally long, equally congested and equally scenic. The woman fell into the convention of driving on one of these roads, and today her car was rear-ended as she waited at a stoplight. Compare her regret to the regret she would have felt if she had decided today, for no particular reason, to drive on the other road and the same accident were to happen. This woman can easily imagine choosing her conventional road but finds it harder to imagine choosing the unconventional road. Her pain of her regret is likely greater when she deviates from her convention. Cikovsky would have been able to reduce her regret further if choosing cash over options was her convention in other work she had done. Cikovsky would have been able to reduce her regret even more if she could have shirked her responsibility altogether, perhaps blaming her choice on her husband.

Get-even-itis

Some investors are experts at shifting responsibility, assuming responsibility when choices turn out well and shirking it when choices turn out poorly. This expertise underlies the brokers' lament: "When a stock goes up, investors say that they bought the stock. And when it goes down, investors say that their brokers sold them the stock." Shifts of responsibility underlie "moral hazard." Some bankers assume responsibility for risky loans that turn out well, enjoying both bonuses and pride, while they shift responsibility to the government that bails them out when risky loans bring disaster. Some investors pocket the profits of risky investments that turn out well and sue their brokers when risky investments bring losses.

Investors with paper losses pose a difficult problem for brokers, especially when these losses were generated by following the brokers' recommendations. In the early 1980s, a former student of mine referred me to a manual by LeRoy Gross, a broker's guru, who described the reluctance to realize losses as the "get-even-itis" disease. Investors do not want to realize losses, Gross wrote, because they do not want to give up hope of getting even. "The "get-even-itis" disease has probably wrought more destruction on investment portfolios than anything else. . . . Investors who accept losses can no longer prattle to their loved ones, "Honey, it's only a paper loss. Just wait. It will come back." Investors all over the world are reluctant to realize losses on stock investments, testifying to the universality of our aversion to the pain of regret. The reluctance to realize losses is evident among investors in the United States, Japan, Finland, Israel, Portugal, Australia, China, and Taiwan.[3, 4, 5, 6, 7, 8, 9]

RELUCTANCE TO REALIZE LOSSES

The reluctance to realize losses is terrible news for stockbrokers who miss commissions when their clients do not trade. But that reluctance is great news for managers of terrible mutual funds; these managers continue to collect their fees from investors who fail to realize their losses and move on to better funds. The last of Steadman's mutual funds investors continued to hold on losing shares bought 20 years before. Losses were sure to multiply in future years because Steadman Funds had an annual expense ratio of 25 percent. Still, said a Steadman investor, he "never wanted to sell it at a loss."[10] Indeed, losing mutual funds tend to persist in their losing streaks in part because their investors are reluctant to vote with their feet, realize their losses, and move on.[11]

The reluctance to realize losses has always been with us. Humphrey Neill dedicated his 1931 investment book to his losses, with a deep appreciation for the knowledge that each loss has brought him.[12] "The one thing that retards success in trading, more than any other," wrote Neill, "is the unwillingness of many of us to accept losses, cheerfully and quickly. . . . For heaven's sake," he added, "you do not need to have a love affair with your stock just because you bought it. Love is sometimes fickle, you know."[13]

Framing Gains and Losses

We can frame gains as losses and losses as gains by varying the "reference point." We can frame a 4 percent raise as a gain, when the reference point is our previous income, or as a loss, where the reference point is the 8 percent increase we were hoping for. Here is the framing of gains and losses in the 1973 episode "The Hot Watch," in *All in the Family*, a television sitcom. Archie Bunker buys for $25 a watch from Matt, a street vendor, who presents it as a $300 Omega watch. The watch's hands stop moving soon after, and the watchmaker delivers the bad news. The watch is a fake, an "Onega," worth $8. It would cost $21 to repair.

> *Archie:* I hate to admit, but it looks like I have been took.
>
> *Son-in-Law Mike:* It ain't that bad.
>
> *Archie:* What do you mean 'it ain't that bad,' this watch is same as two weeks' take-home pay.
>
> *Daughter Gloria:* How do you figure that, daddy?
>
> *Archie:* 'How do you figure that daddy?' . . . Two weeks take-home pay is same as 300 dollars.
>
> *Mike:* What? You only spent 25 dollars on an 8-dollar watch . . . You are only out 17 bucks.
>
> *Archie:* Use your brains, Matt told me it's a 300-dollar watch, I paid 25 for it, 25 dollars and 300 dollars, 275 dollars I am out.
>
> *Mike:* You are wrong!
>
> *Archie:* I ain't wrong you dumbbell, I am right.
>
> *Mike:* All right, you want to be right, I will show you how you can be right. You spend the 21 dollars, you get the watch fixed. You already spent 25 dollars, so for a 46-dollar investment you got your 300-dollar watch fixed.
>
> *Archie:* Maybe you got something there. . . .
>
> *Wife Edith:* But the watch is still only worth 8 dollars. . . .

We adapt to both gains and losses, but we tend to adapt to gains more quickly than to losses. When the price of the stock we have bought for $50 increases to $60, we are likely to set our reference price to $60, registering a subsequent decline to $56 as a $4 loss rather than a $6 gain. Rates of adaptation vary from person to person in one country and they vary among people of different countries. People in China and Korea adapt more quickly to both gains and losses than people in the United States.[14] Time tends to heal the wounds of losses. Investors display a stronger tendency to come to terms with losses incurred years ago than with losses incurred weeks ago. Expectations about future prices affect the rate of adaptation as well. Investors are more likely to come to terms with past investment losses when they expect that these investments would inflict further losses.[15]

Reluctance to Realize Losses in Real Estate

Homeowners are notorious in their reluctance to realizing losses, and so are banks holding mortgages on these houses. Homeowners and banks are reluctant to realize their losses in the financial crisis that still engulfs us in the second decade of our century. The prices of houses in Paramount, California, shot up from $200,000 in 2003 to $500,000 in 2005. But by 2007 few buyers were ready to pay $500,000 for a Paramount house and few could afford to pay such price. Gary Endo, a Paramount real-estate agent, said, "We're going through this transition where sellers can't accept that prices are falling. They're still caught up in this idea that their property is worth more than it is. It's just strange."[16]

But what seems strange to Mr. Endo is quite normal. Houses sell quickly in boom times at prices that exceed list prices. Yet in bust times, houses sit on the market for months and years at list prices higher than they could possibly fetch. Many sellers withdraw their houses from the market rather than sell them at prices lower than the prices they have set in their minds. Homeowners say the market is slow, we'll just hold on and wait. In truth, it is homeowners who are slow. They are slow to reconcile themselves to the fact that today's reasonable prices are lower than the prices they have set in their minds. Realtors often refuse to represent such reluctant homeowners, knowing that they are not likely to persuade them to reduce their prices and realize their losses.

In 1992, when the Boston condominium market in Boston was at its bottom, owners offered condominiums at prices that exceeded reasonable selling prices by more than a third. Buyers responded with a buying strike, and fewer than a third of condominiums sold within 180 days. The market recovered in 1997 when condominiums were offered at only one-tenth above likely selling prices. Buyers came back and more than 60 percent of condominiums sold within 180 days.[17]

Reluctance to Realize Losses Fuels Scams

Lottery promoters capitalize on our aversion to regret as they encourage us to keep on buying. "Don't let your number win without you," says a lottery slogan.[18] A lottery commercial shows a lottery ticket blowing out of a farmer's hand into the nearby cow pasture. Next, the farmer sees one of his cows riding in the back seat of a luxurious stretch limousine. We see the farmer's expression of the pain of regret as he realizes that his cow won the jackpot that should have been his.

Perpetrators of scams also capitalize on our reluctance to realize losses. The immediate attraction of Nigerian 419 scams is akin to the attraction of a stock that is sure to zoom. People who are scammed, like investors, neglect to ask, "Who is the idiot on the other side of this trade? Why would anyone offer me millions for nothing?" And, as with investments, the reluctance to realize small losses escalates to a reluctance to realize large losses. This is the sad story of John Worley.

Worley, a decorated Vietnam veteran, ordained minister, and practicing Christian psychotherapist, received an e-mail from "Captain Joshua Mbote" offering a share of a $55-million-dollar windfall. Worley was suspicious enough to check the legitimacy of the offer with a lawyer, who warned him that the offer was a scam. Ironically, the lawyer's fee turned out to be the beginning of Worley's downfall. He plunged into the scam in an attempt to break even by gaining from "Captain Joshua Mbote" what he had paid to his lawyer. Instead, Worley's losses mounted as he sent more and more money to Mbote and his confederates. In the end, Worley was convicted of fraud, for depositing into his bank account fake checks he received from Nigeria and sending to Nigeria the proceeds of these checks. He was sentenced to two years in prison, and ordered to repay the nearly $600,000 he sent to Nigeria.[19]

In his manual for brokers, LeRoy Gross recommended an ingenious remedy for the reluctance to realize losses by merging two mental accounts, one in which the losing stock resides, and another in which a newly purchased stock would reside. "Transfer your assets" are "magic selling words" spoken by brokers to their investors. The words make investors think that they are not realizing a loss when they sell their losing stocks, only "transferring" their money from one stock to another.[20] The mere transfer of money obscures the realization of losses and alleviates the regret that comes with such realization. The contemporary magic words for inducing investors to realize their losses are "harvest your losses." Harvesting losses bring to mind plucking juicy peaches while strolling in an orchard rather than realizing rotten losses while bent over our portfolios.

I practiced a variation of the transfer-your-assets mental trick some years ago when my wife and I arrived at the Rome airport for a vacation that would takes us all the way to Milan, with many stops along the way. The clocks in Rome showed ten in the morning, but we felt as if we were awakened from deep sleep soon after midnight California time. I withdrew 300 euros from an ATM, stuffed them into my wallet without looking, and we hurried to collect our luggage. A sign at the carousel warned us against solicitations for rides into the city and advised us to take only a white taxi. It also said that the fare into Rome should be approximately 42 euros. The taxi driver was friendly, making small talk. Here is the Coliseum, he said, and over there is the Vatican. Taxi drivers are known as a bit crafty with tourists, and I was on guard. I expected the fare to exceed 42 euros and it did; the meter showed 52 euros. Well, I thought, this is the fate of a tourist, and placed the difference between 42 euros and 52 euros in a mental account labeled "payment for a guided tour of Rome."

I drew two 50 euro notes from my wallet and handed them to the driver. "You only gave me 20," he said a moment later, showing me two 10 euro notes. It didn't seem quite right but it must have been my mistake, I thought. I gave the driver another 50-euro note. He gave me back change and I left a tip. Once in our room I checked my wallet again and fully realized that the driver had pretended I gave him two 10-euro notes instead of two 50 euro notes, thereby cheating me of 80 euros. I was outraged. Here I am, fresh in Rome, and I'm already a loser. I went on and on until my wife said, "Now listen, if you're going to go on like that, we won't have much of a vacation in Rome. Why don't you pretend that we went out, had a wonderful meal at a great Roman restaurant, and paid 80 euros?" It took a while for her advice to sink in, but in time it did. I transferred the 80 euros from the "I am a loser in Rome" mental account to the "vacation in Rome" mental account, accepting the loss, and then our vacation was wonderful indeed.

NO-MENTAL-LOSS INVESTMENTS

Circumstances can make losses vanish as well as magic words. The circumstances of December are different from those of other months since December brings to mind taxes, and newspapers are full of urgent advice about cutting taxes, including the realization of losses. What is framed as a loss in November is framed as a gain, in the form of a tax deduction, in the following December. Framing losses as tax deductions makes it easier to realize them. This is what Martha Stewart did when she realized her losses in December 2001.

There is nothing rational in the role that December plays in the realization of losses. Investors receive no more tax benefits from realizing losses in December than they receive from realizing them in November or October. Indeed, it makes rational sense to realize losses as soon as they occur rather than wait until December. The real advantage of December is the balm it brings, easing the pain of regret that accompanies the realization of losses. "We did not realize losses," we lie to ourselves, "We only shortchanged the taxman, saving some taxes." The personal circumstances of investors matter as well, providing incentives to overcome the disposition to realize gains quickly but postpone the realization of losses. A study of German taxpayers revealed that high-income investors subject to high marginal tax rates are quicker to realize losses and slower to realize gains than investors with lower incomes and marginal tax rates.[21]

Some investments belong naturally to several mental accounts, facilitating transfers from losing mental accounts into winning ones. Houses are prominent examples of such investments and so is art and gambling money. Our houses, like our stocks and bonds, reside in mental accounts we label investment. But our houses also reside in mental accounts we label place-to-live. The place of our houses in two mental accounts gives us options. When our houses gain value we place them in the investment mental account, taking pride in our gains. But we transfer our houses into the place-to-live mental accounts once they have lost value. We mitigate our pain of regret at the loss saying, "After all, we need a place to live." The same transfer from one mental account to another is true in art. We place paintings in investment mental accounts when they have gained value, taking pride. But we place them in the "looks-beautiful-over-the-sofa" mental account when they have lost value, mitigating regret. Money for lottery tickets, slot machines, and other gambles belong in an entertainment mental account and in the investment mental account. We congratulate ourselves for making a wise investment when we win, and when we lose we say, "Las Vegas was great fun."

Some investments give us options to obscure losses or postpone their realization. We frame them as "no-mental-loss" investments. The realistic selling price of a particular house is the $200,000 price it would fetch from today's buyers. That realistic price might well be lower than the $300,000 we paid for it five years ago. When we sell this house at its realistic price. we realize a $100,000 loss. Yet we can frame this house as a no-mental-loss investment in two ways. First, we can postpone selling our house. Second, we can obscure our loss by avoiding any information pointing to it. We can avoid looking at the zillow.com Web site, which estimates the value of our house at $200,000. We can avoid hearing the story of our neighbor who just sold an identical house for $200,000.

We are pretty good at avoiding information about investment losses, sparing us the regret that accompanies facing them. Bradford Roth, a Chicago lawyer, came into a Fidelity Investments branch to make a deposit to his checking account following a major decline in the stock market in 2008, but he did not check the balance of his retirement account. "The less you know," he said, "the better you feel."[22] Many investors in the United States, Israel, and Sweden follow Roth's method. Swedish investors are more likely to look up the balances of their portfolios on days when they know from general news that the stock market went up than on days when they know that the market went down.[23] This way they savor the pride of portfolio gains while shielding themselves from the regret of portfolio losses by pretending that the general decline in the stock market was accompanied by no losses in their own portfolios. Israeli investors prefer certificates of deposit issued by banks over Treasury bills, even though Treasury bills offer higher returns. They do so because certificates of deposit display no daily prices, making it easier for investors to keep themselves blind to losses. Investors in Treasury bills find it harder to keep themselves blind to losses because daily prices of Treasury bills are displayed in newspapers and on the Internet.[24]

Bonds as Safety Nets and Trampolines

Zero-coupon Treasury bonds pay no interest. Instead, we buy them at a discount. For example, we might buy a zero-coupon Treasury bond maturing in 20 years for $45,000. The bond promises to pay us $100,000 when it matures, but its price might go higher or lower than $45,000 during its years, depending on changes in interest rates. The no-mental-loss benefits of zero-coupon Treasury bonds are reflected in their description as safety nets with the bounce of a trampoline. If the price of the bond exceeds $45,000 a year or two later, we can realize a gain, enjoying the bounce of a trampoline. But we can pretend that we have sustained no loss if the price of the bond declined to $35,000 a year or two later, since we do not have to realize our loss and have a safety net in the $100,000 we are sure to receive in 20 years.

We hear the importance of the expressive and emotional benefits of no-mental-loss investments in comments about the advantage of buying individual Treasury bonds over mutual funds containing Treasury bonds. Individual bonds have specific maturity dates, such as in three years, while bond mutual funds contain many bonds with varying maturity dates, perhaps some with two years to maturity, some with three, and some with four. Holders of individual bonds have greater no-mental-loss benefits than holders of bond mutual funds since they have the option to wait till the maturity date of each of their individual bonds and receive what they have been promised. In contrast, holders of bond mutual funds have no such option since mutual funds have no maturity dates. The prices of mutual funds are set at the market price at the end of each day, moving up or down. Holders of bond mutual funds are never assured that they will not incur a loss when they sell, no matter how long they wait.

Never Break the Buck

Money market funds were introduced in the early 1970s to circumvent a regulation that limited the rate of interest banks could pay for deposits smaller than $100,000. They soon turned into substitutes for bank savings and checking accounts. Money market fund investors received checkbooks similar to bank checkbooks and could write checks for use everywhere. But money market funds were not a close enough substitute for checking accounts because they lacked the no-mental-loss benefit.

Investors who deposited a dollar in a checking account were assured that they would be able to withdraw a dollar the following day, week, or year. But money market fund investors had no such assurance. A dollar invested in a money market fund one day might be worth 98 cents the following day. Investors who contemplated buying a television set for $500 would have had to withdraw 510 shares of the money market fund if its share price declined from $1 on the day of the purchase to 98 cents when their check was cashed. The extra ten shares registered as a loss in the minds of money market investors, and money market fund executives were soon hearing their unhappy voices. In 1977, following much lobbying by mutual fund companies, the SEC approved the use of an accounting method for money market funds such that the price of their shares remains at $1 even when the value of the shares deviates from it. Managers of money market funds promised not to "break the buck" and, at last, they seemed to have acquired the no-mental-loss benefits of checking accounts.

The Buck Is Broken

The promise of managers of money market funds not to break the buck was sincere but not guaranteed. The small print always said that the buck might be broken. Still, managers of money market funds kept their promise for many years, on occasion paying from their own pockets so as not to break the buck when the value of the funds' shares fell below $1. But when the financial crisis arrived in 2008 the managers of Reserve Primary Fund announced that their fund contained securities of bankrupt Lehman Brothers and they must break the buck and set its shares to 97 cents. The development "is really, really bad," said Don Phillips of Morningstar. "You talk about Lehman and Merrill having been stellar institutions, but breaking the buck is sacred territory."[25] This breaking of the buck was prominent among the events that led Henry Paulson, America's Secretary of the Treasury and Ben Bernanke, chairman of its Federal Reserve Bank, to recommend drastic measures, including government insurance of money market funds, fearing the panic that would ensue if money market fund investors raced to withdraw their money, further destabilizing the financial system.

The demise of Reserve Primary Fund is ironic because Bruce Bent, one of its founders, opposed buck accounting when it was considered in the 1970s. Bent feared that buck accounting would compel managers of money market funds to buy risky securities in attempts to provide higher returns than their competitors. Bent vowed not to buy such risky securities, but he broke his vow under the pressure of competition. This is why Reserve Primary Fund held securities in Lehman when it went bankrupt. What started as an attempt to turn money market funds into no-mental-loss investments ended with very real losses.

LOSSES MAKE US ANGRY

Anger joins regret and pride on the list of emotions that animate our attitudes toward investment gains and losses and our decisions to realize them. Losses make us angry, and anger propels us to take revenge by getting even. This is true in our investments lives and in our personal lives as well. "I do hold grudges," said Terry Garnett, a senior vice president of Oracle Corp and a personal friend of its CEO, Larry Ellison, before Ellison fired him. "Am I motivated by that? Absolutely." Anger propelled Garnett to vow there would be a day of reckoning. He strove to get even from his new position at Ingres Corp., a software company trying to outdo Oracle.[26]

The desire to get even following losses and the anger they provoke amplify our ambitions. Workers at a Chinese factory produced more when incentives were framed as getting even from losses than when the same incentives were framed as gains.[27] Sometimes rejection letters from colleges and universities register as crushing losses, including the rejection letter sent to Warren Buffett from Harvard's Business School. Years later Buffett, the chairman of Berkshire Hathaway, said that the letter crushed him at the time but, in time, all turned out well. Buffett enrolled at Columbia's Business School instead, where he studied with Benjamin Graham and David Dodd. In 2008 his family gave Columbia $12 million.

Sadness and disgust join anger, regret, and pride in the emotions that affect our perceptions of losses and our decisions to realize them. Anger drives us to hold on to our losing investments and fight our losses, whereas sadness urges us to change our circumstances by selling our losing investments, and disgust compels us to expel our losing investments. People exposed to images that elicit sadness are willing to sell what they have at lower prices, and people exposed to images that elicit disgust are more inclined to trade away what they have than people not exposed to such images.[28, 29]

PROFESSIONAL INVESTORS AND AMATEURS

Professional investors are no more immune to cognitive errors and emotions than amateur individual investors and they are no more eager to realize their losses. Yet professional investors have learned to recognize their reluctance to realize losses and devise methods to counteract that reluctance. One professional investor said:

> I have a hard and fast rule that I never let my losses on a trade exceed ten percent. Say I buy a ten-dollar stock. As soon as it goes to nine dollars, I must sell it and take a loss. . . . You have to be man enough to admit to your peers that you're wrong and get out. Then you're alive and playing the game the next day.[30]

Trading companies regularly construct systems that mandate traders to close their positions at the end of each day or even before they leave for lunch during the day. This compels traders to realize their losses. Investment companies sometimes rotate managers, facilitating the realization of losses. Newly appointed mutual fund managers are ready to realize losses left behind by departing mutual fund managers.[31]

When Bankers Are Reluctant to Realize Losses

Investors who are reluctant to realize their losses can go bankrupt, but bankers who are reluctant to realize their losses can bankrupt their banks. This is what Nick Leeson did to Barings Bank, Britain's oldest merchant bank, the bank that financed the Napoleonic wars, the Louisiana Purchase, and the Erie Canal. Nick Leeson was hired by Barings Bank in Singapore in 1992 and almost immediately made unauthorized positions in Japanese stocks and bonds. He lost his early bets but was reluctant to realize his losses. Instead, Leeson hid his losses in a fictional account he created and continued trading, hoping to get even. Unfortunately, Leeson kept losing, digging his hole deeper rather than climbing out. His losses amounted to two million British pounds in 1992, mushroomed to 23 million a year later, and then to 208 million in 1994. In the end, Leeson's losses amounted to 827 million British pounds and Barings Bank was sold for a single British pound. Leeson has learned his lesson, now that he is out of jail. Now he realizes his losses quickly and does not risk more than he can afford to lose. Leeson bolsters his self-control by following a rule that compels him to realize his gains or losses at the end of each day, thereby limiting his ability to hide losses and postpone their realization.[32]

The collapse of the Amaranth hedge fund provides another example of the disastrous consequences of the reluctance to realizing losses. Nicholas Maounis, who founded Amaranth, made Brian Hunter co-head of the energy desk in 2005 and gave him authority over his own trades. When Amaranth lost money in trading convertible bonds, its mainstay, Maounis was reluctant to make peace with his losses, realize them, and move on. "Do something" former traders quote Maounis saying to Hunter, "We need you." But energy trades brought only additional losses and increasing reluctance to realizing them. The fund, which had $9.2 billion, lost $6.5 billion of it in less than a month. "Amaranth's demise is not due to some complicated quantitative reason—it's about human failing and frailty," said Hank Higdon, who runs New York–based Higdon Partners LLC, a recruiter for hedge funds and other money management firms.[33]

When Corporate Managers Are Reluctant to Realize Losses

Corporate managers are as reluctant to realize losses as individual investors and professional ones. On December 7, 1981, Lockheed Corporation announced that it had decided to terminate the production of its L-1011 Tristar jumbo jetliner. Lockheed started the Tristar program in 1968 in partnership with Rolls Royce, hoping to compete with Boeing's 747 and McDonnell Douglas' DC-10. The L-1011 program was known to be a loser for many years and would have bankrupted Lockheed if not for a government bailout.

I remember reading the news about the termination of the Lockheed jetliner project while on a trip paid for by a short course on finance I taught to Lockheed engineers at our campus. "Rational decisions to continue or terminate investment projects," I said to my Lockheed students, "depend on likely future costs and revenues. Past costs are 'sunk costs,' which should play no role in such decisions." I illustrated the general principles of rational decisions with the example of the Lockheed L-1011.

Lockheed's shareholders celebrated the L-1011 termination decision. The news was announced on December 7, 1981, after the close of the stock market, but on the following day Lockheed's share price increased by 18 percent. Evidently, Lockheed's shareholders expected that Lockheed would continue to throw good money after bad, and were pleasantly surprised by its rational decision to stop. I hasten to add that I claim no credit for Lockheed's wise decision.

More recently, in 2008, Toshiba announced that it was terminating its HD DVD project and ceding victory to Sony after a two-year battle with its Blu-ray format. Toshiba's cost of dropping HD DVD would be in the hundreds of millions. But the money Toshiba spent on the HD DVD project was already sunk. Toshiba had nothing to gain from throwing good money after bad and much to gain from realizing its loss. The inevitability of termination of the HD DVD project became evident to Toshiba's executives on Monday, February 18, after Wal-Mart decided not to stock discs and players using the Toshiba format. Toshiba's share price increased 5.7 percent following its decision to terminate its HD DVD project.[34]

Later, Atsutoshi Nishida, Toshiba's chief executive, said that he started thinking about terminating the HD DVD project when Warner Bros. announced its support for Blu-ray. "We took a little time before reaching a final decision," he said, "so we could give people a chance to voice their opinions and we could consider all the ramifications and consequences of pulling out, such as how it would affect consumers and us. . . . One has to take calculated risks in business, but it's also important to switch gears immediately if you think your decision was wrong." Nishida was able to integrate the mental account of the HD DVD into Toshiba's other mental accounts. Asked whether the termination of the HD DVD project was a blow to Toshiba's growth he said, "It was just one avenue of growth. It was one of 45 strategic business units that we have. This just means we now have 44."[35]

Our anger at losses and our reluctance to realize them are nothing compared with our anger at taxes and our reluctance to pay them. This is the subject of the next chapter.

CHAPTER 11

We Want to Pay No Taxes

"Nowhere on any tax form does it say you can't be crafty," winks an advertisement by an investment company, offering tax-free mutual funds and the picture of a smiling man next to a swimming pool. "How to send less to the IRS," promises an advertisement by another investment company. Few of us like to pay taxes and most of us have blueprints for ideal tax systems in which we pay less. The message we send to our elected officials was summarized succinctly by Senator Russell B. Long: "Don't tax you, don't tax me, tax that fellow behind the tree!"

High returns are the utilitarian benefits of tax-free funds; investors who send less to the IRS keep more of their investment returns. But tax-free funds and other tax-saving investments have expressive and emotional benefits as well. We express ourselves as high-income investors, with status as high as our tax brackets. We express ourselves as smart, savvy, wily and crafty, which is what it takes to avoid taxes. Pride at avoiding taxes is emotionally satisfying, but the emotions accompanying taxes extend to anger and hatred. We are angry when taxes rob us of personal freedom or when they are wasted by politicians and bureaucrats. "Well, Mr. Big Brother IRS man, let's try something different, take my pound of flesh and sleep well," wrote Andrew Joseph Stack III in February of 2009, just before flying his plane into an IRS office building, killing an IRS employee and himself.[1]

TAX-BREAK SPECIALS

Anger over taxation by a foreign government was the cry of the 1773 Boston Tea Party where American colonists, animated by anger, tossed into the Boston Harbor a shipload of tea taxed by the British government.

Still, we do not like taxes even when imposed by our own governments. Commenting on a *Wall Street Journal* article about taxes, one taxpayer wrote: "I drive to work. I paid tax on the car I drive, the gas it uses, and on the maintenance to keep it up. At work, I earn money. This money is taxed by the state and federal government. . . . I go out for lunch and guess what, it's taxed as well. . . . Should I die, taxed again. . . ."[2]

My mechanic sent a postcard offering "Tax Break Specials," saving me the cost of sales taxes. He must know that his typical customers prefer small savings in the form of tax breaks to more substantial savings in the form of cash discounts. We dislike taxes so much that we are willing to forego $5,000 to save $4,000 in taxes. For instance, imagine circumstances where you earn an annual salary of $50,000 before taxes at an American company. Now pretend you are offered a position at one of two European branches at a $75,000 salary. The good thing about Country A is that your daily commute will be 60 minutes shorter than in Country B. The bad thing about Country A is that food would cost you $5,000 more than in Country B. Which country would you choose? Now imagine identical circumstances except that the bad thing about Country A is that you would pay $4,000 more in taxes than in Country B. Which country would you choose? The first of the two circumstances was presented to one group of people and the second was presented to another group. It turned out that more people in the United States and Britain chose country B when they could save $4,000 in taxes than when they could save $5,000 in the cost of food.[3]

TAX EVASION AND AVOIDANCE

"Angry affluents" fight the taxman with a scheme in which life insurance premiums they pay are tax deductible while tax-free benefits go to their heirs.[4] "I hate the IRS," said cardiologist John McCartney. "I don't want to give [the IRS] another penny of my money, and this plan helps it go to my kids and grandkids, and to the causes I feel are important." The desire to help children by avoiding taxes sometimes backfires, igniting anger and splitting families. A trust and estate lawyer told me of parents who placed a parcel of land in a trust, shared equally among their children. The parents considered the trust as no more than a tax dodge, while the children saw it as a gift. Some years later the parents wanted to sell the land and asked the children to sign documents approving its transfer back into their hands. One son, now married, was reluctant to sign. "You did not speak like that to your mother before you married *that* woman," said the mother. Tears and family estrangement followed.

John McCarthy, a California businessman, admitted using a UBS Swiss account to hide more than $1 million from U.S. tax authorities. UBS employees told him that "a lot of United States' clients don't report their income and just take it off the top." McCarthy avoided as much as five years in prison by helping prosecutors pursuing enablers of offshore tax evasion. He was sentenced instead to six months of home detention and three years of probation. Two others were not as lucky. Robert Moran and Jeffrey Chernick who used UBS accounts to evade taxes were ordered to prison.[5]

Trouble also came to Leona Helmsley who ran her empire of luxurious Manhattan hotels with an iron fist that earned her the sobriquet "Queen of Mean." Helmsley was a bit too wily and crafty, and so her tax maneuvers led to a prison term for tax fraud. A housekeeper testified that Helmsley said, "We don't pay taxes. Only the little people pay taxes." But Helmsley continued to insist on keeping her distance from the little people. She sued when a cemetery announced plans to build an affordable mausoleum, large enough to hold the remains of more than 2,000 people, near the palatial mausoleum where her late husband and son were put to rest. Helmsley claimed that the mausoleum for the masses would disrupt the serenity she was promised for her family's eternal resting place.[6]

Nothing may be certain except death and taxes, but the death tax, also known as the estate tax, was abolished for those dying in 2010. Not everyone is willing to let nature take its course. "I have two clients on life support, and the families are struggling with whether to continue heroic measures for a few more days," said Joshua Rubenstein, a lawyer with Katten Muchin Rosenman. "Do they want to live for the rest of their lives having made serious medical decisions based on estate-tax law?" Some heirs are quite willing to live the rest of their life with such decisions. They have been granted permission by those nearing death to consider estate taxes when making end-of-life medical decisions. "We have done this at least a dozen times, and have gotten more calls recently," said Andrew Katzenstein, a lawyer with the Proskauer Rose law firm. Death by euthanasia qualifies for exemption from estate tax, and one of Katzenstein's clients was considering a trip to Holland for that purpose.[7]

Donations combine the expressive and emotional benefits of charity with those of tax avoidance. The urge for charity is greater than the urge to avoid taxes when we decide how much to donate to charities whose missions are human services, public and social benefit, and health. The amounts we donate to such charities vary little when tax rates change. The urge for charity is weaker and the urge to avoid taxes is stronger when we decide how much to donate to private foundations, private educational institutions, arts and culture charities, environmental charities, and animal-related charities. The amounts we donate to these charities decline when the tax benefits of donations decline.[8]

"Giving when you are alive can give you tremendous fulfillment," said Claude Rosenberg, an investor who made his fortune by investing for others. He established the New Tithing Group to show people how much they can give without endangering their own financial security. Rosenberg noted that American donors did not harvest all the tax benefits available to them, such as the benefits of donating appreciated investments rather than cash; he devised a calculator that optimizes both charity and tax savings.[9]

Harvesting tax benefits from charitable giving is legal even if it shortchanges the taxman, but charitable giving is no defense when it is funded by tax evasion. Finn M. W. Caspersen donated millions to Harvard and Princeton and pledged $30 million to Harvard Law School, the largest single donation in the school's history. Yet authorities were gathering information that Caspersen was using a secret offshore bank to evade as much as $100 million of taxes. Caspersen chose suicide over fines and possibly prison. "He made everything right for so many people, and that is why this is such a tragedy," said Susan Wachter, a friend.[10] Yet the story of Caspersen is a puzzle as much as it is tragedy. Why would a man evade taxes, risking fines, prison, or worse, only to give away that money to universities? Perhaps it is because Caspersen believed that universities would use the money better than the government. Or perhaps it is because evading taxes is a sport, where pride goes to the crafty. Or perhaps it is because universities receiving $30 million donations etch the donors' names over entrances of new buildings while the taxman etches nothing but a canceled check.

WHO COMMITS TAX EVASION

Not everyone evades taxes and not everyone evades taxes by the same proportionate amount. Some people are less honest than others, and some, hoping that they will not be caught, are willing to gamble on that hope. The propensity to evade also depends on different opportunities and rewards for evasion. People who receive their income in cash find evading taxes easier than people who receive their income in checks, and people who stand to gain thousands by evasion may succumb to temptation more easily than people who stand to gain only hundreds.

Most of the gap between taxes owed by Americans and taxes paid comes from underreported income. The IRS estimates that only a small fraction of wages and salaries, which are subject to withholdings and information reports, is not reported. But self-employment business income is not subject to withholding or information reports, and the IRS estimates that more than half of it is not reported.[11] Danes are a bit more honest than Americans, but they too underpay their taxes when they can get away with it. Tax evasion amounts to less than 1 percent of taxes due on income subject to withholding and information reports but it amounts to more than a third of taxes due on self-reported income.[12]

Fear of audits deters tax evasion. An independent poll conducted for the IRS found that 96 percent of respondents agreed that "it is every American's civic duty to pay their fair share of taxes" and 93 percent agreed that everyone "who cheats on their taxes should be held accountable." But when asked what factors influence their decision to pay taxes honestly, 62 percent answered "fear of audit" and 68 percent said it was the fact that the IRS already knows their income from reports by third parties.[13] The same is true in Denmark. Taxpayers who were audited in the past report substantially higher income, and so do taxpayers who receive letters threatening audits.

Culture affects tax evasion. Tax evasion is greater in the United States than in Denmark, and it is greater in Greece and Italy than in Sweden and the Netherlands. "The core of the problem is that we don't have a culture of civic society," said Stavros Katsios, a professor at Greece's Ionian University. "In Greece, complying with the rules is a matter of dishonor. They call you stupid if you follow the rules." *Fakelaki* is Greek for "little envelopes" of bribes. Taxpayers who owe 10,000 euros bribe tax inspectors with 4,000 euros, pay 2,000 euros to the state, and keep 4,000 euros for themselves.[14]

WINNING THE TAX GAME

"Doubtless the time will come when all the states will recognize the necessity of working out, along sensible and scientific lines, the problem of the taxation of investment securities,"[15] wrote the *World's Work* in 1914. But that time has never come nor is it likely to ever come. The tax game is an endless tennis game in which taxpayers are on one side of the net and governments are on the other. Governments devise schemes to lob the tax ball into the taxpayers' side of the court, and taxpayers learn to lob it back, avoiding taxes or evading them. Clever accountants and tax lawyers look for loopholes in tax laws and devise schemes to exploit them. In time, governments close old loopholes but invariably open new loopholes. And the tax game goes on.[16]

The desire of investors to win the tax game was as great a century ago as it is today. The *World's Work* comment was prompted by a clergyman asking for directions to tax-exempt investments. "Government bonds," he had sensibly pointed out, "were a sort of investment luxury which few people could really afford to buy. They bore low interest rates. . . ." The problem in the clergyman's case, therefore, seemed to be to find something in the category of "exempt" stocks, on which the yield would be good and the risk negligible."

The story of the clergyman also illustrates the common tendency of taxpayers to hit the tax ball into the net, losing more than they had hoped to gain. The clergyman's banker hesitated but finally recommended the stocks of two established companies, each paying substantial dividends, Boston & Maine Railroad and Western Union Telegraph. Everything went well for several years until the two companies reduced their dividend before canceling them altogether.

Partnership Tax Games

General partnerships existed for ages and they were often used for investments. All partners participate in the management of such partnerships and are responsible for its debts. Limited partnerships are different. Management is in the hands general partners, whereas limited partners have no role in the management of the partnerships and only limited responsibility for the partnerships' debt. Tax laws made limited partnerships difficult to market to ordinary investors before 1981 by restricting the types of investors who qualify. But a 1981 revision in the law changed the game, opening a mass marketing loophole. Investors rushed in before a 1986 revision in the law closed that loophole, handing the game to the government and turning investors into losers.

Limited partnerships created accounting losses for their investors, offsetting taxable income and slashing tax bills. They promised that no real losses would follow accounting ones. An investor wrote to *Money* magazine in 1996, "I have two limited partnership investments that I bought in 1984 and want to unload. They are 10 units in Consolidated Resources Health Care Fund II, which cost me $1,000 each and 80 units of Phoenix Leasing Income Fund VII, which originally cost $250 apiece. Is there any way I can sell them?" *Money* magazine delivered the bad news. The $10,000 invested in the first limited partnership has dwindled to $400. The $20,000 invested in the second has dwindled to $212. The unfortunate investor would have to pay a $199 trading fee and a $50 back-end fee if he wished to cash his $212 investment in the second partnership.[17]

Governments initiate some tax games by imposing different tax rates on different kinds of income. Tax rates on wages and salaries are different from tax rates on dividends or capital gains, and taxes on corporations are different from taxes on individuals. Taxpayers play the tax game by switching income from where it is subject to higher tax rates to where it is subject to lower tax rates. General partners of hedge funds and private equity funds are one group of investors who play this switching tax game against the government.

The general partners of hedge funds and private equity funds are its managers, such as the executives of Kohlberg Kravis Roberts, a private equity fund. Limited partners are the outside investors in the funds, including individual investors and pension funds, such as CalPERS, the giant pension fund of California's state employees. General partners commonly take a 2 percent fee on the investments they manage plus a 20 percent cut of the profits they generate. The 2 percent fee counts as regular income but general partners have been counting their 20 percent cut, called "carried interest," as capital gains. The distinction matters because the top federal tax bracket for regular income is 35 percent, scheduled to rise to 39.6 percent, whereas the top federal tax bracket for capital gains is only 15 percent.

The government wants to compel general partners to count carried interest as regular income, paying the higher regular income rate rather than the lower capital gains rate. This would cost general partners almost $25 billion during the coming decade, transferring that money into the hands of the government. When that happens, "people will try to figure out how to get around this," said Francois Hechinger, a tax partner at BDO Seidman. General partners are positioning themselves to strike the government's tax ball when it crosses the net. The government knows that general partners are skillful at striking the tax ball and is devising clever moves to strike it back. These moves include a 40 percent penalty on general partners who employ a scheme later ruled illegal. General partners are rumored to plan their next strike at the tax ball, selling their carried interest to others and investing the proceeds so gains count as capital gains.[18]

Tax Shelter Games

FLIP, OPIS, Boss, and Son of Boss are tax shelters invented and marketed by the KPMG, the accounting firm. FLIP stands for Foreign Leveraged Investment Program and OPIS is Offshore Portfolio Investment Strategy. Clever tax shelters bring their designers both money and pride. KPMG awarded paperweights shaped like light bulbs to employees with good tax-shelter ideas.[19] It earned $124 million from shelters that cost the government more than ten times that in lost taxes. Some KPMG partners warned the firm that its tax shelters crossed over the line onto the wrong side of the law, but to no avail. An e-mail from Mark Watson, a KPMG technical tax advice partner, said that KPMG used "stealth reporting" on tax returns to deceive the IRS. Another e-mail warned that "we are filing misleading, and perhaps false," tax returns. Jeffrey Eischeid, a supervising partner at the tax shelter unit, insisted in testimony before a Senate committee that the shelters were legitimate investments. "I certainly viewed them as investment strategies that also had tax avoidance benefits," he said. "Do you see anything about investment attributes in your memo?" pressed Senator Carl Levin. Eischeid was silent for some moments before he finally said "I don't know how to change my answer." "Try an honest answer," retorted Levin.[20]

KPMG's tax partners were quite explicit in their calculation of the utilitarian costs and benefits of their tax violations. Gregg Ritchie, a KPMG tax partner, noted in an internal memo that the firm would earn $360,000 from each shelter but pay only $31,000 in penalties if a shelter was discovered by the IRS. It turned out that his accounting was faulty. He neglected to add to the cost column the potential loss of career and perhaps prison time.[21]

EMC Corporation is the world's biggest maker of storage computers, and Richard Egan, its founder, was one investor in the Son of Boss tax shelter. Egan was the newly appointed American ambassador to Ireland when KPMG constructed the shelter for him in 2001 and 2002, aware that the IRS warned against it in 2000. The shelter "involved creating transactions with offsetting positions, which by itself meant that there was no economic risk," said Howard Medwed, a lawyer.

Egan used the shelter to avoid paying more than $62 million of taxes on more than $327 million of capital gains from EMC shares and options. "None of the participants in these complex transactions believed that they were real business transactions, with any purpose other than tax avoidance," wrote U.S. District Judge Dennis Saylor in 2010 as he ruled that Egan crossed the legal line. Saylor added that "the transactions at issue were real only in the sense that a performance by actors on stage is real. No one watching Macbeth believes that they are witnessing the murder of a Scottish king, and the actors do not believe it either."[22] Egan committed suicide in 2009 and Michael Egan, his son, said that he is not likely to appeal the 2010 decision "It was important to my father at the time," he said.[23]

KPMG agreed to pay $456 million to avoid criminal prosecution over its sale of tax shelters such as the one used by Egan, but it does not refrain from designing and promoting tax shelters. "KPMG in Belgium has built up a distinct reputation in the tax-shelter regime for Belgian audio-visual works," says its 2010 Belgian Web site. "The tax shelter is an important media-specific tax break that provides corporate investors, within certain limitations, with an exemption from their retained tax profits equal to

150 percent of the investment made, in view of financing the production of a Belgian audio-visual work."[24]

A search for status animates tax dodgers as much as a search for money. Leona Helmsley, the Queen of Mean, had more money than she could have spent in many lifetimes. In the end she left much of it to her dog. Yet her tax dodging elevated her status above that of the "little people" who pay taxes. The search for status extends much beyond tax dodging and that search is the subject of the next chapter.

CHAPTER 12

We Want High Status and Proper Respect

An investor cut me off when I mentioned mutual funds. "I'm into hedge funds," he said. The utilitarian benefits of hedge funds include a promise of returns higher than risks, but hedge funds promise expressive and emotional benefits as well. The expressive benefits of hedge funds include status and sophistication, and their emotional benefits include pride and respect. Hedge funds open their doors only to the rich, making it easy for investors to brag about their riches without appearing to brag. An employee at a British hedge fund told me about a group of investors who protested when the fund lowered its minimum investment from a million pounds to half a million. "Now they'll have to consort with the working class," he said. A marketing agent for hedge funds in Silicon Valley told me about prospective investors feeling slighted when she mentioned the $250,000 minimum investment. "Don't you think that we can invest more than that?" asked one.

High returns bring wealth, and wealth elevates status. But hedge funds elevate status even when they detract from wealth. Hedge funds are like exclusive clubs, and exclusivity enhances status. Mere millionaires are consigned to commercial flights, albeit in first-class cabins, but hedge fund investors can dream about the exclusive world of private planes that depart when they command. "Exclusivity and secrecy were crucial to hedge funds from the first," wrote John Brooks in 1973, describing the go-go 1960s. "It certified one's affluence while attesting to one's astuteness"[1]

STATUS INVESTMENTS

Conversations about the benefits of hedge funds and private equity investments are difficult because we are reluctant to admit that we are attracted to anything beyond their utilitarian benefits. We are especially reluctant to admit that we seek status. "The fees paid to private equity managers have been a source of great frustration," said Joseph A. Dear, chief investment officer of CalPERS, the California Public Employees' Retirement System. But he expects utilitarian benefits, even if modest, from his private equity investments. "We don't expect 20 percent," said Dear. "We expect 3 percent more than public markets, net of fees."[2]

Dear might be realistic, but the evidence suggests that he is unrealistically optimistic. One study found that while some private equity funds provided extra returns, even spectacular returns, most did not. The returns of private equity funds, on average, were no higher than those of the S&P 500 Index once fees are subtracted.[3] Another study found that, on average, the annual returns of private equity funds exceeded by 3 percentage points the returns of other investments with similar risks. But the returns of private equity funds lagged once fees are subtracted.[4]

Yet another study found that although hedge funds do tend to provide the utilitarian benefits of extra returns, investors dissipate such extra returns as they switch from fund to fund, seeking the best. Annual returns to investors in hedge fund were on average 4 percentage points lower than the returns of the funds themselves. The gap between the returns of the funds and the returns of their investors expanded to 9 percentage points among "star" funds with the highest returns.[5]

Tasting the Status of Wine Investments

Private equity and hedge funds are not the only investments conveying status. Wine is a status investment, especially in Europe. The Vintage Wine Fund, managed in Britain but domiciled in the Cayman Islands, expects "high capital appreciation by investing in fine wines from regions including Bordeaux, Burgundy, the Rhone Valley, Tuscany, Piedmont, Champagne, and Portugal."[6] Demand for wine splits into two parts, claims the Vintage

Wine Fund on its Web site. "The U.S. seems mainly focused on wines in the second tier, such as Gruaud Larose 2000. . . . Heading in the other direction—East—are the first growths with Lafite and Carruades de Lafite still leading the way. . . ." Still, first-tier wines attract some American vintners, and prestigious American wine labels now substitute for a European coat of arms. Paul Hobbs, a California winemaker, chose to sell his 1999 Beckstoffer Cabernet Sauvignon at $135 a bottle, limiting buyers to six bottles. Christian Miller of Motto Kryla & Fisher, a wine industry consulting company in St. Helena, California, said: "The thing you're paying for as you move up [in price] would be prestige, scarcity, and to some extent intensity of flavor."[7]

Watching the Status of Movie Investments

Movies are also status investments. A glossy IndieVest brochure I recently received suggested: "Your membership may require an acceptance speech," showing a gaggle of cameras poised to take the pictures of investors accepting their awards. The brochure mentions the utilitarian benefits of investments in movies. The movie *Crash,* for instance, made $170 million on a $7.1 million investment, and *Juno* made $229 million on a similar investment. The brochure adds that investments in movies help diversify our portfolios. But there is more to investments in movies than utilitarian benefits, says the brochure. "You'll also enjoy the exclusive benefits of being an IndieVest Executive Producer, seeing your name on screen in each of your film's end credits, attending exclusive cocktail receptions with cast members, going on the set during your film's production, and being a VIP at your film's U.S. premieres."

IndieVest accepts investments only from "accredited" investors, people whose wealth exceeds $1 million or whose annual income exceeds $200,000. People without this kind of money can invest in films or rock bands on the Kickstarter Web site. The makers of the film *Person of Interest* were soliciting investments of $5 or more toward their $5,000 goal, which would help them "build a small summer/fall tour schedule, playing one night screening events in venues large and small, building a community around the film." Reviewers have described the film as "an elegant grunge," and "this generation's *Taxi Driver!*" The filmmakers asked people to join them "in the belief that art, and especially film, can still be a transformative experience, bringing people together, almost like nothing else, in shared exploration and exchange of ideas, philosophies, and cultures." Those who invest $50 will receive a limited edition T-shirt yet to be designed but "assured to be very cool." Those who invest $100 will also receive free tickets to a screening "if we come to your neck of the woods."[8]

Looking at the Status of Art Investments

Paintings are investments, and their expressive and emotional benefits are on display in the distinction between originals and fakes. High-quality fake paintings have all the utilitarian benefits of original paintings; they add color to otherwise blank walls and are pleasing to the eye. Yet they are lacking in expressive and emotional benefits. Han van Meegeren, on trial for a Vermeer painting he forged said, "Yesterday this picture was worth millions of guilders, and experts and art lovers would come from all over the world and pay money to see it. Today, it is worth nothing, and nobody would cross the street to see it for free. But the picture has not changed. What has?"[9] The expressive and emotional benefits of the picture have changed. Once exposed, fake paintings cannot express status, elicit pride, or provide entrance into the rarified club of art connoisseurs and members of museum boards.

It is ironic that when it comes to art, it is art historians, not investment professionals, who want to separate utilitarian benefits from expressive and emotional ones. Lisa Jardin, herself an art historian, challenged that separation in her study of Renaissance art. "It is curious how reluctant we are to include acquisitiveness among the defining characteristics of an age which formed our aesthetic heritage,"[10] she wrote. Jardin illustrated her challenge in a discussion of the Master of Liesborn's *Annunciation* painting, depicting the Virgin surrounded by "a burnished brass platter, an ornate candlestick, a small stoppered bottle and an oriental-style metal pitcher, a carved chest with metal hinges and doors, an elaborately tiled floor, an ornate desk and settle, a canopied bed with red brocade hangings, and embroidered cushion." Was the Renaissance admirer of this and similar lavish Renaissance paintings "encouraged to want to be in the Virgin's spiritual likeness, or was he or she expected to be seduced by all that lavishness to want to inhabit her surroundings, wonderfully cluttered as theses are with the booty of international trade?"

Expensive paintings expressed high status in the time of the Renaissance and they express it in our time. Today it is successful hedge fund managers who buy expensive paintings. The prices of paintings increase when top incomes increase, when income inequality increases, and when stock prices increase.[11] The ups and downs of the prices of Russian art are especially sensitive to the ups and downs in the price of oil, reflecting the ups and downs of the fortunes of the Russian oligarchs.[12] Pablo Picasso's painting *Nude, Green Leaves and Bust* sold at a Christie's auction for $106.5 million to a buyer, likely a Russian oligarch or a hedge fund mogul. Christie's would not disclose the identity of the buyer, but its chief spoke about the "depth of buying from Russia, China, and the Middle East."[13] Steven Cohen, the founder and manager of SAC Capital Advisors, bought Willem de Kooning's *Police Gazette,* an abstract 1955 landscape, for $63.5 million. Kenneth Griffin, managing director and chief executive of Citadel Investment Group bought *False Start,* a seminal 1959 painting by Jasper Johns, for $80 million.[14]

Investors who cannot invest millions in a single piece of art can buy shares of an art fund, where minimum investments range from $100,000 to $250,000. The Fine Art Fund Group's Web site promotes its utilitarian benefits. "The objective is to . . . build long-term capital growth for investors and provide diversification for a client's investment portfolio." But the Web site promotes the expressive and emotional benefits as well. "Enjoyment of the art itself is not compromised," says the Web site, "as investors are given the opportunity to borrow works of art."[15]

The Fine Art Fund Group is frank about the mixing of utilitarian, expressive, and emotional benefits, and young members of boards of art museums, symphonies, and operas are grateful for the new frankness about that mix. "There are a lot of people like myself, in the 30-something and 40-something age group, who want to give something back, but aren't sure what is expected," said Alicia Cooney Quigley, managing director of the Monument Group, an investment company. "It was a relief," she said, when the statement she received from the Boston Lyric Opera specified that a

$10,000 annual donation is expected. Yet Richard Feigen, an art dealer who, by profession, regularly mixes utilitarian, expressive, and emotional benefits, is uneasy. Feigen was concerned that members of art boards are too focused on the fiscal aspects of art and too little on the aesthetic aspects. "Board members are less appreciative of connoisseurship and more interested in the bottom line."[16]

Acquisitions of expensive art mark status ascents and their dispositions mark descents. Disposition of art marked the descent of Richard Fuld, Jr., chairman and chief executive of bankrupt Lehman Brothers, and his wife, Kathy, a well-known collector of modern art. Lehman's stock plunged from $86.18 in February 1997 to 33 cents in September 2008, prompting the Fulds to place much of their art collection on auction at Christie's, including *Study for Agony I,* a 1946 drawing by modern master Arshile Gorky.[17]

STATUS DISPLAYS

While wealth is absolute, status is relative. Would you prefer to live in a society where you earn $50,000 while others earn $25,000, or would you rather live in society where you earn $100,000 while others earn $250,000. Many prefer to be relatively wealthy in a poor society than relatively poor in a rich society.[18] Our happiness depends on how our socioeconomic group is doing relative to the average in our geographic area. This is especially true for people whose group has above-average income.[19] We gain status by pulling ourselves up or pushing others down. In the first stage of one experiment players engaged in bets that resulted in different winnings of real cash, creating inequality among them. Players could see on computer screens how much they and each of the other players were winning, but they did not know the identity of the other players. Next, they were given the option to "burn" other people's money anonymously, but at a cost of burning some of their own money. Despite this cost to themselves, almost two-thirds of people chose to burn other people's money they considered to be undeserved windfalls.[20]

Chief executive officers who are part of wide social circles of fellow CEOs receive higher pay than CEOs in narrow social circles, and the availability of information about the pay of fellow CEOs intensifies competition for pay and status.[21] The rich accumulate more wealth than they or their heirs can reasonably consume, perhaps because accumulated wealth brings status. Wealth boosts self-confidence and applies balm when one is slighted by others.[22] Indeed, the mere act of counting money calms distress and restores self-confidence. In one experiment some people were asked to count $20 bills. Next, each was placed in a group that slighted them by excluding them from the group's activities. Other people were placed in the same situation, where they felt socially excluded, but they were asked to count slips of paper beforehand rather than $20 bills. People who counted money felt less distress when slighted by social exclusion than people who counted mere slips of paper. Moreover, the social exclusion of people who counted slips of papers intensified their desire for money, to serve as balm on their social wounds.[23]

David Tepper left Goldman Sachs in 1993 to found Apaloosa, his hedge fund, after he was repeatedly passed over for a Goldman Sachs partnership. Money provided balm to wounds of slights. In 2004 Tepper donated $55 million to Carnegie Mellon University, and its business school is now the Tepper School of Business. The school's new logo bearing Tepper's name was displayed all around him on banners, posters, T-shirts and lampposts at the dedication ceremony on campus. "Not bad for a kid from Peabody High School," he said.[24] Tepper could have derived some utilitarian benefits from his $55 million but he must have derived even greater expressive and emotional benefits by donating the money, enhancing his self-esteem, status, and pride in being able to contribute to a university, its students and its professors.

Traps in Status Displays

Status displays are complicated by our desire to obscure them. We might want to mention our investments in hedge funds, knowing that hedge funds signal high status. But a loud expression of status, like a display of an oversized logo on a Gucci bag, can bring embarrassment rather than esteem. Canvas tote bags embroidered with the number 11968 were popular several summers ago among the wealthy in Manhattan's upper-eastside. This is the ZIP Code of Southampton, a prestigious summer spot. Jane Holzer, a socialite who owns such a bag and a similar Palm Beach one, tried to obscure her display of status when asked why the Zip Code is embroidered on her bag. "I liked the bag itself, the shape, the happy colors," she said.[25]

Envy

Displays of status are also complicated by empathy toward those of lesser status and by fear of envy-induced backlash. Mechanics at vehicle emission testing stations have opportunities to bend the law for customers whose cars would otherwise fail the tests. Most mechanics are more willing to help customers with standard cars than customers with luxury cars, and both empathy and envy affect that willingness.[26] Brigitte Graulich, the wife of a restaurant owner, no longer buys two designer handbags a month as she did before the recent financial crisis and recession, even though her family's income did not decline. "I think everyone's changed, rich or poor," she said. "You feel sympathetic for other people who lost their jobs. I feel guilty spending too much. . . . I'm more about keeping my logos inside."[27] We can assuage guilt by associating our search for status with good causes, such as healing the environment.[28]

A Montblanc ad features actor Nicolas Cage wearing a status-elevating Montblanc Timewalker Chronograph. "Helping others gives success true meaning," the ad reads. "Nicolas Cage and Montblanc have made a joint commitment to social responsibility. With your purchase of Montblanc Timewalker you are supporting a significant donation to Heal The Bay." The wrong association, however, can inflict wrath rather than assuage guilt. Montblanc attempted to tap India's growing luxury market with an 18-carat gold-and-silver Mahatma Gandhi fountain pen selling for more than $20,000. Gandhi, the leader of India's struggle against British colonial rule, promoted hand-spinning thread as a symbol of self-reliance and independence from Britain. The pen was shaped to evoke hand-spun cotton cloth, with six meters of gold wire around it. Instead, it evoked outrage. "You can't market luxury using India's holy cows," said Suhel Seth, a managing director of a New Delhi marketing consulting company. "It boomeranged, and it always does." Montblac was forced to apologize and halt the sale of its Gandhi pens.[29]

Schadenfreude

Envy is a precursor to schadenfreude, our joy at the misfortune of those whose status exceeds ours. One group of students in an experiment watched a video of an aspiring medical student with a BMW, an attractive girlfriend, and a wealthy family. He boasted of his ability to get straight As with hardly any studying. Another group watched a similar video except that now the aspiring medical student was of modest means, and had no girlfriend and no car. That student got only Bs despite much studying. Students envied the wealthy person more than the one of modest means. In the end, neither student made it into graduate school, but the groups reacted differently in each case. They expressed greater schadenfreude when they found that the wealthy student was not going to medical school than when they found that the student of modest means was not going there.[30]

The glee of schadenfreude was evident when Martha Stewart was found guilty of obstruction of justice related to insider trading and sentenced to jail. Stewart seemed very much like the student who gets As with little effort, a woman with celebrity friends who is able to arrange her life, home, and dinner parties at levels of perfection unattainable by those who can barely get Bs with much effort. The verdict "is a victory for the little guys," said Chappell Hartridge, one of Stewart's jurors. He added that the jury was turned off by the celebrities who showed up to support Stewart, including Bill Cosby and Rosie O'Donnell. Jurors saw their presence as "a little bit of an insult," Hartridge said. "Was that supposed to sway our decision?"[31]

STATUS DISPLAYS AROUND THE WORLD

Status displays vary across countries and within them. More educated and cosmopolitan upper-middle-class secular women in Turkey emulate Western lifestyles, especially American ones. Perfect command of English ranks high among the status symbols of this group, along with college education in the West. Less-educated upper-middle-class women signal their status through expensive goods deemed prestigious by upper-class Turks and find satisfaction in public deference.[32]

Water buffaloes are the status symbol of the Torajan society in Indonesia. Traveling in Indonesia, I saw buffalo horns nailed to a post in front of a house. The guide explained that status is measured by the number of horns and their size. "How do you think we measure status in the United States?" I asked a fellow traveler standing next to me. "By the length of the home's driveway," he answered. We know the status of our peers and neighbors even when their homes have no long driveways or buffalo horns. Governments of developing countries that seek to identify the poor for social insurance and aid face a problem since they have little information about people's incomes. Governments have attempted to overcome the problem in two ways. One involves observing assets that are hard to hide, such as homes or television sets. The other calls for each person to rank all people in the village from the richest to the poorest. A field experiment in 640 Indonesian villages showed that people rank themselves in the hierarchy no differently than they are ranked by others, and distribution of aid based on rankings was greeted with more satisfaction than distribution based on hard-to-hide assets.[33]

STATUS COMPETITIONS

Sometimes the rich subvert the emblems of status. Henry Paulson, then a Goldman Sachs partner and more recently the U.S. secretary of the Treasury, wore an inexpensive Casio watch. "We are not told whether this is because he is so obviously rich that he does not need to show off or because he hopes that his nonchalant attitude to material possessions will win him admiration," wrote Lucia van der Post.[34] An inexpensive watch on the wrist of a man who can obviously afford an expensive one says, "I'm too smart to be fooled into buying an expensive watch when an inexpensive one shows the same hour." Investors in low-cost index funds often wear their funds as the investment equivalents of Casio watches. Index fund investors say, "I'm too smart to pay extra for funds that are likely to deliver lower returns than index funds."

Few of us willingly engage in status competitions with hedge fund managers. We prefer to enter into status competition we are likely to win. But opting out of status competitions is not always easy. We can hardly opt out of status competitions within our families, illustrated by H. L. Mencken who defined a wealthy man as one who earns $100 more than his wife's sister's husband. Mencken's quip was confirmed in a study of employment decisions. Women are more likely to seek employment when their sisters are employed.[35] Silicon Valley, where I live, is home to many affluent families. The average house here costs about four times the average price in the United States, and the proportion of tax returns reporting income in the $200,000 to 500,000 range is double its overall proportion in California. Silicon Valley multimillionaires are rich in money, obviously, but they care a great deal about their status as well. Gary Kremen's $10 million net worth places him above 99.5 percent of Americans, but he doesn't feel rich. Kremen, founder of dating site Match.com, said "You're a nobody here at $10 million. . . . Everyone around here looks at the people above them. . . . It's just like Wall Street, where there are all these financial guys worth $7 million wondering what's so special about them when there are all these guys worth hundreds of millions of dollars."[36]

Some, including 33-year-old James Hong, do manage to opt out of the status competition. Hong, a co-founder of Hotornot.com, another dating site, found that the site's success allowed him "a very comfortable life without ever needing to get a job—freedom money, as they call it." Yet he also found himself envious of Max Levchin, his best friend and a founder of PayPal, whose net worth is probably in the tens of millions. Hong opted out of the status competition by replacing his Porsche Boxster with a Toyota Prius. "I don't want to live the life of a Boxster, because when you get a Boxster you wish you had a [Porsche] 911. And you know what people who have 911s wish they had? They wish they had a Ferrari." But opting out is not easy. "The only way I've dealt with it over time is to consciously decide not to care. Still, every now and then, when I hear they're getting a certain valuation, I think, 'I need that, too.' There's a little devil inside all of us that says, 'Why not you?'"[37]

SIGNALING STATUS

The poor search for status as the rich do. Many of the poor devote larger shares of their spending on visible status goods such as clothing, jewelry, and cars. Consequently, they save little and invest even less. Banks and mutual fund companies that open branches in poor communities are likely to enhance savings and investment since they offer people opportunities to be seen going in and coming out of these branches, turning invisible savings and investments into visible status goods that might displace some spending on clothing, jewelry, and cars.[38] Prepaid cards serve the poor as credit cards serve people with higher means. Prepaid cards look like credit cards but money charged to them is prepaid rather than paid later, as in credit cards. Interviews with users of prepaid cards revealed that these cards are appreciated for their utilitarian benefits as a convenient payment method. But they are also appreciated for their expressive and emotional benefits, conveying status similar to that of credit card holders.[39]

The status of cars and the signals they convey vary over time. Hummer SUVs signaled power after the 1991 Gulf War, and their drivers spoke derisively of the Toyota "Pious." The popularity of the Hummers declined along with the popularity of the Iraq War and the increase in the price of gasoline. The Prius was now the car that tells the neighbors, 'I'm smarter than you are.' Yet status symbols in Iraq are different from those in the United States. An Iraqi Hummer dealer said "Iraqis love them because they're really a symbol of power." The Hummer satisfies *hasad thukuri*, as the dealer called it in Arabic. In English it is "penis envy."[40]

The status of investments and the signals they convey vary over time as well. The financial crisis of 2008 and 2009 inflicted great losses on private equity and hedge fund investors. The public equities in Harvard's endowment, available to all investors, lost more than 28 percent during the 12 months between July 2008 and June 2009, but its private equities, available only to the prominent few, lost more than 31 percent. This lowered the status of private equities. In 2005 Bear Stearns allowed investors with only $250,000 to invest in funds normally accessible to those investing $1 million or more. Ronald Greene, a 79-year-old retiree, lost $280,000 in the Bear Stearns High Grade Structured Credit Strategies Fund. The e-mail Greene received from his broker in 2005 touted the performance of the fund and said that "it will accept smaller investments this month on a limited basis."[41] The status of private equity and hedge funds was damaged further by new awareness of their high fees, low liquidity, Ponzi schemes, and insider trading. Private equity and hedge funds are more humble now, as befits lower status funds, willing to share more information with their clients and reduce their fees.

We signal our status and esteem to others, but we also do it for ourselves, to promote our self-esteem. Socially responsible portfolios are private so they offer little benefit in signaling social responsibility to other people. Yet socially responsible portfolios offer great self-signaling benefits, where investors signal their social responsibility to themselves. We observe self-signaling in life and in experiments. People in one experiment were asked to place an arm in a container of cold water until they could no longer tolerate the pain. Subsequently, they were told that recent medical studies have discovered an inborn, incurable heart disease in some people that makes them prone to illness and early death. Furthermore, this bad heart condition can be identified by the ability to withstand cold water after exercise. Next, people were divided into two groups, one was told that the bad heart condition is associated with an *increase* in tolerance to cold water after exercise and the other was told that the condition is associated with a *decrease* in tolerance to cold water after exercise. It turned out that people are willing to subject themselves to the discomfort of cold water so as to signal to themselves that they do not have a bad heart condition. Those who were told that the bad heart condition is associated with low tolerance to cold water kept their arm in the water longer than those who were told that the bad heart condition is associated with high tolerance to cold water.[42]

WOMEN WANT RESPECT

The respect accorded to today's women investors falls short of the respect accorded to men. "As wealth management clients, women are both significant and undervalued," concluded the Boston Consulting Group, based on a 2010 survey of women investors. "Aside from not taking women seriously in general, [wealth managers] should be focusing on generating the best returns for the client, regardless of gender," said an American woman interviewed for the survey. "I don't need a tea party," she added. "Banks are spending their marketing budgets on men by sponsoring sports such as football or rugby," said a New Zealander woman. "Male clients also get invited to corporate boxes at games, but as a woman I don't get that kind of treatment."[43] The respect accorded to women a century ago was also short of the accorded to men. Indeed, disrespect, coupled with condescension, was blatant.

"A woman in Massachusetts wrote to me a little while ago, in very great distress," read a story from the *World's Work* in 1911. Of course it took only a little persuasion and a few cold facts to demonstrate to her that what she thought was a cyclone was merely a summer breeze. Her letter and her trouble, however, are merely types. They are an extreme illustration of the facts that make difficult the transaction of investment business with women and with constitutionally frightened men."[44]

The *World's Work* derided women investors not only as constitutionally frightened, but also as naïve and less skillful than men. "I think that the majority of women investors are more apt to be misled by specious argument, by appearances and by the element of plausibility than are men," said another 1917 story in the *World's Work*. Apparently, that was the reason why a woman should search for a man. "The real guardian of a woman's fund is an honest and skillful man, and probably the simplest recipe for safety is to find the man."[45]

In 1930 George Frederick wondered if condescension toward women investors, perhaps rooted in "old-fashioned chivalry," has gone a bit too far. "Nowadays women are not the swooning, weak, and helpless things they used to be. Eleven million of them earn their own living . . . they are independent and unafraid, and despise the old cages and cautions which have hobbled them. Their 'weakness' was largely a man's imagination."[46] Still, Frederick could not resist a bit of condescension himself a few pages later. "Quite obviously," he wrote, "women are less competent to use their own judgment in investments than men. Very few women should attempt to make their own investment analyses. It is not unfair to say that they have not the same coolness of judgment, as a rule, as men."[47]

Condescension toward women investors was on display in a 1953 *Business Week* article about a Los Angeles Stock Exchange campaign to "educate the public in corporate securities, and to get more of the securities business that originates in the Los Angeles area placed under its brokers." The caption under a photograph says "Ladies signed up in large numbers for this Community Investment Course had time for a good gab at intermission."[48]

The image of women investors had changed little by 1965, when women were portrayed in an Investment Company Institute brochure as maturing from nursery to wedding dress, and on to leisurely retirement. "The woman who looks ahead knows that today's nursery rhyme is succeeded by tomorrow's college textbook," said the brochure, "[T]his season's prom gown will be replaced by next year's wedding dress . . . and that the frantic pace of activity eventually subsides in the leisure of retirement years, when there is time for travel and the pursuit of pleasant pastimes." The brochure went on to tell women not to bother with the economics and statistics of investing: "By and large, women are not followers of investment trends. Women have the savings instinct but most find little pleasure in poring over complicated charts and forecasts, and hesitate to invest." This is why the Investment Company Institute recommended mutual funds to women.

"Investing in a mutual fund can satisfy the woman's rational urge to put money aside yet not confuse her with mountains of statistics."

Women pushed back in the 1970s. Women and Money '77: Financial Freedom for Today's Woman was a conference funded by a brokerage firm. The conference was described as "a one-day 'learning experience,'" covering what every woman should know (but was never told) about money. Patricia Carbine, publisher and editor-in-chief of *MS* magazine, was there to tell more than 500 women packing the auditorium that money might be the root of all evil, but "the root of all evil feeds the tree of life."[49] This pushback continues today.

The mostly male community of Japanese investors ridicules the many thousands of Japanese housewives who ventured into online trading of currencies as "Mrs. Watanabes," or "Kimono traders." But buying and selling British pounds or Australian dollars appeals to these women because it nurtures hopes of financial independence. Mayumi Torii is now famous in Japan, writing books about online trading and speaking about it on television, but she ventured into trading to "stand on my own economically," she said. This was when she had to support herself and her son after a divorce. "I never want to feel that vulnerable again."[50]

SMALL INVESTORS WANT RESPECT

Small investors crave the respect accorded to large investors and their status. Small investors felt excluded from the outsize returns of Harvard's and Yale's private equity and hedge funds, as if pressing their noses at windows of clubs they could not enter. Some wrote to the SEC protesting their exclusion from hedge funds because their incomes are lower than $200,000 and wealth is less than $1 million. Why should athletes with big signing bonuses, pop stars, and heirs to family fortunes have access to hedge funds when they don't "even come close to the sophistication I have," wrote Gregory Kapraun. "Force all the very wealthy to invest only in mutual funds and see how that flies," wrote Arnold Peterson, an orthopedic surgeon.[51] Even investors with many millions are occasionally made to feel like small investors. Goldman Sachs analysts offer stock tips to the likes of Citadel Investment Group, SAC Capital Advisors, and other favored clients, but George Klopfer was unaware of the trading tips, and he was angry when he found out. "I was at the end of the food chain," he said as he pulled out most of the $20 million in his Goldman Sachs account.[52] Young investors crave respect and status as well. Anish Vora and Nirav Patel, two high school juniors, established the school's Stock Club. "Me and Anish, all our idle conversation is about stocks, that or girls. A lot of our friends crack on us, but I don't care." "They think it's for geeks," said Anish with a note of defiance and self-respect. "They can try to call us a geek, but I'm 18 times richer than them." [53]

We gain self-respect when we stay true to our values, and we respect others who stay true to their values. We derive expressive and emotional benefits from staying true to our values, especially when we forego utilitarian benefits for them. We stay true to compassion when we share the little we have with those who have less. We stay true to our society and religion when we forego high returns from investments that violate our social or religious values. Staying true to our values is the topic of the next chapter.

We Want to Stay True to Our Values

Sergey Brin, cofounder of Google, drove the company out of China in 2010. A few years earlier, Google agreed to live by censorship conditions set by the Chinese government, but the Internet search corporation remained troubled by China's censorship and its suppression of dissidents. Cyber attacks aimed at e-mails of Chinese dissidents pushed Google beyond its threshold, moving the company to withdraw its search engine from China.

Brin sacrificed the utilitarian benefits of money when he drove Google out of China. Google lost business when China Unicom Ltd. reacted to Google's decision by canceling its plan to install Google's search functions into new mobile-phone handsets. And Google lost employees who defected to rivals. But Brin and his Google colleagues gained the expressive and emotional benefits that come with staying true to their values. China's actions reminded Brin of the totalitarianism of the Soviet Union where he was born, manifested in policemen searching his home, and anti-Semitic discrimination against his father. "I think that at some point it is appropriate to stand up for your principles," said Brin, "and if more companies, governments, organization, individuals did that, I do think that the world would be a better place."[1]

Every one of us faces the choice of sacrificing utilitarian benefits for expressive and emotional ones. Some, like Brin, choose to do so, while others do not. Executives in several of Google's neighboring companies were baffled by Google's decision to sacrifice money for values.

SOCIALLY RESPONSIBLE INVESTING

Socially responsible investors are prominent among those willing to sacrifice utilitarian benefits of investments for expressive and emotional ones. Indeed, I was drawn into studying socially responsible investors years ago because they defy the premise that investors care only about the utilitarian benefits of investments. I have met some of these people at conferences, such as SRI in the Rockies, which are frequented by socially responsible investors. They are passionate serious investors, eager to profess their values to fellow investors and as comfortable with one another as old friends.

Some social responsibility communities express a single value, such as protection of the environment, while others express several values, such as avoidance of tobacco, alcohol, and gambling. The differing values are reflected in the many alternatives to the term "socially responsible investing," including environmental, societal, and governance (ESG) investing, sustainable investing, green investing, ethical investing, mission-based investing, values-based investing, and religion-based investing.

The Range of Values

We observe the range of values of socially responsible investors in the appalled reaction of Paul Hawken, the cofounder of Smith & Hawken, to the Calvert Social Index Fund's holdings of Microsoft, which he criticized for dominating software markets, and by Sierra Club's holdings of Outback Steakhouse, which he criticized for promoting cattle production that leads to overgrazing and ecological damage. And we observe the range of trade-offs among social responsibility values in the reaction of Amy Domini of the Domini Fund. Hawken criticized the Domini Fund for straying away from strict social purity by including in its portfolio companies such as McDonald's, but Domini defended her inclusion of McDonald's as a good choice, even if an imperfect one. "I personally may prefer slow food to fast food. I personally prefer the ambiance of organic over nonorganic. But I don't have a mandate from the public to avoid fast food. . . . When I look at McDonald's versus [other companies in] the fast-food industry, I see them on a path toward human dignity and environmental sustainability. I can live with myself for investing in McDonald's."[2]

Reader Phil Thompson wrote to the editor of *Consumer Reports* about his concern that the Vanguard Calvert Social Index Fund, recommended by *Consumer Reports,* holds stocks of Microsoft, Pfizer, Intel, and IBM, which offshore U.S. jobs. "I'm not sure I see what is socially conscious about putting Americans out of work," he wrote.[3] Carl Goldstein has sparred with one socially responsible mutual fund over its exclusion of companies that produce nuclear power. "The fund thus shuns a source of electricity that is abundant, domestic, safe, virtually carbon-free and efficient," he wrote, "Yet this fund will invest in companies linked to the production and use of coal. How socially responsible is that?[4]

Range of Benefits for Socially Responsible Investing

I have learned the wide range of utilitarian, expressive, and emotional benefits of socially responsible investments in interviews with many socially responsible investors.[5]

Respect for employees matters most to a video producer. "I don't like big-box stores very much, but when I happen to be in one, I tune to its general vibe. If employees are unhappy, there's a reason for it. . . . I am appalled by incredibly high CEO salaries, and the increasing gap between rich and poor in the United States. People need a living wage, they need health insurance—all of that is important to me."

An owner of military-related companies distinguishes between the products of companies and their behavior. The type of company, he said, whether military, tobacco, or gambling, has nothing to do with holding the board and the leadership of a company accountable for socially responsible behavior. "Being a good corporate citizen also includes the way companies treat community issues and the environment and support the communities where they reside, not just by hiring the people but by contributing to community causes."

Investors in socially responsible stocks are drawn to their benefits by families, religions, books, and life experiences. "Although I was raised secularly for the most part," said an education consultant, "my core values come from my family's religious tradition, that is, that Jewish people believe in social justice. My grandfather emigrated from Eastern Europe when he was 14. He was one of the founders of a major union local and then went on to start his own business. When I was a teenager, I was doing some work for him when there was a strike at his business, and he told me I couldn't cross the picket lines. My mother said, 'You have to go to work and help him,' but my grandfather said, 'You can't do that.' Those are the experiences and the key framework that led me to emphasize feminist and workers' rights in my investing."

Socially responsible investors regularly express their social responsibility in donations of money and time to community and volunteer work, promotion of socially responsible resolutions at shareholder meetings, and direct investments in projects such as housing for low-income people. These provide consistency between the utilitarian benefits of investments and their expressive and emotional benefits and illustrate the conflicts among them.

"The church is involved in community work and volunteerism, much beyond investment," said the member of the Church of the Brethren. "We have active programs under way in several countries, including the Dominican Republic, Brazil, and India, where we work directly on issues such as education, social justice, and community health."

"I've participated in boycotts against American and international corporations in support of issues such as infant health in third-world countries and fair labor practices," said a student. "In the last few years, I've also become much more conscious of the choices I make as a consumer. I buy organically and locally grown products. I'm also considering buying a car, and would prefer one that runs on bio-diesel fuel. . . . In addition, making charitable contributions is a constant part of my life . . . One of my primary charities is involved in providing micro-credit in developing countries, and another advocates for the rights of women and children in policy matters such as abortion and minimum wage."

Religious Origins of Social Responsibility Investing

The origins of the socially responsible investing movement are in religion. In the mid-1700s, John Wesley, the founder of Methodism, noted that the use of money was the second most important subject of New Testament teachings and taught these to his congregation. Weapons and slavery offended the religious tenets of the Quakers who settled North America, and the Quakers refused to invest in them.[6] Many of today's socially responsible mutual funds are premised on religion. The MMA Praxis mutual funds are sponsored by Mennonite Mutual Aid (MMA), which serves as the stewardship agency for the Mennonite Church. The Ave Maria Catholic Values Fund eliminates from its portfolio stocks of companies associated with contraceptives and abortions. Ave Maria disposed of the stock of the Eli Lilly pharmaceutical company when it began offering benefits to unmarried partners of its employees.[7] Mormons, whose traditions prohibit tobacco or alcohol, are less likely to own stocks of companies associated with tobacco and alcohol.[8]

Religious Investors Today

Islamic finance raises the issues of morality in financial dealings, attempting to guide investors into merging of the spiritual with the worldly, promoting social goals, and restraining material ones.[9] The Amana Funds avoid bonds and other interest-paying investments because they violate the Islamic prohibition on interest or *riba*. Chicago's Devon Bank offers an Islamic financing program that enables observant Muslims to buy houses in a manner that avoids interest payments or collections. And the design of the increasingly popular *Sukuk* bonds makes them compliant with *shariah's* prohibition on paying or collecting interest.

Mutual funds following the tenets of Judaism are still scarce, although Clal Insurance offers a mutual fund that excludes the stocks of companies that violate the Sabbath, and the Department of the Treasury in Israel has agreed to let savings and pension institutions establish funds that follow the strictures of Judaism. These include keeping the Sabbath, refraining from producing or marketing non-Kosher food, and refraining from improper payment or receipt of interest.[10] A list of the principles of proposed Jewish mutual funds includes improving society through philanthropy, community activities, and medicine.[11] The rabbinical court followed by many ultra-Orthodox Jews goes further, prohibiting investment in all Israeli companies. "Investors in Israeli companies," said the court, "are full partners in violations of Torah prohibitions, including, not only violations of the Sabbath and provision of non-Kosher food, but also obscene advertisement and filthy television programs."[12]

A survey of the values of religious and nonreligious investors shows many similarities but some differences as well.[13] The top four concerns for both groups are sweatshops, product safety, high executive compensation, and the environment. But opposition to adult entertainment and abortion products ranks higher among religious investors than among nonreligious ones. There are also differences among members of different religions. Evangelical Christians are more likely than Catholics or Protestants to avoid companies associated with adult entertainment, abortion products, gambling, alcohol production, and equal family benefits to homosexual employees, whereas Catholics and Protestants are more concerned about companies' environmental records.

Civil Rights Origins of Social Responsibility Investing

While the origins of the social responsibility movement are in religion, much of today's social responsibility movement was born in the impassioned 1960s, when struggles for civil rights, women's rights, anti-war, and pro-environment policies served to escalate awareness of social responsibility. Opposition to apartheid in South Africa was a rallying cry that brought many into the socially responsible investing movement in the late 1970s, and the movement continues to grow today as emphasis shifts to protection of the environment and improving corporate governance. "Back in the 1970s, it was human rights and South Africa," said a nun at a Roman Catholic order. "The environment was not really on the list at that time." The Order now avoids companies contributing to global warming.

"WE WANT TO DO GOOD. WE ALSO WANT TO DO WELL."

Socially responsible investors care about expressive and emotional benefits of their investments, but most care about utilitarian benefits as well. You know," said to me one financial advisor, "socially responsible investors will retire someday and they too will need income in retirement." The member of the Church of the Brethren said: "People from the church ask us fairly regularly whether we give up anything in terms of returns by narrowing the focus of our portfolio through [social responsibility] screens. . . . Often it's phrased just that bluntly: "How much does it cost me to invest with you and exclude those things from my portfolio?"

The reality of the trade-off between returns and social responsibility was also conveyed to me by the video producer who said, "My husband and I became involved in socially responsible investing early on. . . . We didn't have enough money then to have a portfolio manager. So we bought socially responsible mutual funds, which actually performed very badly at that point, and we ended up leaving them. . . . [Afterward], we bought plain . . . funds and looked the other way. However, we didn't feel comfortable investing that way; I didn't even want to look at how those funds were invested. So we always kept an eye toward returning to socially responsible investing. Then, as the result of an accident . . . I received a large settlement. The minute I was in a position to hire an investment manager, I said, 'Let's invest in a socially responsible way. . . . I consider it a luxury that I now have the ability to invest more in line with my values.'"

Arthur Ally founded the Timothy Plan mutual funds, which takes its name from a letter written by the apostle Paul, to cater to conservative Christians. Its flagship, the Timothy Plan Small Cap Value Fund, performed near the bottom of its category for several years and many investors lost faith. "There were those that thought if they invested in Timothy they'd have top returns, the Lord would bless them," said Ally. When that didn't happen, some of them went to better-performing funds."[14] Yet, on average, socially responsible investors remain more loyal to their funds than other investors when performance falters, less likely to withdraw their money.[15]

Providers of socially responsible portfolios understand that socially responsible investors care about all the benefits of their investments, utilitarian, expressive, and emotional. Calvert presented in an advertisement a photograph of an investor saying, "Truth be told, I'm as financially ambitious as I am socially conscious." Calvert's advertisement went on to say: "We hear you. You want to do good. You also want to do well. That's why we manage Calvert mutual funds with Double Diligence. It's our disciplined process for finding stocks with strong growth potential and avoiding those at risk from unethical business practices. So you can invest for your goals without compromising your values."

The investor in Calvert's advertisement typifies most socially responsible investors. A Yankelovich survey found that only 20 percent of American investors would consider investing in socially responsible mutual funds if their returns were lower than those of conventional mutual funds.[16] A survey of Swedish investors in socially responsible funds found that 19 percent were primarily concerned about social responsibility, 29 percent were primarily concerned about profits, and 52 percent were concerned about both social responsibility and profits.[17]

SIN STOCKS

The values of the rich and powerful bear special scrutiny. Meg Whitman, a California gubernatorial candidate and the former chief of eBay, is a billionaire, listed as the 326th richest American. A *Los Angeles Times* article noted that "Meg Whitman has invested her vast wealth in firms that sought to profit from the country's credit crisis, in venture capital and hedge funds open only to the wealthy, and in oil, gas, healthcare and other concerns seeking to influence state policy."[18] Another *Los Angeles Times* article excoriated Bill Gates for stocks held by his foundation. Although Justice Eta, a 14-month-old Nigerian baby, was immunized against polio and measles thanks to the Gates Foundation, Eta also suffers from respiratory trouble blamed on fumes and soot spewing from a nearby oil plant, whose investors include the Gates Foundation.[19]

Some car owners claim the high moral ground with environmentally responsible Prius hybrids, but others attempt to claim it with Hummers, expressing their rugged individualism and personal freedom. One Hummer owner wrote: "Grow up and join us Americans that believe in our freedom. . . . Stop trying to oppress others that don't share your beliefs, color, and religion."[20] And while socially responsible investors derive expressive and emotional benefits by excluding stocks of tobacco, alcohol, and gambling companies, other investors derive these benefits by embracing the same stocks. The Vice Fund earned high returns by investing in stocks of companies associated with the military, tobacco, alcohol, and gambling. Dan Aherns, the manager of the Vice Fund, delighted in needling socially responsible investors. "I don't think coffee liqueur is going to be the downfall of society."[21] Aherns' needle penetrated deep into Pax

World Funds, which were among the earliest socially responsible funds. Pax was compelled by its no-alcohol policy to sell Starbucks shares when the company set up a deal to launch a coffee liqueur with whiskey maker Jim Beam. Pax also sold its Yahoo! shares because Yahoo! had business ties to Internet gambling. In the end, Pax decided to drop its zero-tolerance policy against alcohol and gambling.

SEEKING BALANCE BETWEEN INVESTORS

Trade-offs between utilitarian, expressive, and emotional benefits are complicated when they involve trade-offs among investors, not only within each investor. A public pension fund that foregoes profitable real-estate investments or divests itself of profitable stocks of tobacco companies might enhance the expressive and emotional benefits of its socially responsible members, but other members might prefer to forego these expressive and emotional benefits and keep the utilitarian benefits of high returns. In 2010 CalPERS, the giant pension fund of California's state employees, was considering a policy that would prohibit investment in real-estate deals in which rent-controlled apartments are converted to apartments that would be rented at higher rates. The policy document stated that "affordable housing is an important aspect of CalPERS real-estate-investment strategy."[22]

In 2000, Philip Angelides, a board member of CalPERS at the time, pressed for divestment of tobacco stocks. "I believe you can make money and do good for society at the same time," he said. But Christopher Palmeri of *Business Week* disagreed. "The purpose of a pension fund is to provide income for its members. . . . Muddying the waters with a social agenda can mean poor results in both areas." And where does doing good end? "I'm against making investment decisions based on someone's idea of what is good or bad for society, because I don't know where that train stops," said William Crist, CalPERS board president. "Do we one day ban investments in alcohol, handguns, and rap music?"[23] Yet Mary Wells, director of the Council for Responsible Public Investment, said that CalPERS is ultimately funded by Californians' tax dollars, and most Californians disapprove of investing public pension money in tobacco stocks. "Why does Christopher Palmeri think it's so wrong for CalPERS to listen to its funders?"[24]

Pension funds, especially public pension funds, bear expressive costs when they invest in real-estate deals that reduce affordable housing or in "sin" stocks of tobacco, alcohol, and gambling companies. Pension funds tend to divest themselves of such stocks.[25] University endowment funds bear similar costs. Santa Clara University, my university, is a Catholic Jesuit university. John Kerrigan, who manages the university's endowment fund, listed the values that guide it: the sacredness of life that guides the fund to avoid investments associated with abortion, euthanasia, or tobacco; human rights; opposition to discrimination; opposition to nuclear weapons; and protection of the environment. Sometimes questions arise. A group of students questioned an investment in a mining company they considered environmentally irresponsible. "We don't want to do anything that violates the university's policies, or something that would embarrass the university," said Kerrigan.

The expressive costs of investing in tobacco stocks are high for universities and they are especially high for organizations, such as the American Medical Association, which strive to educate the public about the dangers of smoking and offer help at quitting. Opposition to tobacco is fairly recent, dating to the second half of the twentieth century. People smoked conspicuously in the 1950s, even when television cameras were on, but today's smokers get dirty looks from passersby as they stand outside office buildings. Opposition to alcohol was more prominent than opposition to tobacco in the first half of the twentieth century, reflected in the prohibition of alcohol in the United States, which lasted from 1920 to 1933. The triggering event in the changing of attitudes toward smoking was the accumulation of medical evidence about its health risks since the 1950s. Opposition to smoking found its way into investment practice as socially responsible funds adopted anti-tobacco screens. In 1996 the American Medical Association prodded the mutual fund industry to give up tobacco companies' stocks and bonds, threatening to publish an annual list of offending funds and praising funds that sign no-tobacco pledges.[26]

I was on a panel presenting evidence to the CalPERS board in 2000 as it was deliberating divestment of tobacco stocks. My evidence was based on studies comparing the returns of socially responsible mutual funds to the returns of conventional mutual funds. That evidence indicated that, on average, the returns of the two groups of mutual funds were approximately equal, supporting Angelides' belief that "you can make money and do good for society at the same time." Yet more recent studies show that the equal returns of socially responsible and conventional funds come from a balance of two opposite forces. Stocks of companies that rank high on social responsibility criteria such as employee and community relations earn returns higher than stocks of companies that rank low. This indicates that investors in stocks of companies ranked high on employee and community relations enjoy not only the expressive and emotional benefits of investing in the stocks of such companies but also the utilitarian benefits of high returns. Yet stocks of companies associated with activities regularly shunned by socially responsible investors also provided higher returns than stocks of other companies. Shunned companies include those associated with tobacco, alcohol, gambling, firearms, military, and nuclear operations. This indicates that socially responsible investors sacrifice utilitarian returns for the expressive and emotional benefits of excluding the stocks of tobacco companies and those of other shunned companies.[27]

Socially responsible investors who invest by the "best-in-class" method can enjoy high utilitarian returns along with high expressive and emotional benefits. Investors who use the best-in-class method select the most socially responsible companies in each industry, including the tobacco industry and other industries usually shunned by socially responsible investors, rather than exclude entire industries. This method might work for some socially responsible investors, but not for all. Not every socially responsible investor can stomach stocks of alcohol-producing companies, or sleep quietly at night knowing that firearms produced by companies whose stocks he owns are used in war.

Alcohol and gambling are shunned by many socially responsible investors but not by all. And while wars are hardly popular among investors, whether socially responsible or conventional, few investors advocate turning all swords into plowshares. The proportion of investors shunning tobacco is higher than the proportion shunning alcohol or gambling, but even its social stigma is nothing like the stigma of sex-related companies. The expressive costs of investments in such companies regularly exceed their utilitarian benefits. Friendfinder, Inc. operates social networking sites that attract many registrants and $200 million in annual revenues. The company's main site, Adult Friendfinder, helps people meet others for sexual liaisons. That makes investors queasy. Venture capitalists find it tough to take sex-related companies public, and universities and endowment funds are reluctant to approve sex-related investments.[28]

Some investors refrain from socially responsible investing because they believe that they can contribute more by direct social responsibility action than by buying stocks of companies deemed socially responsible. Some refrain from it because they are unsettled by the absence of clear lines that distinguish perfectly pure companies from those that are not as pure. Some fashion themselves as vice investors, needling socially responsible investors. Yet other investors believe that there is no need to apply social responsibility criteria in the selection of investments because companies are driven to social responsibility by their pursuit of profits. This belief is longstanding. The *Literary Digest* of 1927 quoted J. Edward Baker of the New York bond house of Stone and Webster and Blodget, Inc.: "A good security, judged by the best business tests, will meet the highest requirements of Christian ethics."[29] But the *Digest* also quoted a critical response in the *Christian Advocate:* "Just when we want [Baker] to tell us whether it is ethical to hold stock in a company which pays us 9 percent and underpays its girls, or in a corporation which cuts melons, and at the same time pares wages to the quick . . . just at these points he becomes vague and unconvincing. . . . Absolute security and liberal dividends are enough to establish the investment value of a stock, but the Christian Church feels more and more keenly that it must ask other questions after the investment house has come to the end of its list."[30]

INVESTING IN PHILANTHROPY

Socially responsible investors regularly combine doing good through their investments with doing good directly, through philanthropy, sacrificing the utilitarian benefits of donated money for its expressive and emotional benefits. Socially responsible mutual funds facilitate philanthropy. Pax World investors can donate some or all their capital gains or dividends to Mercy Corp., and Calvert investors can contribute their money to affordable housing, micro-finance, and fair trade coffee.

Some investors want to engage in major philanthropic ventures and have the means to do so. Charter schools are favorites among hedge funds managers. John Petry and Joel Greenblatt, partners in the hedge fund Gotham Capital, established Success Charter Network to raise money for charter schools. Petry and Greenblatt sacrifice the utilitarian benefits of the money they contribute but derive great expressive and emotional benefits from their philanthropy. "You can't talk to Petry without talking about charters," said another hedge fund manager recruited into Success Chapter Network. "You get the religion fast."[31]

Other investors engage in micro-credit, providing loans to the poor to establish or expand businesses, buy refrigerators, or pay school tuition for their children. There is concern that loans that provide money for consumption rather than enterprise would entice people to borrow too much. Yet the evidence indicates that, on average, poor people benefit from consumer loans.[32] Micro-credit can be profitable to its providers, raising concerns that the poor would be exploited by lenders charging high interest rates. "We created micro-credit to fight the loan sharks; we didn't create micro-credit to encourage new loan sharks," said Muhammad Yunus, who pioneered micro-credit by lending money to basket weavers in Bangladesh and won a Nobel Peace Prize for his work. "Microcredit should be seen as an opportunity to help people get out of poverty in a business way, but not as an opportunity to make money out of poor people."[33]

Peter Peterson, a founder of the Blackstone Group investment company, had more than $1 billion when he retired at age 81. The utilitarian benefits of money held little attraction for him. "The idea of trying to make the money grow felt empty to me," he wrote, "so buying a yacht was out of the question." But the expressive and emotional benefits of philanthropy held much attraction. "Almost all the [billionaires] I most admired were major philanthropists: Warren Buffett, Bill Gates, Mike Bloomberg, George Soros, Eli Broad—each with a passion to do good, each getting so much pleasure from giving their money away. I decided that's what I wanted to do." Peterson's passion is in meeting America's key fiscal-sustainability challenges and this is the focus of his foundation. He donated to it $1 billion, the vast majority of his net proceeds from Blackstone. Peterson explained his large contribution with a story about Joseph Heller and Kurt Vonnegut at the home of a wealthy hedge-fund manager. "Joe, doesn't it bother you that this guy makes more in a day than you ever made from *Catch-22?*" "No, not really," Heller said. "I have something that he doesn't have: I know the meaning of enough."[34] Peterson concluded that he personally had far more than enough. This, however, is not every investor's conclusion.

WHY SOME AVOID SOCIAL
RESPONSIBILITY INVESTING

Many refuse to join the ranks of socially responsible investors. A banker told me: "I work in corporate finance, making bank loans to investment-grade corporations for working capital, leveraged buyouts. . . . [T]here are not many industries that we shy away from. We finance tobacco companies, defense contractors, gaming and casino companies, all the sins certainly. Capitalism is a wonderful thing, and—frankly—it all boils down to that. When I go to my grave, will I regret making those loans or investments? I don't think so. I think there's certainly a difference between one's moral life and one's professional life. If we all had options, we'd all be out helping poor people and spending more time with our children. So this is what you do to make a living, and this is what you deal with, so get on with it."

The banker is not oblivious to society. "My wife and I joined the Unitarian Universalist Church, a church that has a social responsibility aspect to it," he said. "Volunteerism is a major part of the church, whether helping the community, educating the children, helping the church financially, or working in the soup kitchen." But social responsibility does not extend to the banker's investments. International mutual funds are among his investments. "Do I investigate the companies in those international funds and determine whether they are paying their workers fair wages? Absolutely not—I have not done that."

There is now much evidence that people derive expressive and emotional benefits by accumulating wealth and keeping it. Increased wealth increases happiness, overturning the old evidence that increased wealth does not increase happiness once wealth has reached a fairly modest level.[35] But Bill Gates, Warren Buffett, and Peter Peterson are not alone among those who gain more expressive and emotional benefits by giving away money than all benefits, utilitarian, expressive, and emotional they would have by keeping it. In one experiment, experimenters gave money to people with instructions to spend it by 5 P.M. that day. Some were told to use the money to pay bills or treat themselves to a gift. Others were told to use the money to buy someone else a gift or to donate it to charity. It turned out that those who gave to others increased their happiness by more than those who spent it on themselves. It also turned out that people are not very good at predicting the effects of giving on their happiness. A significant majority thought that they would be happier by spending the money on themselves rather than on others, but this is not how they felt afterward.[36] Another study, conducted among adults, children, and primates, demonstrated that the relation between happiness and giving resembles a virtuous circle. Happier people give more and giving increases happiness. Advertising these happiness benefits of charitable giving may have the perverse effect of decreasing charitable giving by corrupting expressive and emotional benefits with utilitarian benefits.[37]

THE VALUE OF PATRIOTISM

We express our patriotism when we fly the flag, we feel pride when our nation's athletes win the gold in the Olympic Games, and we are members of one community when we stand together and sing the national anthem. We derive expressive and emotional benefits from patriotic food and patriotic investments alike. Frankfurters were turned into hot dogs when Americans fought Germans in World War I, and French fries were briefly turned into Freedom fries by Americans unhappy with the opposition of the French to the war in Iraq. Likewise, Liberty Bonds expressed patriotism in World War I, War Bonds expressed patriotism in World War II, and Patriot Bonds conveyed patriotism after the September 11, 2001, terrorist attacks. Patriotism was summoned again in 2009, during the financial crisis. Bailout funds would give ordinary Americans a chance to buy the troubled assets of banks and profit along with bankers when the recovery arrives.[38]

The sting of investment losses is especially painful when accompanied by a betrayal of patriotism. DHB Industries produces bulletproof vests used by American soldiers fighting in Afghanistan, yet David H. Brooks, the chief executive officer and chairman of the company, stands accused of defrauding shareholders for luxuries such as a $100,000 American-flag belt buckle encrusted with rubies, sapphires, and diamonds. Patriotism coupled with a desire for high returns compelled Michael Adair to invest most of his retirement savings in DHB shares, and most of these savings vanished as the price of DHB's shares plummeted. "This is a trial of greed," said Adair, "I'm hoping to get some justice."[39]

In 1908 patriotism was called upon to battle socialism. The *American Review of Reviews* of that year encouraged its readers to become new owners of the corporations by buying their shares. "The more people there are with money invested, the sounder is the general financial situation and the less chance is there for Socialism to spread."[40] Some Americans, such as Joseph Goodman, a columnist at *Forbes* magazine, believed that President Franklin Roosevelt combined socialism, totalitarianism, and class war in his New Deal. He recommended the stock of Public Service of New Jersey in 1939, not only because its dividend yield exceeded seven percent, but also because its operations were entirely confined to the State of New Jersey. This gave the company an advantage in that "it is free from the attacks and schemes of designing New Dealers in Washington." Goodman elaborated on his distaste for the New Dealers: "Frankly, the trend toward totalitarianism in this country disturbs me more than foreign war threats. The present Administration has built up a huge vote-getting political machine with funds from the public Treasury and has created class hatred along lines more or less familiar to the .dictatorship countries abroad. Just how an investor can protect himself against ominous developments of this type is beyond my knowledge."[41]

The threat of communism augmented the threat of socialism as the Cold War followed World War II, and Keith Funston, the chairman of the New York Stock Exchange, urged Americans to defend capitalism from communism by buying American stocks. "A nation of share owners is our strongest defense against the foreign 'isms' that would sap our vitality and eventually turn us over to the evil enemy we know as communism. We can preach the virtues of capitalism until we are blue in the face, but one stock certificate in the name of Joe Public is a stronger argument than all the oratory of which we are capable."[42]

India and Pakistan have drawn on patriotism in their rivalry since their founding in 1947, and that rivalry continues today. When India exploded a nuclear device in the late 1990s, Pakistan followed. India and Pakistan also expressed their patriotism in the battle over currencies. Both India and Pakistan attempted to keep identical exchange rates for their currencies even when there was virtually no trade between them. People in both countries considered exchange rates as matters of national pride and measures of their leaders. The major devaluation of the Indian rupee in 1966 created havoc in the ruling elite of the Congress Party, and Indira Gandhi capitalized on that havoc to seize power within the party.[43]

Investors who concentrate their investments in their home countries gain the expressive and emotional benefits of patriotism while they lose the utilitarian benefits of global diversifications. Financial advisors warn investors against mixing investments with patriotism. "Common sense dictates spending your money where you make it," wrote the *Literary Digest* in 1930, "but it is foolish to let any sense or urge of civic obligation make you invest in local enterprises whose real financial status you can seldom ever find out until a receiver is appointed."[44] Patriotism waned in the 1990s and investors indeed focused on their personal needs rather than on their civic obligations. Marketers of U.S. Savings Bonds, the successors of the War Bonds of World War II, found few takers. "The focus groups were very negative to patriotic and emotional appeals," said Wes Ball of the Ball Group, a research and advertising company. "They wanted to know 'What's in it for me? How would it help them reach their goals?'"[45]

Patriotism was revived by the attacks of September 11, 2001. The targets of the 9/11 attacks extended to the symbols of American life, including capitalism, yet financial advisors warned investors against "patriot rallies" to prop up the stock market. Still, patriotism continues to affect investment behavior. How proud are you to be a citizen of your country? Investors in countries with high proportions of proud citizens are more likely to invest large proportions of their portfolios in stocks of their own countries.[46] Moreover, the pattern of stock returns following World War II, the Korean War, and the more recent War on Terror indicates that investors gravitate toward stocks with patriotic names when wars elicit patriotic feelings.[47] In contrast, liberalism mutes the voice of patriotism. Countries whose citizens express strong economic and social liberal ideals are more willing to buy stocks in countries other than their own than investors in countries where citizens express only weak economic and social liberal ideals.[48]

Americans are increasingly polarized by values into left and right, Democrats and Republicans. Blog readers gravitate toward blogs that accord with their views and few read blogs of both left and right.[49] Mutual fund and hedge fund managers who make campaign contributions to Republicans invest larger proportions of their portfolios in stocks of companies shunned by socially responsible investors, such as companies associated with tobacco and guns, than managers who make campaign contributions to Democrats. Democratic-oriented managers tilt their investments toward stocks of companies with social features such as excellent employee relations and clean environmental records.[50] Republican-oriented institutional investors overweighed their portfolios with Bush stocks during the 2000 United States presidential election whereas Democratic-oriented institutional investors overweighed their portfolios with Gore stocks.[51] Republicans are more optimistic than Democrats when they are in power, perceiving the stock market as offering higher returns with lower risk, while roles are reversed when Democrats are in power.[52]

Conservative investors in Finland are more likely to buy stocks than liberal investors.[53] Conservative American investors have a special affinity for gold as their hedge against the chaos that would follow inflation brought about by liberals. Conservative investors often quote the words of Alan Greenspan in 1960, who went on to become chairman of the Federal Reserve Bank: "In the absence of the gold standard, there is no way to protect savings from confiscation through inflation. . . . This is the shabby secret of the welfare statists' tirades against gold."[54]

Some investors value social responsibility while others do not, some are patriotic while others are not, some lean right while others lean left, but all value fairness. The quest for fairness is the topic of the next chapter.

CHAPTER 14

We Want Fairness

Soccer was not played fairly on a level playing field in Brazil and outrage was palpable when two referees accepted bribes to favor one team over another. "If you can't even trust in the score of the game to be honest, then what hope is there for us?" asked Jorge Luiz Costa, a street sweeper in Rio de Janeiro."[1]

We want to play on level playing fields in sports, investments, and every other field. We want fair stock markets where our chances at winning depend on our skills, savvy, or even luck, not ones where our chances are diminished by those who have fast computers or inside information. We want to be treated fairly by financial advisors and money managers. And we are willing to sacrifice utilitarian benefits for the expressive and emotional benefits of fairness. We boycott stores that treat their employees unfairly even when we pay higher prices at other stores and we forego profits to avoid financial advisors whose fairness we suspect. Cooperating members of groups are eager to punish free riders because they consider them unfair. The eagerness of cooperators to punish free riders deters free riding and increases cooperation.[2]

THE ULTIMATUM GAME

Imagine that I am holding $1,000 in cash, facing you and a person behind a curtain. You will never know the identity of the person behind the curtain, and he or she will never know your identity. I ask the person behind the curtain to make an offer for the division of the $1,000 between the two of you, perhaps $500 for each of you or perhaps $1 for you and $999 for him or her. But the offer is an ultimatum, not open to counteroffer or negotiation. This is known as the "ultimatum game." If you accept the offer, I will divide the money as offered. But if you reject the offer, I'll keep the $1,000 and neither of you will receive anything. Suppose that the person behind the curtain offered you $1. Do you accept?

Researchers have played ultimatum games with people all over the world, from people in Pittsburgh, Pennsylvania, to the Polynesian Lamalera and the Amazonian Machiguenga. Considerations of utilitarian benefits alone would lead the person behind the curtain to offer a tiny fraction of the total pot of money, such as $1 out of $1,000. The same utilitarian considerations would lead the person on the other side of the curtain to accept the offer. After all, $1 is better than nothing. But outcomes of ultimatum games show that the expressive and emotional benefits of fairness regularly trump the utilitarian benefits of money. Indeed, people regularly turn down offers lower than 20 percent of the total pot of money. They say to themselves, "I'd rather burn the money offered to me for the satisfaction of also burning the money of the unfair person behind the curtain."

FAIRNESS AMONG BANKERS AND HOMEOWNERS

Thoughts about fairness has been prominent on our minds in the recent financial crisis. Banks and homeowners alike face the trade-offs between utilitarian, expressive and emotional benefits as they contemplate mortgage loans and fairness. Homeowners who owe more than the values of their houses engage in "strategic default" when they choose not to make payments of their mortgages even though they have enough money for these payment. Josh Bartlett is one homeowner whose mortgage is several times the value of his house. "Yes, I'm defaulting," he said. "Yes, I'm walking away."

Homeowners who pay their mortgages on time greeted with anger news that the government will assist homeowners who cease payments. Is it fair to ask homeowners who honor their mortgage obligations to pay for defaulting ones? In turn, defaulting homeowners are angry at banks they consider unfair. Jason Welsh bought his house for $100,000 a decade ago, renovated it, and refinanced it with a $240,000 mortgage. The house is worth no more than $100,000 today but Welsh's bank refuses to accept his offer to pay $150,000 for it. "I call. I try to get help. They just say I don't qualify. And they're willing to sell it to somebody else for $100,000 out from underneath me. It's just upsetting that there's supposed to be help out there, and there is none." But Bert Ely, a banking consultant, argued that a fairness-driven political backlash would accompany bailing out defaulting homeowners. "It's unfair to those folks who, in fact, have made their mortgage payments," he said.[3]

Defaulting homeowners pay utilitarian costs in lower credit scores that would hamper future borrowing, including mortgage borrowing. Fannie Mae, the giant mortgage finance company, announced that it would not grant new mortgage loans to homeowners who default on mortgages they could afford to pay. "Walking away from a mortgage is bad for borrowers and bad for communities, and our approach is meant to deter the disturbing trend toward strategic defaulting," said Terence Edwards, Fannie's executive vice president for credit portfolio management.[4] Yet for many homeowners the expressive and emotional costs of strategic defaults are even greater than the utilitarian costs. Most choose to pay rather than default. Approximately five out of six homeowners continue to make the monthly payments on their mortgages even when their houses are worth no more than half the amount they owe on their mortgages. Homeowners who consider it unfair to default are much less likely to default. Social norms and stigma matter as well. Homeowners in neighborhoods where many have chosen strategic default are more likely to default than homeowners in neighborhoods where few have chosen strategic default.[5]

Fairness Among Investment Professionals

Outrage about the unfairness of bonuses paid to bankers and investment professionals propelled some to sacrifice the utilitarian benefits of time and money for the emotional benefits of expressing their anger. A pastor whose sister-in-law was facing foreclosure and a laid-off steelworker with a wife and five children were among many who traveled by bus to Fairfield County, one of the wealthiest places in America, to deliver a letter to Douglas L. Poling, an A.I.G. executive. The government rescued A.I.G. at a $180 billion cost to taxpayers, yet more than 400 of its employees, including Poling, have been paid at least $165 million in bonuses.[6] "They're all about themselves," said the pastor about the A.I.G. executives. "The more they can get, the more they want."

Outrage over bankers' bonuses also animated President Barack Obama. "I did not run for office to be helping out a bunch of, you know, fat-cat bankers on Wall Street," Obama said.[7] Many considered Obama's outrage too mild and too late. The *New York Times* said in an editorial: "President Obama seems genuinely, if belatedly, upset about the way America's voracious bankers leveraged hundreds of billions in taxpayer bailouts to line their pockets with multibillion-dollar bonuses while American businesses starve for credit. Before he gets over his anger, he might want to take a look at how the British found a way to realign the fat-cats' boundless greed with the public interest: slapping a hefty windfall tax on their bonuses."[8]

Investment professionals make tempting targets for public outrage and mockery, not only because they earn high incomes, but also because their contributions to the welfare of the rest of us are not as easy to explain as the contributions of butchers, bakers, and candlestick makers. Tom Wolfe mocked Sherman McCoy, the "master of the universe" bond trader in his novel *The Bonfire of the Vanities*. McCoy's wife explained to their daughter how bond traders make their money: "Daddy doesn't build roads or hospitals, and he doesn't help build them, but he does handle the bonds for the people who raise the money. . . . Just imagine that a bond is a slice of cake, and you didn't bake the cake, but every time you hand somebody a slice of the cake a tiny little bit comes off, like a little crumb, and you can keep that. . . . If you pass around enough slices of cake, then pretty soon you have enough crumbs to make a gigantic cake."

Quelling Outrage over Unfairness

Public outrage about perceived unfairness has consequences for bankers, investment professionals, and corporate executives. Lloyd Blankfein, the chief executive of Goldman Sachs described its work as "God's work," and some expected him to defy public outrage and accept as much as a $100 million bonus. But Blankfein accepted only a $9 million bonus. "It was certainly less than expected," said Mark Borges, a compensation consultant. "While the fact that he's making this much won't sit well with people out of work, it seems Goldman is being sensitive to the political considerations and optics of this amount."[9] Indeed, a study of patterns of executive pay found that outrage over executive pay has led to lower executive pay. A 1993 law limited the tax deductibility of corporate salaries exceeding $1 million. And a 2004 ruling by the Financial Accounting Standards Board made stock options granted to executives less lucrative. Moreover, executive pay is lower in states where residents consider income inequality unfair.[10]

Arthur Levitt, the former chairman of the Securities and Exchange Commission, regards Regulation Fair Disclosure (FD) as his great accomplishment while in office. Levitt understood the desire for fairness and chose the name Regulation Fair Disclosure to appeal to the public and "make our opponents think twice about fighting it."[11] The regulation compels corporate executives to release information to everyone simultaneously rather than leave ordinary investors in an information dark while the favored Wall Street few receive a head start in the investment race. Levitt recounted the great pressure against Regulation Fair Disclosure from Wall Street. "As I walked to the SEC's public room . . . an aide rushed to hand me a pink message slip: *Hank Paulson is trying to reach you from China. He strongly urges you to vote no.*" Levitt was not surprised by the message. "Paulson, the chairman of the investment bank Goldman Sachs Group . . . and the rest of the securities industry thought I was about to apply the executioner's noose to Wall Street's way of life."[12] The SEC received more than six thousand comments on the proposed regulation, almost uniformly negative from the industry and almost uniformly positive from the public, and Regulation Fair Disclosure was enacted.

DECIDING WHAT'S FAIR

Debates about fairness tend to be long because we bring into them our perceptions of fairness and leave with the same perceptions. A study of Swedish business school students revealed that 44 percent are strict egalitarians, 38 percent are liberal egalitarians, and 18 percent are libertarians. Strict egalitarians believe that fairness requires that all inequalities between people be eliminated, even when some people produce more than others. Libertarians argue that fairness requires that each person receive what he or she produces. Liberal egalitarians are in the middle, arguing that fairness requires that inequalities resulting from factors outside people's control, such as disability, should be eliminated, but not inequalities resulting from factors within people's control, such as laziness.[13]

Differing perceptions of the rules of fairness are evident in the debate about high-frequency trading, superfast computerized trading used by hedge funds, such as Renaissance Technologies, Wolverine Trading, and Goldman Sachs. Well-programmed computers, placed close to the stock exchange, help high-frequency traders win their race against ordinary traders hampered by slow telecom lines. Arthur Levitt argued against restrictions on high-frequency trading in *Wall Street Journal* article.[14]

To some, the rule of fairness is the rule of freedom. Free markets address all fairness concerns in the libertarian fair world. A *Wall Street Journal* reader expressed a libertarian perspective on the fairness of high frequency trading in a letter to the editor following Levitt's article: "The market itself will address the perceived unfairness, as the "victims" who are creating these short-term opportunities realize that they, and not their counterparties, are the ones to blame for the profits being taken from them. They will change or force their executing brokers to change their strategies to be cleverer and less predictable in their approach to trading."[15]

To some the rule of fairness is the paternalistic rule of protection not only from others, such as high-frequency traders, but also from ourselves. According to the paternalistic rule, we need protection from ourselves because we tend to surrender to the temptation of trading against high-frequency traders as we surrender to the temptation of door-to-door salesmen hawking vacuum cleaners. Buyers of vacuum cleaners, drapes, cabinets, and other products sold at buyers' homes have the right, by law, to cancel a signed contract within a three-day cooling-off period even if they were hot and foolish enough to sign that contract.

Yet to some the rule of fairness is the rule of equal power, embodied in level playing fields. In that fair world, powerful traders who boost their speed with superfast computers would be slowed down to the speed of powerless traders who have equal savvy but lack such computers. This is the perception of another reader of the *Wall Street Journal* in the comments section following Levitt's article: "There should be a level playing field—if you are getting better prices because your server is closer to the market server, then the advantage is completely artificial and brings no value with it. It's seems parasitical to interpose a third party in a trade because that third party has a geographically advantaged computer as opposed to any market savvy."

Are Spinners Fair?

Disagreements about rules of fairness are also evident in discussions of the practice of spinning. The practice involved investment bankers who allocated lucrative shares in initial public offerings (IPOs) to executives whose business they were courting. An investment banker courting the business of Joseph Cayre allocated 100,000 shares of Pixar Animation Studios to him when Pixar went public. Cayre sold the shares that day for a $2 million profit. Christina Morgan, the managing director of investment banking at Hambrecht & Quist at the time, saw nothing unfair in spinning. Allocating hot IPOs to corporate executives, according to Morgan, is neither illegal nor immoral. It's a business decision. "What we're talking about is trying to solicit business," she said. "What do you think about taking them out to dinner? What do you think about that? We throw lavish parties with caviar. Is that not trying to influence them, their behavior? I suggest that it is"[16] But James Penrose was incredulous at Morgan's perception that spinning is fair: "Are [investment bankers] really unable to see any distinction between a golf outing or a dinner with a favored client and a payoff of several hundred thousand dollars?"[17]

Andy Kessler, like Christina Morgan, saw nothing unfair in spinning. Kessler's fund was allocated some MP3.com shares at $28 per share when shares of the company were sold to the public. "I must have owned them for an excruciatingly long 45 seconds," wrote Kessler, "then sold them for $60. . . . So, who was buying this garbage? It was small investors who placed orders with no limits at Fidelity or E-Trade or Schwab. These gamblers were the real villains, and the victims. And no, I don't feel bad dumping my shares on them—a fool and his money . . ."[18]

Are Credit Card Issuers Fair?

The Credit Card Accountability, Responsibility and Disclosure Act of 2009 favors cardholders over credit card companies. Perceptions of fairness can be discerned in the signing ceremony for the Act on May 22, 2009 when President Obama recounted stories he heard during the presidential campaign from people "choking backs tears" as they recounted credit card predicaments imposed by unforeseen medical bills or mortgage payments. Obama accused credit card companies of writing contracts "designed not to inform but to confuse." Noting that one provision of the law requires credit card companies to inform customers in advance of changes in payment due dates, he added his personal experience as a cardholder: "This always used to bug me."[19] The Act restricts fees charged by credit card companies and limits their ability to increase the interest rates they charge.

Advocates of strict credit card regulations tend to hold paternalistic notions of fairness. They argue that fairness calls for protecting cardholders, not only from credit card companies but also from themselves. Poor cardholders have little power when unemployed or facing onerous medical bills. Moreover, many cardholders cannot understand the contracts they sign and are unable to muster the self-control necessary to stop spending before high interest rates and penalties are imposed. Advocates of lenient credit card regulations tend to hold libertarian notions of fairness. They argue that fairness calls for the right to freedom of choice. Credit card companies do not force anyone to hold their cards. All the terms of the cards, including the criteria determining penalties and interest rate increases, are noted in pages that accompany cards, even if in small print and words that only lawyers can comprehend.

Changes in regulations over the decades reflect shifts in the tug of war between cardholders and credit card companies, and shifts in the resonance of notions of fairness. Cardholders were relatively powerful until the late 1970s as usury laws limited the interest rates charged by credit card companies. But a 1978 Supreme Court decision opened the door to changes favoring credit card companies. Over time, credit card companies introduced increasingly complex contracts specifying late fees, penalties, and interest rates. Penalties that rarely exceeded $15 soon exceeded $30. Clauses in contracts gave credit card companies wide discretion in resetting interest rates. Introductory 9.9 percent interest rates were soon reset above 20 percent, sometimes surpassing 40 percent. The 2009 law shifted some power back to cardholders, yet the tug of war continues.

Are Bankers Fair?

Banks are not blind to their recent setbacks in the tug-of-war, where power shifts to their customers. Bank of America moved to abolish overdraft fees even before a Federal Reserve Bank regulation went into effect. "Believe it or not, that $35 fee that the bank charges you when you overdraw your account is actually a "service" that your bank is offering you," wrote a mocking customer online.[20] Eliminating overdraft is costly to Bank of America and its fellow banks since overdraft fees on debit purchases and ATM transactions amounted to about $20 billion in 2009 alone, and overdraft fees covering checks and recurring bills added $12 billion. "A few years back, I used to work in a small bank and I remember a customer who owned a lawn-care company who seemed to be in there every day," wrote another customer on the same Web site. "He was bad with a checkbook at best. He bounced checks left and right, and I still remember my boss bragging about how much money he had made off that guy. Over a thousand dollars in a year—all in overdraft fees." Banks were finally forced to listen. "What our customers kept telling me is 'just don't let me spend money that I don't have,'" said Susan Faulkner, Bank of America's deposit and card product executive. "We wanted to help them avoid those unexpected overdraft fees."[21]

FAIRNESS, LAW, AND SELF-INTEREST

Fairness and the law make up a two-way street where the law affects perceptions of fairness while perceptions of fairness shape the law. Legislators change the law and judges modify their interpretation of the law when perceptions of fairness change. Differing perceptions of the rules of fairness push some close to the legal line or over it. Listen to a telephone conversation between two Enron Corporation traders in 2000, during California's energy crisis.[22]

> *Tim:* He steals money from California to the tune of about a
>   million—
> *Person 2:* Will you rephrase that?
> *Tim:* O.K., he, um, he arbitrages the California market to the
>   tune of a million bucks or two a day.

Investment professionals tend to be closer to the libertarian end of rules of fairness than to the paternalistic end. They tend to favor free markets and are suspicious of regulations. Some of that tendency is rooted in self-interest and some in ideology. Tom, an Enron trader, provides an extreme example of that tendency as he railed against regulations imposing price caps on electricity:

> *Tom:* It's just [expletive]. It's completely [expletive]. It . . . it just goes against everything our country's about.

Matt, another Enron trader, expresses the same sentiment, equating regulations with socialism.

> *Matt:* Tell you what—you heard this here first: When Bush wins . . .
> *Tom:* Caps are gone.
> *Matt:* That [expletive] Bill Richardson, he's [expletive] gone. The [expletive], ah, Clinton, he's [expletive] all these [expletive] ah, socialists are gone.

The tendency to tilt perceptions of fairness toward self-interest is universal, extending far beyond the tendency of Enron traders. Teachers negotiating with boards of education compare their salaries to those of teachers in better-paying districts and conclude that the salaries offered by their boards are unfair. Boards compare the salaries of their teachers to those in lower-paying districts and conclude that the salaries they offer are generous beyond fair. Differences in perceptions of fairness between teachers and boards often lead to teacher strikes.[23]

Kathleen Treanor, whose four-year-old daughter was killed in the Alfred P. Murrah Federal Building in Oklahoma City in 1995, agreed that it is fair to compensate the families of the victims of the 9/11 attacks. Indeed, she asked the Red Cross to let her come to New York to comfort 9/11 grieving families. Treanor never expected compensation for her family's loss, not even when her family lost the farm of her father-in-law who was killed along with his wife and Treanor's daughter. "I didn't really buy into this whole victim-compensation idea," she said. But Treanor changed her mind when she heard about the planned 9/11 compensation fund. "Why is it right for a New York stockbroker's widow to be given millions of dollars and not a poor farmer's family in Oklahoma?" she asked. "Why is my daughter worth less than these people?"[24]

PERCEPTIONS OF FAIRNESS AROUND THE WORLD

People in each country differ in their perceptions of fairness, but differences in the perceptions of fairness across countries are often more pronounced. Such differences are rooted in culture, the body of shared values, beliefs, and attitudes. Beliefs about fairness, reflected in attitudes toward income redistribution, are one example. Taxes are low and little income is distributed in countries where people believe that high incomes are the outcome of hard work rather than more luck, and that people are entitled to enjoy the fruits of their work. In contrast, taxes are high and much income is distributed in countries where people believe that high incomes are the outcome of luck rather than more hard work.[25] People in European countries tend to have a more positive attitude toward income redistribution than people in the United States.[26] And people in former socialist countries tend to favor income redistribution more than people in Western nations.

Perceptions of the fairness of prices also vary with culture. American consumers tend to perceive prices as fair if they pay a lower price than others and unfair if they pay a higher price. This is true whether they compare the prices they pay to the prices paid by friends or by strangers. Chinese consumers, in contrast, care more about the prices they pay relative to the prices paid by friends than relative to strangers. Moreover, American consumers are bothered if they pay higher prices whether they are loyal customers of a store or first-time customers. Yet Chinese consumers are more bothered if they pay higher prices when they are loyal customers.[27]

Fairness is part of the social capital of a country, and social capital matters in financial markets because investors consider not only the available information when assessing the trade-off between risk and return but also how much they trust the accuracy of the information and the fairness of markets. People who do not trust the fairness of the stock market are less likely to invest in it.[28] In one experiment, wallets containing approximately $50 in local currency, together with photographs, names, and phone numbers, were "dropped" in the streets of various countries. The proportion of wallets returned in each country was highly correlated with levels of trust in these countries.[29]

Disparity of information among traders is common. Owners of used cars often have inside information, such as about faulty transmissions, unknown to potential buyers. Corporate executives often have inside information, such as about disappointing earnings, unknown to potential traders. Corporate executives who exploit inside information violate the law while car owners who exploit inside information do not violate it, but perceptions of the fairness of insider trading in the car and stock markets do not always correspond to the law. The particulars of insider trading law were clarified by the U.S. Supreme Court in a case involving James O'Hagan, a partner of the law firm of Dorsey & Whitney. O'Hagan's firm helped Grand Met Company acquire the Pillsbury Company. O'Hagan bought shares and options of Pillsbury and sold them later for a large profit. The Supreme Court ruled that O'Hagan violated insider trading laws.

One case in a survey presented a simplified version of the O'Hagan case to finance professionals and students in eight countries and asked them to judge the fairness of "Paul Bond" who plays the role of O'Hagan.[30]

The proportion of finance professionals and students who judged Bond's insider trading as fair was higher in Italy, Turkey, Tunisia, and India than in Australia, Israel, The Netherlands, and the United States.

Yet judgments of fairness vary by context, whether stocks or cars. Another case in the survey presented "Peter Jamison," who sold his car without disclosing his inside information about a defect in the car's transmission. Students in Italy, Turkey, Tunisia, and India judged Jamison's use of inside information in the car market as *less* fair than they judged Bond's use of inside information in the stock market. For example, only one-quarter of Italian students judged Bond's use of inside information in the stock market as unfair, but almost two-thirds of them judged Jamison's use of inside information in the car market as unfair.

Still, while some judgments vary across countries, other judgments seem universal. Inside information gives insiders power not available to outsiders, and wealthy insiders have even greater power. People of all eight countries believe that it is unfair to use that power. Some finance professionals and students read a case in which "Larry Woods" is a high income executive who trades on inside information in the stock market while others read the same case except that now Larry Woods was an intern earning a low hourly wage. Professionals and students in every country judged Larry Woods the executive less fair than they judged Larry Woods the intern.

The *desire* for fairness is universal even if we disagree about the *rules* of fairness. And the desire for fairness begins early in life. Children protest "It's not fair!" soon after they learn to say Mommy and Daddy. We invest in our children our love and our money, and we teach them fairness in words and behavior. Investment in children is the topic of the next chapter.

CHAPTER 15

We Want to Invest in Our Children and Families

"There are no bounds for what you do for your children," wrote Jack Grubman, a star stock-research analyst at Citigroup in the boom years of the late 1990s. We invest our money, energy, and hopes in our children, as we nurture, guide, and provide for them. We derive expressive and emotional benefits from our investments in our children, proud of their accomplishments and comforted by their love. Sometimes we derive utilitarian benefits as well, as our children care for us in old age and support us with their money.

Grubman wanted to get his twins into the 92nd Street Y, a prestigious Manhattan preschool.[1] What he did for his children included recommending that investors buy AT&T's stock when, in truth, he believed that investors should sell it. Grubman recommended AT&T's stock at the request of Sanford Weill, Citicorp's chief executive, who wanted to enlist Michael Armstrong, AT&T's chief executive and a Citicorp director, in a power struggle with Weill's Citicorp rival. Grubman removed his recommendation for AT&T's stock soon after that rival, John Reed, was ousted from Citicorp.

Grubman described his actions in an e-mail. "I used Sandy [Weill] to get my kids in the 92nd Street Y preschool (which is harder than Harvard) and Sandy needed Armstrong's vote on our board to nuke Reed in a showdown. Once the coast was clear for both of us (i.e., Sandy clear victor and my kids confirmed), I went back to my normal self [on AT&T]."

Parents have always invested in their children. A 1929 advertisement by the National City Company shows a father in an armchair with two little children playing with a toy train at his feet. "Invest today for their tomorrow," said the advertisement. "Good securities are among the surest and the least troublesome income producers you can possibly leave to your dependents."[2]

Judah ibn Tibbon, a twelfth-century physician, described his investment in his son in his will:

> You know, my son, how I swaddled you and brought you up, how
> I led you in the paths of wisdom and virtue. I fed and clothed you;
> I spent myself in educating and protecting you. I sacrificed my sleep
> to make you wise beyond your fellows and to raise you to the highest
> degree of science and morals. These twelve years I have denied
> myself the usual pleasures and relaxations of men for your sake,
> and I still toil for your inheritance.[3]

Rich parents invest in their children by buying $6,500 Tiffany teapots. Tiffany's advertisement says: "For Your Children's Children."[4] Poor parents are attracted to affordable bonds they can buy with as little as $50, and they are especially attracted to bonds they can buy for their children.[5] We invest for our children when we purchase baby formula. Mead Johnson Nutritionals places into college savings accounts 1 percent of the amount paid for formula.[6]

British children receive a head start from their government in the form of the United Kingdom's Child Trust Fund. Children receive 250 British pounds placed in savings accounts when they are born, and a similar amount when they are seven years old. Poor children receive more. Parents can choose an interest-bearing account, or one of two stock accounts, one invested more conservatively and one invested less conservatively. Subsequently, parents, other members of the family, and friends can add to the accounts.[7]

Parents are especially concerned about investments in children's education and about helping them start households. A survey of employees of academic institutions found that 86 percent of them believe that it is important to provide for children's education, and 85 percent of them consider helping children start households. Only 60 percent of them consider it important to providing a bequest to their children. Still, parents who plan to leave bequests to their children spend between $4,000 and $9,000 less than parents who do not plan to leave bequests, and they accumulate more savings. Parents also plan to leave larger bequests amounts when they believe that their children are not likely to earn much money[8, 9]

Men and women do not always agree about what they can spend on themselves and what they must invest their children.[10, 11] And they often differ in how much they invest in sons and daughters. That difference is evident in the outcomes of the expansion of the South African social pension program to the black population in the early 1990s. Grandmothers devoted more of their pensions to granddaughters than to grandsons. The weight and height of granddaughters increased in households where grandmothers received pensions, but there was no such effect on grandsons.[12]

INVESTING IN EDUCATION

It is every parent's hope that their children will be educated at fine schools, and that the family will be able to afford to pay for it. Parents invest in the education of their children all over the world, and the desire of parents to help their children get into Harvard is universal. *Harvard Girl* was a bestseller in China, selling more than a million copies. The book, written by the parents of Liu Yiting, a teenager from China's northern coal-mining city of Taiyuan, describes how their daughter got into Harvard and offered advice to other parents who want to invest the same hopes and money in their children.[13] The BBC offers MUZZY, a foreign language program for children as young as one year old. "Today, MUZZY. Tomorrow, a top college!" says an advertisement. It displayed pictures of MUZZY alumni, Jonathan at age four and now at Columbia, Debbie at age two and a half and now at Harvard, and Emily at age six and now a Brown graduate.[14]

Erin Stawarz, the mother of three young children, knows the likely tuition costs that await her. Stawarz's income is too low to afford college savings for her children, so her parents stepped in to help, opening college savings plans for the two oldest boys, ages five and three, and contributing when they can. Ron Waltz, Stawarz's father, recalled that college cost roughly $9,800 in 1994, when his first daughter enrolled at the University of Illinois. He paid $13,000 when his second daughter started at the University of Iowa, and he paid $20,000 during her senior year. "I can only imagine the task of educating kids 15 years from now," he said. "There are big challenges out there in the future for these kids."[15]

Entitled Children

Poor and middle-class parents worry that they might not have enough money to pay their children's college tuition, while rich parents worry that generous allowances might create in their children a sense of entitlement. Large gifts of wealth can extinguish all desire for financial independence and accomplishments because they contain magic erasers of failures in school, work, marriage, and investments. James E. Rogers, the chief executive of the Cinergy Corporation, the utility holding company, is a rich father, some $500 million rich. But he understands the dangers of unearned wealth. "Leaving children wealth is like leaving them a case of psychological cancer," he said. Mr. Rogers intends to use most of his money to promote education.[16]

One wealthy investor, widowed after a long marriage, was alerted by an offhand remark by his son-in-law to the danger that his will, which bequeathed his estate, would be contested when he dies: "If we have 50 million, we want 75," said his son-in-law. As a precaution, the man videotaped the execution of the new estate plan when he remarried and accepted the recommendation of his lawyer to get a letter from a psychiatrist attesting to his sanity. "[The] thought that my will would be challenged is frightening, humiliating, and embarrassing and, now that I have talked to more of my friends about this, I find that this is not that unusual."[17]

Some Korean adult children feel entitled as well. Reverse mortgages allow Koreans to tap into the equity in their houses for income during their lifetimes, at the cost of leaving less of their houses to their children. Some Koreans have sufficient income during their retirement years without a need to generate additional income from reverse mortgages, but others who would have wished to increase their incomes by reverse mortgages find that their children resist that wish because they are concerned about reduced inheritances.[18]

PROMOTING FINANCIAL INDEPENDENCE IN CHILDREN

We want our children to be financially independent when they turn into adults. Children want it as well, associating adulthood with financial independence. "I [began to think of myself as an adult] maybe when I was like 20," said one young woman. "And really, like, got out of my parents' house and started, like, living, I mean working to pay the bills." Another young woman said " [I began to think of myself as an adult] Um, probably at 21 . . . I finished school. Finally working. Taking care of myself. And no longer dependent on my parents."[19] Yet financial independence is not easy to reach. Large proportions of Americans middle-class and upper-class sons and daughters receive financial assistance from their parents well into their 30s.[20] Financial contributions from parents to children between the ages of 18 and 34 average $2,200 per year and many young adults receive financial support even when they are employed. Alison Riccardi had $50,000 in loan debt when she graduated from college but found no more than a part-time job. Her parents pay $1,300 each month for a Manhattan apartment she shares with her fiancé. "I am really lucky to have their support," said Alison. "I know friends that parents cut them off when they graduate and they flounder really hard for a while."[21]

Allowances from parents to children are not only for candy and movies but also for lessons about spending, saving, investing, and growing into financially independent adults. Some parents offer lessons in straight allowances. One wrote, "I give one dollar for every year of age, every two weeks." Another wrote, "Depends on the prices at the moment. . . . I give them enough for one movie a week and some for music. . . ." The world of cell phones, credit cards and the Internet complicates allowances. One mother found the following charges by her 14-year-old son:

$ 2.99 . . . MLB Baseball
$ 4.99 . . . ESPN BottomLine
$ 7.99 . . . Tetris
$ 0.25 . . . eBay bid alert
$ 3.98 . . . Guy Stuff bikini girl wallpaper
$32.67 . . . iTunes downloads[22]

Some parents replace allowances with payments for chores or accomplishments. One wrote, "I prefer to provide jobs for my children. . . . The other day my 4-year-old worked nonstop for four hours cleaning my office, stamping envelopes, sharpening pencils, etc. He wouldn't stop because he wanted to buy a Shamu doll." Another wrote, "We don't give allowances. The kids' job is getting good grades in school, and we pay them on report card day. A C [grade] is not rewarded. Bs are rewarded with a specific dollar amount each and As are worth twice that."[23]

Do allowances promote financial independence in children as they grow into adults? Economic self-efficacy underlies financial independence, and Jeylan Mortimer studied it in a survey of more than a thousand ninth graders and their parents in 1988 and follow-up surveys through 1997, six years after their scheduled graduation from high school. She found that payment for chores enhanced economic self-efficacy in children as they matured into adults, but allowances detracted from economic self-efficacy. Allowances, it seems, are perceived as entitlements, promoting dependency rather than self-efficacy. Mortimer also found that children with a relatively high grade point average are more likely to develop economic self-efficacy, and so are children who grow up in families with relatively high incomes and where parents have at least some college education. Listening to parents as they discussed their work did not affect the economic self-efficacy of their children, and neither did children's visits to parents' workplaces. But discussions of work with parents did promote economic self-efficacy in their children.[24]

Yet parents transmit to their children savings and investment habits as children observe and mimic their parents. These habits explain much of the persistence of wealth over the generations.[25] Parents and children continue to share investment information even after children have grown into adults and moved away. The likelihood the investors would invest in the stock market is 30 percent higher if their parents or children have invested in the stock market in the previous five years.[26]

Children Strive to Please Parents

Children are keenly attuned to parents, attempting to quiet parents' fears and accomplish what parents could not. We listen intently to our parents' words, even when they do not say them aloud. We watch our parents, learn from them, and try to please them. Most of the lessons we learn from our parents are worth adopting, but some are best avoided.

Tom Perkins, a founder of the venture capital firm of Kleiner, Perkins, Caufield & Byers is a very wealthy man. He owns a 900-year-old, moated estate in England, a Bentley, a $450,000 Porsche Carrera GT, an Aston Martin, and two yachts. "Analyze that for us," asked Lesley Stahl in a television interview. "Why do you have to have the biggest and the first . . . ?"

"You know, I'm no psychiatrist," said Perkins, "but it probably comes from my childhood and the attitude of my parents." Perkins, who grew up during the Depression, continued: "My mother wanted things in life that my father couldn't provide—that were bought by money. . . . The fact that we didn't have any money was very, very evident always in my life. . . . She talked about it all the time."[27]

The desire of children to please their parents and the sadness that sometimes accompanies it are starker in a D. H. Lawrence's allegorical story, "The Rocking Horse Winners," than in Tom Perkins' real one. Paul, a young boy, lives in a house "haunted by the unspoken phrase: There must be more money! The must be more money!"

"Mother," said the boy Paul one day, "why don't we keep a car of our own? Why do we always use uncle's, or else a taxi?"

"Because we're the poor members of the family," said the mother.

"But why are we, mother?"

"Well—I suppose," she said slowly and bitterly, "it's because your father has no luck."

Paul, anxious to please his mother, discovers that he can foresee horse-race winners as he furiously rides his rocking horse. Yet Paul's mother never has enough and the house now screams, "There must be more money! Oh-h-h; there must be more money. Oh, now, now-w! Now-w-w—there must be more money!—more than ever! More than ever!"

The story ends sadly when Paul falls gravely ill as he rides his rocking horse and dies. "My God, Hester," says Paul's uncle, "you're eighty-odd thousand to the good, and a poor devil of a son to the bad. But, poor devil, poor devil, he's best gone out of a life where he rides his rocking horse to find a winner." [28]

Stephen Manes tells a lighthearted version of Lawrence's cautionary tale in *Make Four Million Dollar$ by Next Thursday*.[29] Jason, the young boy, is following a get-rich-quick formula he found in a book, planting a dollar bill sprinkled with coins.

"What do you want with four million dollars, anyway?" his mother asked . . .

"Why do you play the million-dollar lottery every week?" he asked . . .

"Good question. You got me, pardner."

"Well?" Jason pressed.

"I guess the idea of getting rich quick is pretty hard to resist," said his mother . . .

"You just wait," Jason told her. "After Thursday, I'll give you some of my money. Maybe you'll be able to stop working so hard. . . ."[30]

The three stories share one lesson. Parents who fail to teach their children a balance between money and life might see children grow into adults lacking that balance.

Financial Education and Trading

Schools are much less effective than parents in teaching financial literacy and inculcating saving and investment habits in children. High school education in financial literacy had little effect on financial knowledge and even less on financial behavior. Children who score well on financial literacy tests come from well-off, well-educated families, and children cite their parents as their primary source of information on financial matters.[31] Some financial education is imparted through stock market games where students pick up stocks for hypothetical portfolios. But such games teach trading more than they teach investing and they might give children a false sense of confidence in their trading skills.

Some children become hooked on trading. Jordan Webb, a 19-year-old college student, has been trading since he was 15. "My cell phone has stock quotes on it," he said. "I definitely hate being away from a computer. I feel really weird if I don't know what my stocks are doing."[32] Children's trading confidence inflates with the stock market and deflates with it, and some children who follow game money with real money regret it. Avery Maxwell, an 11-year-old student invested $500 saved from birthday and Christmas gifts in a mutual fund that lost almost half his money in 2008. "I don't want to open it," said Avery of the monthly financial statement from the fund. "I'd feel, like, sad." Michael Ashworth a 13-year-old fellow student said: "I'll be honest with you. Before all this, I asked my mom to get me stocks for Christmas, but then I told her not to do it. I asked for a parakeet instead."[33]

I use a stock market game in my undergraduate and graduate investment classes and I play along with my students, buying and holding a broadly diversified index fund, containing the stocks of more than three thousand companies. My return is usually higher than the average return among my students because I do not trade, saving me costs that weigh down my students' returns. And the risk of my portfolio is usually lower than the average risk in the portfolios of my students because my portfolio is better diversified than that of my students. Boarding a plane one day I encountered a former student who came in first in the stock market game a few years before. The win emboldened him enough to try trading a real portfolio as he traded in his game. It did not work very well, he admitted with a sheepish grin.

PARENTS AND CHILDREN ACROSS CULTURES

Children expect parents to invest in them and parents expect returns on their investments when children turn into adults, but the nature of these returns vary across countries and cultures, and they vary among families within one country and culture. Can parents expect more than the expressive and emotional benefits of the pride they take in their children and the affection of their grandchildren? Can parents expect utilitarian benefits from their adult children, including financial support and personal care in old age? One woman joined a Web discussion about cultural differences between Asian-American and European-American families. "My boyfriend's parents are Asian and I'm white American. Last week we were discussing how much money he should give to his parents when he visits them next month. This week, my parents were visiting and gave me an unexpected (and unnecessary) financial gift. I would never think of giving my parents money unless they needed it. He would never think of accepting money from his parents unless he needed it. It struck me as ironic and as a good illustration of the cultural differences concerning parent–child relationships and financial support."[34]

But another woman wrote: "I am a white American but some of these . . . comments boggle my mind. My mom supported me through college even though it ate into her retirement savings. This means I owe her. Period."

A man from India wrote: "It is pretty common in India. [S]ometimes it is to show appreciation for what parents have done for children but many times children are much better off than their parents and children would like their parents to have the a similar standard of living. I have seen cases where it is voluntary and [cases] where parents kind of force it on their children. In my case both parents and in-laws are doing financially okay. But the expectation is that if there is a need then we will need to support them and my wife and I will have no issues with it."

A man from Israel wrote: "I grew up in Israel where it's quite common and expected that older parents will come live with their children after a certain age. They're not seen as a burden but as a welcome addition to the household. The parents help with household activities and help take care of children and grandkids."

A woman from Nigeria wrote: "This is a common thing also in Africa. We are expected to give back in appreciation for all that was done for you. . . . My husband is also Nigerian so we do think about the future of us eventually taking care of two generations."

And a man from Asia wrote: "Cultures and circumstances always mold a person's thinking. Without going into debt, it would be fine to give back to parents regardless of your background really. Even in the US now the "sandwiched" generation has to deal with supporting two generations at once."

Indeed, many in the United States belong to the sandwiched generation, caught between caring for parents and for their own children. Elizabeth Rodriguez, a 58-year-old woman, left her job, sold her house, and depleted her savings to care for her 97-year-old father. The costs are mounting: "A shower chair, body cream with no alcohol, new shoes . . . You don't stop and calculate. You just buy what you have to buy." Sometimes children are the only defense elderly parents have against scammers who exploit their loneliness and impaired thinking to steal their savings. Yet children are caught between the urge to protect their parents, turning into the parents of their parents, and the wish to let parents maintain the dignity of their independence.[35]

Remittances from adult children to parents, spouses, and children are the lifeblood of many families in developing countries. Remittances amounted to almost 12 percent of the gross domestic product of the Philippines in 2008.[36] Migrants from relatively poor African countries remit more than migrants from relatively rich African countries, and men remit more than women, especially when they have left a wife behind.[37] Turkish immigrants in Germany remit to families left behind, and remittances are especially high when they are spent on education and investment. Remittances to Asia plunged during the 1997 Asian financial crisis but rebounded a year later. Remittances declined during the more recent global crisis but they are likely to rebound and grow, even if at a slower pace.[38]

Facing the Expectations of Families and Friends

People who remit to families abroad find it more difficult to accumulate savings for themselves than people who keep all their money for themselves. People who feel compelled to share what little they have with family and friends face the same difficulty. The problem often calls for ingenious solutions. When Rolf Engelbrecht, an American missionary, first arrived in Guinea, West Africa, he was amazed to see "ruins" of old mud brick houses standing around in villages and across the countryside. He soon learned that these are savings accounts rather than ruins. "You see," wrote Engelbrecht, "in Guinean culture it's like this: If you have any cash on hand and your relatives find out about it (which they almost certainly will), they are entitled to come over and "ask for help," meaning a financial handout. Since you are socially obligated to comply with their request, it becomes very hard to save up money for a special project like buying a wife, building a house, or hiring someone to carve a dugout canoe for you." The solution is to open a savings account by laying a foundation to a house. Bricks are added whenever cash comes into the household, making it out-of-bounds to hungry relatives. But the process is so slow that sometimes substantial trees grow in the middle of these works in progress.[39]

CEMEX, a cement-making company in Mexico, established a successful savings program for poor families, which resembles the Guinean saving accounts encountered by Engelbrecht. Families make small periodic payments for construction materials they can use later to expand their small homes. CEMEX delivers building materials to the sites of homes after families make some payments for the materials but before they pay for all of them. The program is useful to combat temptation to spend the money now rather than save it, but it also useful in removing money that families might feel obliged to share with extended families and friends.[40]

FAMILY STRIFE AND EMBARRASSMENT

My parents would say, "When parents give to children all smile, but when children give to parents all cry." They were fierce in protecting their financial independence. Jean Ley, a 62-year-old woman, could not protect her financial independence when she lost her job, leaving her with little savings. She was grateful for the support of her son, Matt. "If my family weren't able to help me out at this point, I wouldn't have a home," she said. "And I would be struggling."[41] But Matt said, "I think money changes everything . . . It's a cliché, but when you lend money to a friend, when you lend money to family, it changes things."

That change of everything is evident in the voice of Josh Maeir, an experienced software engineer, who found himself out of a job and dependent on his mother and his in-laws. "It feels strange to become dependent after all these years," he said. "My mother and my in-laws help out because they can, because they're generous, and because they really care about us. But there are some strings. . . . Once, when we hired an electrician to fix a ceiling fan, it turned into this big deal because my in-laws considered it to be an extravagance."[42]

Dividing the Estate

We usually leave estates when we are gone, whether by plan or by default. But how should we divide our estates among our children and between them and the surviving spouse? The rules for the division of estates vary from country to country, revealing differences in religion, culture, and notions of fairness. In the United States parents can divide their estates among their adult children as they wish, even excluding one or more of their children. But under Islamic law the freedom of parents to divide their estates is limited to one-third of the estate. The other two thirds are divided in accordance with *Shari'a*. Sons usually receive twice the share of daughters, mainly because of disparity in the economic burdens on men and women. Men are obliged to use their shares of estates to support their families, while women are free of that obligation. Moreover, the assets of women remain theirs after they marry while the assets of men, including inherited assets, are shared in marriage.[43]

In the United States more than 96 percent of parents plan to divide bequests equally among their children, while less than half of Japanese parents plan an equal division of bequests among their children. Indeed, most American parents follow their plans, dividing bequests equally among their children even when their children differ greatly in schooling, earnings, and visits to parents.[44] More than 32 percent of Japanese parents plan to leave a greater amount to the child who takes care of them in old age, while only 2.5 percent of American parents plan to do so. More than 7 percent of Japanese parents plan to give more to the oldest son or daughter and almost 7 percent plan to give more to the child who continues a parent's business, while such plans are almost absent among American parents.[45]

Bequests are usually met with gratitude, even reverence. A single woman nearing retirement received from her father a bequest of $200,000 worth of a paper-products company stock. This bequest made up the largest portion of her assets and offered her the best hope of financial security in retirement. The woman knew that it was wise to diversify her portfolio by selling some of these shares, but she found it hard to do. "I don't want to lose a penny he gave me. I just don't feel worthy. This was a gift. I didn't do anything here."[46] Joe Thompson held on to the stock of KeyCorp, a bank in the midst of the financial crisis of October 2008. The stock came to Thompson when KeyCorp acquired another bank that his grandfather helped found in Winamac, Indiana. KeyCorp stock is "the family heirloom," said Thompson, held in trust for his 89-year-old mother. But KeyCorp's stock lost 70 percent of its value since early 2007.[47]

Sibling Rivalry

Strife among siblings sometimes follows the death of parents, especially when bequests are not divided equally. James and Virginia Null and their three daughters were very close to one another while their parents were alive, and the three daughters were treated equally. An early will divided the bequest equally among the three, but in a later will their father placed Amy, his middle daughter, above her two sisters. Almost all the father's estate went to Amy when he died, and the two other sisters received next to nothing.

The two excluded sisters sued. Adam Gaslowitz, their lawyer, said "People do things to their families that they would never think about doing to a stranger. You are fighting with your family, and it doesn't get any worse than that." A cartoon taped on his computer shows two men sitting on a cloud with angel's wings. One says "I love this. I have been up here for 11 years and my will is still in probate."[48]

Sibling Rivalry Begins Long Before Bequests Arrive

In the late 1990s, I was at a meeting between a financial advisor and a prospective client, a well-educated man who had just received more than $30 million from the sale of his father's business. His brothers and sisters had each received the same amount. The advisor was trying to help the man build a well-diversified portfolio composed of domestic and international stocks and bonds—a good portfolio that would deliver good returns with relatively low risk over the long run. But the man was distressed. His brothers and sisters had chosen portfolios concentrated in a few stocks, confident that they could pick winners. They ridiculed the man's ideas about well-diversified portfolios, and were sure to laugh at him when they came out ahead. He chose to follow his brothers and sisters.

Another advisor told me of a woman client in her early 50s, an attorney doing advocacy work and philanthropy. Their father sold a family business established 90 years before and gave her and her brother approximately $35 million each. The two established a joint investment portfolio and promised to stay together, but conflicts arose between her and the know-it-all brother. So she split away from her brother and hired that advisor to manage her share of the portfolio. Her portfolio was doing better than her brother's and she was proud to be ahead, smiling as if saying to her brother, "See, I'm not so stupid after all."

People bring to financial advisors their life problems, some as petty as keeping up with siblings and some as pressing as setting aside money for a disabled child. One advisor told me of a couple who said, " Plan for our disabled son's future before you begin planning for our own financial future, so we can rest assured that his needs would be met when we are gone."

We are increasingly responsible for our financial future, yet many of us lack the knowledge to plan that future and follow the plan. We seek information, protection, and advice from financial advisors, government, television, the Internet, and other investors. This is the topic of the next chapter.

CHAPTER 16

We Want Education, Advice, and Protection

Financial advisors feared that the Internet would make them obsolete. Stock prices rose in 1999 as if they had no ceiling, and confident investors found huge amounts of free advice on the Internet. At a meeting with advisors that year I tried to allay their fears, reminding them that patients can find huge amounts of free medical advice on the Internet, yet seek out physicians when that pain in the chest persists. "Good advisors are like good physicians," I said. Good physicians promote health and well-being, and good advisors promote wealth and well-being. Patients leave the offices of good physicians not only with prescriptions that promote their health but also with the sense of well-being that comes from understanding the diagnosis, dire as it might be, and knowing the way forward. The same is true for good financial advisors.

Advisors' fears that the Internet would displace them were allayed when stock prices plunged as if they had no floor and investors' confidence plunged along with prices. "I feel sick," wrote one investor on a Yahoo.com message board. "I feel like a deer caught in headlights. . . . I'm scared to get out now because I have lost so much $."[1] Trading stocks when prices were high was "really a form of entertainment," said Donald Williams, a software company executive, but he looked for a financial advisor when almost half of his portfolio vanished. "I didn't want to make any mistakes with the bulk of my assets," he said.[2] Charles Schwab & Co. promoted do-it-yourself investing in its early years, catering to confident investors who traded a lot but wanted no advice, but now it caters to investors seeking advice. "Talk to Chuck," is today's Charles Schwab & Co. slogan.[3]

Investors are increasingly responsible for their financial future as company pensions disappear. They seek information, protection, and advice from financial advisors, governments, television, the Internet, and fellow investors. Some of the advice they receive is good and some is bad. Some delivers what investors want and some does not. Some sticks with investors and some washes away

FINANCIAL LITERACY

Financially literate investors have the knowledge and skills they need to manage their investments, yet not all investors are financially literate. What are your answers to the following questions from a financial literacy test: Would you agree that "an employee of a company with publicly traded stock should have a lot of his or her savings in the company stock?" Would you agree that "if you invest for the long run, the annual fees of mutual funds are important?" Would you say that "if you start out with $1,000 and earn an average return of 10 percent per year for 30 years, after compounding, the initial $1,000 will have grown to more than $6,000?" Financially literate investors are more likely to be financially ready for retirement, yet many investors lack financial literacy and poor financial decisions follow poor financial literacy.[4]

Teaching Financial Literacy

Many old investors lack financial literacy, failing to understand even the basics of stocks and bonds and the importance of investment fees.[5] Financial literacy among the young is no better. Less than one-third of young adults possess basic knowledge of interest rates, inflation, and the risk-reduction benefits of diversification. Still, financial literacy can be taught and learned. High school students improved their financial literacy by a board game confronting them with real-life problems such as a where to get the money to fix a broken car or a broken arm. The board game of an 11th grader placed him in a life with a $21,000 annual income, a wife, and two children. "I first learned that real life isn't going to be as nice as this game," he said. "I also learned that good budgeting has to be maintained throughout a person's life no matter the income, no matter the living conditions."[6]

Parents and schools can enhance financial literacy. College graduates whose parents own stocks and retirement savings are more likely to know about the risk-reduction benefits of diversification than people with less than a high school education.[7] Soldiers who took financial literacy courses in high school were more likely to have savings accounts and save regularly. Such soldiers were also more likely to pay off credit card balances, have emergency funds, read money management articles. They were also less likely to owe overdraft fees.[8]

The poor who can benefit most from financial literacy are often last in receiving it because they offer few benefits to those who might teach them. Juan Maldonado is an exceptional teacher who helps the poor manage whatever little they have. His work is part of a program to reduce poverty in New York City. "As important as education is, when things get really complicated, that's not enough," said Jonathan B. Mintz, commissioner of the Department of Consumer Affairs. "You need to be able to sit down with a professional who is going to look at your financial problems, at your documents, and help you through the crisis, like folks in higher-income tax brackets do." Maldonado, who grew up poor said: "I learned the value of money very early on. . . . I also learned that saving isn't something poor people care about much." He added: "Savings is really not an amount; it's an activity."[9]

Financial Literacy in Crisis

The benefits of financial literacy were evident when a wave of mortgage defaults heralded the recent financial crisis. Adjustable-rate mortgages with complicated features were widely available in the period leading to the financial crisis, and homeowners lacking financial literacy chose them.[10] Homeowners with better financial literacy chose fixed-rate mortgages. Competence at working with numbers is one aspect of financial literacy, and homeowners with such competence were less likely to default on their loan or face home foreclosures.[11] Still, lessons must be clear if they are to be absorbed. Prospective homeowners who read clear disclosures were more likely to choose well.[12] Comprehensive education is even more effective. The Indianapolis Neighborhood Housing Partnership offered prospective homeowners education and mandatory counseling before they could buy their homes. Education started with a three-hour class on money management practices, continued with one-on-one monthly meetings, followed by an eight-hour class on home buying. Counseling continued even after participants bought their homes to remedy mortgage delinquencies at their early stage. Low to moderate income families who completed the program improved their financial literacy. Such families were also less likely to default on their mortgage loans than families with similar income who did not participate in the program.[13]

Enhanced financial literacy and advice help borrowers avoid mortgage loan defaults, but the success of the Indianapolis partnership at reducing defaults came from more than that. The partnership rated borrowers by their ability to repay mortgage loans and lent money only to borrowers who proved that ability. The partnership protected itself when it declined to lend to borrowers lacking the ability to repay, but it also protected such borrowers from themselves, reducing the likelihood that they would suffer the financial and emotional consequences of defaults and foreclosures. In that, the partnership exercised paternalism, as parents do when they prevent young children from crossing busy streets on their own. Indeed, paternalism motivates much of government programs and regulations.

PROTECTING US FROM OURSELVES AND OTHERS

In 1900, Charles R. Flint, the organizer of the United States Rubber Company, spoke for free markets and libertarianism and against regulated markets and paternalism. "My idea," he said, "is that affairs of trade are best regulated by natural law. The careless banker has lost his reputation; the careless investor has lost his money; and the result of it is, more care will be taken."[14] Yet others were unwilling to leave the protection of investors to the libertarian "natural law" of the marketplace and recommended paternalistic "blue-sky" laws instead. The price of Kansas farmland more than doubled from 1900 to 1910, and the new prosperity attracted sellers of investments so fraudulent that they were likened to pieces of blue sky. Blue-sky laws are paternalistic, empowering regulators to prohibit sellers of investments from charging what regulators regard as excessive fees or selling investments at prices regulators consider too high.

"Cheat me once, shame on you, cheat me twice, shame on me." Free markets and libertarian societies are not without restraint. We prefer to stay away not only from those who have cheated us but also from those who fail to nurture a reputation for honesty and fair dealing. This preference provides an incentive for honesty and fair dealing even in the absence of regulations mandating it.

Reputation can sustain trust in free markets. Jacob Schiff, an investment banker at the turn of the twentieth century, attributed the growth of investment banking in his time and the prominence of firms like his own to "the fact that they have been more honest than those who, thirty and twenty years ago, were among the leading banking firms. Not more honest, as construed in the literal sense of the word, but honest in their respect for the moral obligation assumed toward those who entrusted their financial affairs to them. . . ."[15]

Alan Greenspan, the former chairman of the Federal Reserve Bank, would have preferred to sustain trust with reputation, as Jacob Schiff did. Greenspan said: "In a market system based on trust, reputation has a significant economic value." But reputation did not sustain trust in the years leading to the recent financial crisis. Greenspan added, "I am therefore distressed at how far we have let concerns for reputation slip in recent years."[16]

Regulations can replace trust when reputation slips. Regulations can also replace trust when being cheated once does not put us on guard against being cheated twice, or when even one instance of cheating is one too many, as when predatory lenders lead borrowers into foreclosure or bankruptcy.[17]

Protecting Us with Suitability and Fiduciary Regulations

Suitability and fiduciary regulations are prominent among financial regulations. Brokers who recommend securities to their investors must have reasonable grounds for believing that their recommended securities are suitable for their investors' financial situation and needs. Financial advisors carry even heavier responsibilities as fiduciaries, required to place their investors' interests before their own.

Fiduciary and suitability regulations are paternalistic, shifting away from the libertarian notion that suitability is in the eyes of investors to a paternalistic notion that suitability is in the eyes of their brokers. The

Securities and Exchange Commission illustrated the paternalistic nature of suitability regulations when it concluded that a broker violated them. It does not matter whether investors considered the investments suitable, wrote the Commission. It does not even matter that investors were driven by greed to insist on these investments. What matters is that the investments were not suitable for their investors based on their financial situation and needs.[18]

Protecting Us with Regulations of Leverage

There would have been no housing defaults and foreclosures if homebuyers paid for their houses in full with their own cash rather than leverage their houses through mortgage loans. There would have been no financial crisis if financial institutions did not multiply mortgage leverage in securities backed by leveraged mortgages. But the costs of regulations prohibiting leverage altogether are enormous. Few would be able to buy houses if not for the ability to leverage their down payments through mortgage loans. The leverage debate is not about whether leverage should or should not be allowed but about whether leverage should be allowed without limit. Much of this debate has been conducted in the context of stocks, where leverage is discussed in the language of margins.

Margin on stocks is now set by regulations at 50 percent. Investors who want to buy $1,000 worth of stock must pay a "down-payment" of no less than $500 and can leverage their stocks by borrowing the other $500 from their brokers. Homeowners can leverage their homes with mortgage loans from banks. Yet, unlike stocks, there is no legal limit on the down payment required from homeowners. Years ago, down payments on houses were regularly set by banks at no less than 20 percent, but down payments have dwindled to almost zero in the years leading to the crisis.

Down payments on stocks were as low as 10 percent and leverage was high in the early part of the twentieth century, and speculation facilitated by leverage is among the factors blamed for the crash of 1929. President Franklin Roosevelt wrote in 1934: "The people of this country are, in overwhelming majority, fully aware of the fact that unregulated speculation in securities and in commodities was one of the most important contributing factors in the artificial and unwarranted 'boom' which has so much to do with the terrible conditions of the years following 1929."[19]

Two worries underlie the drive to limit leverage, one about the damage investors can inflict on themselves, and one about the damage they can inflict on others. Limits on leverage were considered necessary to protect investors from the cognitive errors and poor self-control that can lead them to speculation facilitated by leverage. And limits on leverage were considered necessary to protect others from spillovers caused by investors using leverage. We know that both worries were valid in the recent financial crisis.

The Cycle of Investor Protection

Our desire for paternalistic protection from ourselves and others increases when we experience the sad consequences of our own behavior or the behavior of others. Sometimes regulators are effective protectors. "One day, about seven year ago, a well-to-do architect of Paris found in his mail a prospectus which gave rise to an investment experience somewhat out of the ordinary," wrote the *World's Work* in 1913. The investment offered a 26 percent return. "As every experienced investor knows, those figures should have served to put the Frenchman on guard." But the figures did not put the man on guard, and he lost his money. The man sued the directors of the company and won. The magazine added, with satisfaction, that unscrupulous promoters are "finding it increasingly difficult, year after year, to ply its trade successfully under the watchful eyes of Post Office inspectors, or state officials."[20]

Yet at other times regulators fail. The life of the Office of Thrift Supervision comes to an end now that the 2010 financial regulation bill is law. That end is overdue. We, the general public of individual investors and consumers, hope that regulators would fight for us against the interest groups of bankers, lawyers, union members, and employers. But regulators often treat interest groups as customers and constituents to be served rather than as potential regulation-breakers who should be policed.[21] "Our goal is to allow thrifts to operate with a wide breadth of freedom from regulatory intrusion," said James E. Gilleran in 2004, while serving as the director of the Office. John M. Reich, who directed the Office in 2007, canceled a scheduled lunch so he might have lunch with Kerry K. Killinger, the chief executive of Washington Mutual. "He's my largest constituent," Mr. Reich wrote.[22]

Help from Financial Advisors

Good financial advisers are good financial physicians. Good advisors possess the knowledge of finance, as good physicians possess knowledge of medicine, and good advisors add to it the skills of good physicians: asking, listening, empathizing, educating, and prescribing.

Physicians face "noncomplying" patients who do not take their prescribed medicine as instructed, and financial advisors face noncomplying clients who imperil their future by spending too much in the present. Compelling clients to comply is a difficult task when clients are young athletes or actors. "These kids are making serious money," said Scott Feinstein, a financial advisor. "They don't realize the pressure that friends and family will put on them. They don't have the maturity to say no." One young client called to say that he wanted to buy a $35,000 watch. "What time does it say?" asked Feinstein. "Ten minutes after three," answered the client."Mine says ten after three too, and it cost me 60 bucks," said Feinstein. "Put the watch down." [23]

Larry Ellison, the head of the Oracle Corporation, is one of the richest men in the world and a winner of America's Cup sailing competition. But the life of his financial advisor is difficult. Documents in a trial revealed that Ellison lives well. His annual "lifestyle" expenses amount to $20 million. A villa in Japan costs $25 million, a new yacht costs $194 million, and preparations for America's Cup cost $80 million. The documents include emails to Ellison from his financial advisor. One e-mail said "I know this e-mail may/will depress you. However, I believe it's my job to address issues you'd prefer not to confront. You told me years ago that it's OK to raise the "diversification issue" with you quarterly. . . . Well, I'm doing so. View this as a call to arms." [24]

Trust in financial advisors has diminished greatly in the recent financial crisis. Investors have been distressed to find that the values of their investment portfolios have plummeted and that some investors have been paying money to advisors who sent it to operators of Ponzi schemes. "All right, so it was just a matter of time before I wrote to see if you're still working or you ran away to Belize," wrote one of Scott Rodabaugh's clients in late 2008. "People are confused and they're angry," said Rodabaugh. [25]

Some investors expressed their anger in more than worried e-mails. Four German pensioners kidnapped their financial advisor in June 2009 because they suffered losses in their American real-estate investments. The investors tied up the advisor with tape, gagged him, and beat him up, breaking two of his ribs. Afterward, they forced him to sign a statement promising to compensate his investors for their losses. The advisor was eventually freed when his trustee read a secret message in a fax of that statement and alerted the police.[26]

FAIR FEES FOR VALUABLE ADVICE

Fees come between financial advisors and their clients as they come between physicians and their patients. "I have a million dollars in my portfolio," thinks a client. "I don't mind paying a fee for the management of stocks. Stocks are complicated and I cannot manage them on my own. But the management of bonds is easy and cash needs no management at all. Why am I paying you a fee for these?" Financial advisers hope that clients would understand the value of their services and the fairness of their fees, yet fees are difficult to discuss because clients regularly misperceive the value of the services of financial advisors.

Imagine that you are seeing a physician because your stomach hurts. The physician asks many questions, examines your body, provides a diagnosis and concludes with education and advice. The examination, diagnosis, and education are free, says the physician. All you have to pay is the price of the pill you received. That would be $200, please.

Financial advisers act regularly as the physician in this story. Financial advisors frame themselves as *investment* managers, providers of "beat-the-market" pills, when they are, in truth, mostly *investor* managers, professionals who examine the financial resources and goals of investors, diagnose deficiencies, and educate investors about financial health.

Financial advisors are not capricious as they frame themselves as managers of investments when, in truth, they are mostly managers of investors. They respond to the perceptions of investors. Some of my undergraduate students spend a quarter as interns in financial services companies, often assisting financial advisors. "What do you think financial advisors do?" I ask them before they leave for their internships. "Financial advisors are investment managers," they say. "Financial advisors analyze investments just as we have learned in our investments class. Then they recommend investments to their clients." I wait for the term papers at the end of the quarter. "What a surprise," they write, "financial advisors spend most of their time prospecting for new clients and advising old ones."

Financial advisors respond to investor perceptions by framing fees for managing investors as fees for managing investments. "Rule 12b-1 fees" are one example. The fees were originally designed to help mutual fund companies attract new investors and eventually save investors money as funds grow and their costs decline. Yet the fees go to financial advisors who recommended the funds to their investors, and payment to advisors can extend into decades, long after money was placed into the funds. Mary Schapiro, the chairwoman of the Securities and Exchange Commission, is critical of 12b-1 fees. "Despite paying billions of dollars, many investors do not understand what 12b-1 fees are, and it's likely that some don't even know that these fees are being deducted from their funds or who they are ultimately compensating." The SEC is drafting new rules "designed to enhance clarity, fairness and competition when investors buy mutual funds." Yet Robert Kurucza, partner in a law firm serving mutual fund companies, noted the downside of the proposed SEC rule. 12b-1 fees compensate financial advisors for investment advice they continue to provide decades after they have placed clients into funds. Decreased compensation is likely to decrease advice.[27]

WHAT IS GOOD ADVICE?

Financial advisors are hampered by investors' misperceptions of their services. They are also buffeted by differences in the recommendations of investment experts. Diversification is one example. Not all recommended diversification a century ago and not all recommend it today. In 1911 the *World's Work* received a letter from businessman who read an advertisement headed "Diversify Your Investments" and wanted to know if his portfolio was indeed diversified. The analysis of the *World's Work* revealed that while the portfolio seemed diversified, it was not. All the securities in the portfolio were issued by companies in one state and all were bought from "one banking house, a house of the middle class, which maintains a fair selling market in its own securities at all times, but is not a particularly good seller of securities for its customers."[28]

"Do not put all your eggs in one basket" was the diversification advice of the the *World's Work*, but it noted that not all agree. Marsden J. Perry, chairman of the boards of directors of the Union Trust Company of Providence and of the Norfolk Southern Railroad, believed in "putting all his investment eggs in a few baskets, provided he can keep careful watch of those baskets." There is no universal rule for investing, said Perry. "There are as many individual preferences as there are different kinds of investments available. People differ widely in their choice. . . . It depends on the type of mind the individual himself possess, and some prefer dividing their investments over a wide range of business activity, while others are temperamentally unfit to assume the management of such a diversification of interests." Andrew Carnegie advised investors to refrain from diversification and put all their portfolio eggs in one basket and watch that basket. "In my investments I have adhered more to the Carnegie method than to the other," said Marsden, "generally in a few baskets, which I have watched."[29]

More recently an investor wrote about diversification on the Yahoo. com Web site: "I have more shares in Elon then I ever thought I would . . . have definitely broke the rules of diversification with this one. It is scary to be so heavily concentrated, but then I just try and think about other stuff and move on with my day."[30] A fellow investor reassured him: "Congratulations on your independent thinking and action that will put you on the road to great wealth. There are no lasting "rules" of investing! There are however, many planted, restrictive sayings that empower the professional traders who don't live by any rules and take advantage of those who do."[31]

Some are reluctant to offer advice and some are reluctant to accept it. Emerson McMillin was reluctant to offer advice a century ago. McMillin, described by the 1917 the *World's Work* as a "comparatively rich man," started in the gas business soon after his return from the Civil War.[32] Although Mr. McMillin's investments were successful, he hesitated to offer advice. "My own observation," he said, "has led me to believe that few would-be investors really desire advice. They merely want approval of what they have already made up their minds to do." The alternative to good advice is experience, but, McMillin noted, "experience is often a sad teacher."[33]

Investors proud of their opinions are reluctant to seek advice that might contradict them. "Do not buy a stock and *then* ask someone what he thinks of it," wrote Humphrey B. Neill in 1931. "If he disagrees with your judgment, you will not pay any attention to him anyway; and it is a waste of breath to run around looking solely for people who will agree with you."[34]

Some investors are reluctant to accept advice because they have made up their minds, but others are on guard because they suspect the motives of those offering advice. In that, investors are like automobile owners. We suspect that automobile mechanics repair what need not be repaired, and our suspicions are often well founded. The Department of Transportation estimated that more than half of auto repairs are unnecessary.[35] Many mortgage borrowers would have saved themselves heartache, default, and foreclosure if they had been more skeptical of those who advised them. Borrowers with poor financial literacy were charged more than borrowers with good financial literacy, and borrowers who engaged mortgage brokers were charged more than borrowers who engaged banks.[36] Suspicion leads some investors to trust the advice of fellow nonprofessional investors more than they trust the advice of professionals.

Advice from Fellow Investors

Investors seek advice from peers on Web site communities such as Mint, SmartyPig, Cake Financial, Wesabe, and Credit Karma. Investors also seek the expressive and emotional benefits of a community, and the anonymity of fellow members is often an advantage. Marc Hedlund of Wesabe said, "Oftentimes you don't want to talk about stressful financial issues with your friends. Online, you can come in an anonymous way, talk about the things you're struggling with and get feedback."[37] Openness about salaries and financial matters seems odd to elders but natural to their children. "My parents wouldn't have this conversation with friends," said 22-year-old Arielle Green. "For them it's very hush-hush. You don't talk about money, politics, or religion with friends. But in this generation, it's important." And 32-year-old Ilana Arazie said, "If we can talk about how many orgasms we have with our mate, why can't we discuss how much we make?"[38]

"How many people bought at or near the March [2009] low," asked an investor on the Morningstar.com Web site. "I took my shot in October 2008 . . . Too early as per usual . . . made a buy, 10 percent of my portfolio. Was thinking of doubling down on the dip but got scared and did not. Sold in May instead . . . So did anyone bet the farm on the March dip?"[39] A fellow investor responded "I had some jumbo CDs mature late October 2008 and, like you, got in at a good price, but not at the bottom. . . . So, better lucky than smart! . . . One more question, when you did buy? What were your feelings? All aboard? Fearful? Sure? Did not give a damn? SICK TO YOUR STOMACH?"

Another investor, describing himself as Super Newbie, posted his request for advice. Super Newbie had $10,000 to invest but he was stumped: "I have concluded that I want to try this at high risk so I may try and get a high return," he wrote, "But I have no idea where to start."[40] "Here's my 2 cents, kiddo," answered a fellow investor, describing himself as a volunteer sharing what has worked for him in the past but unsure if it would work on the future. "Before you go gambling your dollars into the market . . . let's see if you're qualified." Do you have enough money set aside to pay your bills during the next six months? Are your credit cards under control? Are you saving enough? High risk does not assure high return, wrote another investor. "Let me give you an example. . . . 30 years ago if you had put 10k in Microsoft, you would have been assuming enormous risk. And you would have succeeded marvelously. But what if instead you had dropped 10k into any number of competitors of Microsoft, who have since ceased to exist?"[41]

Offers of advice and their acceptance are complicated because advice judged good by some is judged bad by others, and because advice that satisfies some investors does not satisfy others. "Are expense ratios that important?" asked an investor on the Morningstar.com Web site.[42] "Would you make a case for investing in a fund with a high expense ratio?" One investor wrote "I use exclusively low cost Vanguard funds and always try to keep my expense ratios as low as possible." But another investor disagreed. "Expenses are important but everything is relative. All (but one) my funds have expenses over 1 percent . . . and I still like them."

Some Australian investors sought advice from fellow investors and followed it, avoiding scams. One consulted his brother, who warned him not to touch it. But sometimes distrust of professionals and regulators gets in the way. One investor baited for a scam was told by his accountant that "once you send your money overseas you kiss it goodbye." But he went ahead anyway because "he just had a gut feeling that it might be alright and you take risks at times." Another investor called the Australian Securities and Investments Commission but rejected its warnings, investing anyway because of "resistance to bureaucracy."[43]

Investors want it all. We want good financial education, advice and protection. Yet we are reluctant to pay for it or devote the effort necessary to acquire it. Our desire for good free advice joins our other investment desires, from the desire to play investment games to the desire to win them, from the desire to stay true to our values to the desire for status. Yet what we want is not always what we have. This is where we go next.

CONCLUSION

What We Have

"The trouble is many people don't know how to invest wisely. So everyone should be required to be in the diversified portfolio," said Gregory G. Seals, director of fixed income and behavioral finance at the Chartered Financial Analysts (CFA) Institute.[1] Not everyone agrees. "Nanny Should Keep Hands Off Our 401(k)s" was the heading of Walter H. Inge's letter to the editor, ridiculing Seals' opinion as nanny-state philosophy. "Yes," wrote Inge, "you poor unwashed masses, you sans-culottes, you benighted bumpkins in flyover country. So what if some of you have an IQ of 180 and a Wharton MBA. As nurturing nannies we behavioral finance czars know what is best for you, so everyone is required to obey our investment dictates."[2] The debate between Seals and Inge illustrates two broader debates. One centers on the distinction between what we want and the cognitive errors we commit as we try to get it. The other centers on the right balance between a paternalistic "nanny state" and a libertarian "free state."

Investments offer three kinds of benefits: utilitarian, expressive, and emotional, and we face trade-offs as we choose among them. The utilitarian benefits of investments center on what they do for our pocketbooks. Profits are utilitarian benefits. The expressive benefits of investments are in what they convey to us and to others about our values, tastes, and status. Some express their values by investing in companies that treat their employees well. Others express their status by investing in hedge funds. And the emotional benefits of investments are in how they make us feel. Bonds make us feel safe and stocks give us hope.

It is often hard to distinguish facts from cognitive errors and even harder to distinguish cognitive errors from wants of expressive and emotional benefits. Inge might know his facts when he objects to a requirement that everyone hold a diversified portfolio. Perhaps his 180 IQ enables him to pick a handful of stocks, each sure to turn into the next fabulous Google. Or perhaps Inge's objection to a diversification requirement is founded on cognitive errors. Perhaps he does not understand that there is a loser in every trade. Perhaps he does not understand that he might be that loser since the seller might be an insider who knows that his company is more likely to turn into the next bankrupt Enron than the next fabulous Google. Or perhaps Inge understands that there is a loser in every trade and that he might be that loser, yet he still wants to enjoy expressive and emotional benefits even if he sacrifices the risk-reduction utilitarian benefits of diversification. Inge might want the thrill of trading and the intellectual challenge of picking the right stocks even if trading is more likely to thin his wallet than fatten it.

We should empathize with fellow investors who do not share our wants. Some of us are willing to pay money for the game of golf, including the cost of clubs, balls, and fees. Golf holds no attraction to me; I'd rather read the newspaper in the morning than head for the golf course. Perhaps cognitive errors mislead avid golf players into spoiling a good walk. Or perhaps golf players simply enjoy playing golf as I enjoy reading the newspaper. I empathize with golf's passionate players even if I don't share their passion. Some of us are passionate players of the investment game, willing to pay commissions for trades, subscriptions for newsletters that promise to foresee the market, and fees for mutual funds that promise to beat it. I empathize with their passions as well, even if I don't share them. Yet while I empathize with investors' wants for expressive and emotional benefits, I see no benefit in cognitive errors that mislead us into sacrificing utilitarian benefits for no benefits at all. No benefit comes from foregoing the utilitarian benefits of diversification because we do not understand them. And no benefit comes from failing to make wise choices among utilitarian, expressive, and emotional benefits. We can increase the sum of our benefits if we understand our investment wants, overcome our cognitive errors, weigh the trade-offs between benefits, and choose wisely.

Financial literacy helps us overcome cognitive errors, and education helps us gain literacy. Yet the benefits of financial literacy are limited by our ability to learn and retain what we have learned. Middle-aged people commit fewer financial errors than younger or older ones. Young people lack financial literacy because they have not learned it. Old people lack financial literacy because they do not retain what they have learned. Approximately half of those between the ages of 80 and 89 suffer cognitive impairments that diminish their ability to make wise financial decisions.[3] Cognitive errors are especially costly for older people who have fewer opportunities to replenish their savings through employment. One elderly man, a recently widowed well-educated professional, was cheated out of more than $23,000 by con men who persuaded him that a huge lottery prize awaits him as soon as he pays some processing fees. We, as a society, might choose to leave that man to do what he wants, whether misled by cognitive errors or not, or we might choose to protect him from his cognitive errors at the cost of limiting his freedom. This is the choice between libertarianism at one end and paternalism at the other. The judge considering this man's case opted for paternalism, limiting the man's freedom and granting paternalistic authority to the man's children.[4]

Should government regulations lean toward libertarianism, freeing investors to invest as they wish, or should government regulation tilt toward paternalism, constraining choices to protect investors from themselves and from others? Should government require that all investors diversify their portfolios, even if they have an IQ of 180? Should government protect home buyers from the cognitive errors and emotions that lead them to sign mortgage documents before they have read them because the stack of documents is too high and the emotional pull of homeownership is too strong? And should the government protect us, the neighbors of foolish and emotional homeowners, from the consequences of their likely defaults and foreclosures?

Governments' regulations constrain otherwise free markets. Changes in regulations over time reveal our continuing attempts, through the legislative process, to find the right balance in the tug-of-war between those who pull toward the libertarian free-markets end and those who pull toward the paternalistic regulated-markets end. At the extreme left are those who pull toward completely regulated markets and comprehensive paternalism, and at the extreme right are those who pull toward completely free markets and comprehensive libertarianism. Yet only a few want to pull the tug-of-war rope all the way to the left where most enterprises are owned by the government and regulations constrain most transactions. And only a few want to pull the rope all the way to the right, leaving no role for government. Instead, the tug-of-war is fought mostly in the middle, where groups pull left or right but not all the way to the extremes. Those pulling toward regulations want regulations they consider helpful and effective, such as clear disclosure of information about mortgages, but not regulations they consider excessive, such as prohibiting adjustable-rate mortgages. Those pulling toward free markets want markets to be helpful and productive, such as a free market in derivatives, but not necessarily a free market in cocaine.

The tug-of-war between those who pull toward libertarianism and those who pull toward paternalism goes on because we cannot agree on the perfect balance between them. The awkward balance between them is reflected in a government that provides both Social Security and lotteries. The first is paternalistic, forcing us to save when we are young, and saving us from poverty when we are old. The second is libertarian, giving adults the freedom to spend as much as they want for hope at riches.

Democrats tend to pull toward paternalism whereas Republicans tend to pull toward libertarianism, yet directions of pulls are sometimes reversed. Congress is considering a law that would legalize Internet gambling and tax it. Congressman Barney Frank, a Democrat, supports the law and takes the libertarian side as he champions it. "Some adults will spend their money foolishly, but it is not the purpose of the federal government to prevent them legally from doing it," he said. Yet Congressman Spencer Bachus, a Republican, opposes the law. Bachus was amazed that "after all the talk last year about shutting down casinos on Wall Street," Congress would vote to "open casinos in every home and every bedroom and every dorm room, and on every iPhone, every BlackBerry, every laptop."[5]

Investors who are free of cognitive errors and posses willpower sufficient to resist temptation have no use for paternalism. Indeed, financial resources and self-control enable more than four out of five households between the ages of 59 and 69 to refrain from withdrawing money from their retirement accounts. One such investor wrote: "I worked after school and week-ends as a kid. I also worked summer vacations. Then after the army, I worked for an electric company in Ohio for 40 years with rarely any holidays off. . . . Then I retired at 61 and feel that if I don't start living now, I will run out of time."[6] But others find it impossible to resist temptation because of personality or circumstances. One wrote: "Here on the Oregon coast it seems that every homeless person has a dog (or several). Folks living in tents have cell phones and Facebook accounts."[7]

Light paternalism can nudge in a wise direction people hampered by cognitive errors or insufficient self-control, without restricting the freedom of those who need no paternalism or do not want it. Those who save too little can be nudged toward saving more by automatic enrollment into saving programs, without restricting the freedom of those who choose not to save.[8] And those who save too much can be nudged into spending more by the sad experience of those who spent too little. "I believe one reason many people do not draw on their [savings] when they retire is that they are used to saving," wrote one investor. "My husband always said he wanted to spend all of his money before he died. Yet after retirement, we only tapped our [savings] to buy a new car for cash. . . . Unfortunately, my very healthy husband suddenly became ill and died four months later of lung cancer. . . . So I guess, in addition to factoring in a long life, we should also consider a life cut short and indulge in a few luxuries."[9]

This investor reminds us that investments are about life beyond money, and that we should enjoy all the benefits of investments—utilitarian, expressive, and emotional. We can enjoy these benefits ourselves, indulging in a few luxuries, or we might enjoy them with family, friends, and people in our neighborhoods and faraway continents. But, in the end, we cannot take our investments with us.

Notes

Introduction

1. Brian Stelter, "Gerald Tsai, Innovative Investor, Dies," *New York Times*, July 11, 2008, C10.
2. Donald Jay Korn, "A Matter of Opinion," *Financial Planning* 34, no. 8 (2004): 52–57.
3. Meir Statman, "Quiet Conversations: The Expressive Nature of Socially Responsible Investors," *Journal of Financial Planning* 21, no. 2 (February 2008): 40–46.
4. Suresh Ramanathan and Ann McGill, "Consuming with Others: Social Influences on Moment-to-Moment and Retrospective Evaluations of an Experience," *Journal of Consumer Research* 34 (2007): 506–524.
5. Nathalie Camille, Nathalie, Giorgio Coricelli, Jerome Sallet, Pascale Pradat-Diehl, Jean-Rene Duhamel, and Angela Sirigu (2004). "The Involvement of the Orbitofrontal Cortex in the Experience of Regret," *Science* 304 (May 21, 2004): 1167–1170.
6. *World's Work*, "The Bargain Hunter," October 1911, 14922–14924.
7. Baba Shiv and Alexander Fedorikhin, "Heart and Mind in Conflict: The Interplay of Affect and Cognition in Consumer Decision Making," *Journal of Consumer Research* 26 (December 1999): 278–292.
8. Michael J. Cooper, , Orlin Dimitrov, and Raghavendra Rau, "A Rose.com by Any Other Name" *Journal of Finance* 56 (December 2001): 2371–2388.
9. Meir Statman, Steven Thorley, and Keith Vorkink, "Investor Overconfidence and Trading Volume," *Review of Financial Studies* 19 (2006): 1531–1565.
10. Nerissa C. Brown, Kelsey D. Wei, and Russ R. Wermers, "Analyst Recommendations, Mutual Fund Herding, and Overreaction in Stock Prices," (2009), available at Social Science Research Network (SSRN), http://ssrn.com/abstract=1092744.
11. Peter M. DeMarzo, Ron Kaniel, and Ilan Kremer, "Relative Wealth Concerns and Financial Bubbles," *Review of Financial Studies* 21 no.1 (2008): 19–50.

Chapter 1

1. Janet Whitman, "'May God Spare You No Mercy,' Victim Tells Madoff," *Financial Post* (June 29, 2009), http://www.financialpost.com/story.html?id=1743842.
2. Joe Nocera, "Talking Business: Madoff Had Accomplices: His Victims," *New York Times*, March 13, 2002, http://www.nytimes.com/2009/03/14/business/14nocera .html?_r=1.
3. Steven Syre, "Boston Capital: Madoff's Method," *Boston Globe*, December 16, 2008, http://www.boston.com/business/articles/2008/12/16/madoffs_method/.
4. The Vanguard Group, Vanguard Total Stock Market Index Fund (VTSMX), https://personal.vanguard.com/us/funds/snapshot?FundId=0085&FundIntExt=INT.
5. The Vanguard Group, Inc.,Vanguard Long-Term Bond Index Fund (VBLTX), https://personal.vanguard.com/us/funds/snapshot?FundId=0522&FundIntExt=INT.

6. The Vanguard Group, Inc.,Vanguard Short-Term Bond Index Fund (VBISX), https://personal.vanguard.com/us/funds/snapshot?FundId=0132&FundIntExt=INT.

7. President and Fellows of Harvard College, "Harvard University Fact Book" (Cambridge, MA: Harvard University, 2008), 2007–2008, http://www.provost.harvard .edu/institutional_research/FACTBOOK_2007–08_FULL.pdf.

8. John Bogle, "A Question So Important That It Should Be Hard to Think About Anything Else," *Journal of Portfolio Management* (Winter 2008), 95–102.

9. *World's Work,* "The Bargain Hunter," October 1911, 14924.

10. *World's Work,* "Keeping Out of Investment Trouble," October 1910, 13480–13482,

11. *World's Work* "The Innocent Investor and the Mining Boom," January 1907, 8383–8385.

12. *World's Work,* " Mr. Bush's Advice to the Average Investor," May–October 1917, 596.

13. Lester Pimentel and Daniel Helft, "Kirchner May Heed IMF's 'Pathetic' Advice, Pay Debt," February 21, 2007, Bloomberg, http://noir.bloomberg.com/apps/news?pid=new sarchive&sid=azhC3vZNuM.M&refer=latin_america#.

14. Marco Bertacche and Drew Benson. "Italians May Take 'Anything' to Drop Argentina Bonds (Update 2)," April 26, 2010, Bloomberg, http://www.businessweek.com/news/ 2010–04–26/italians-may-take-anything-to-drop-argentina-bonds-update1-.html.

15. Australian Securities & Investments Commission (ASIC), "International Cold Calling Investment Scams," June 2002, Table 1, 1–64, http://www.asic.gov.au/fido/fido.nsf/byhe adline/02%2F218+International+cold+calling+investment+scams+report?open Document.

16. Larry Light, "Reverse Converts: A Nest-Egg Slasher?," *Wall Street Journal,* June 16, 2009, http://online.wsj.com/article/SB124511060085417057.html.

17. Laura Santini, "Asian Investors 'Accumulate' Big Losses on Risky Contracts," *Wall Street Journal,* November 6, 2008, http://online.wsj.com/article/SB122593605357403861 .html#.

18. Brad M. Barber and Terrance Odean, "Trading Is Hazardous to Your Wealth: The Common Stock Investment Performance of Individual Investors," *Journal of Finance* 55, no. 2 (2000): 773–806.

19. Anders Anderson, "Is Online Trading Gambling with Peanuts?" (2008), available at Social Science Research Network (SSRN), http://ssrn.com/abstract=871435.

20. Illia Dichev, "What Are Stock Investors' Actual Historical Returns? Evidence from Dollar-Weighted Returns," *American Economic Review* 97 (2007): 386–402.

21. Christopher Traulsen, "The Importance of Investing for the Long Term," March 24, 2006, Morningstar UK, http://www. morningstar.co.uk/uk/funds/article.aspx?lang= en-GB&articleID=45274.

22. Ilia D. Dichev and Gwen Yu, "Higher Risk, Lower Returns: What Hedge Fund Investors Really Earn," (2009), available at Social Science Research Network (SSRN), http://ssrn.com/abstract=1354070.

23. Hsiu-Lang Chen, Narasimhan Jegadeesh, and Russ Wermers, "An Examination of the Stockholdings and Trades of Fund Managers," *Journal of Financial and Quantitative Analysis* 35 (2000): 343–368.

24. Malkiel Burton, "The Efficient Market Hypothesis and Its Critics," *Journal of Economic Perspectives* 17, no. 1 (October 2003): 59–82.

25. Burton G. Malkiel and Atanu Saha, "Hedge Funds: Risk and Return," *Financial Analysts* Journal 61, no. 6 (2005): 80–88.

26. CBS, "Tom Perkins: The Captain of Capitalism," *60 Minutes* television program, January 23, 2009, available at Cnet TV, http://cnettv.cnet.com/60-minutes -tom-perkins-captain-capitalism/9742–1_53–50005093.html.

27. Mark Grinblatt, Matti Keloharju, and Juhani T. Linnainmaa, "Do Smart Investors Outperform Dumb Investors?" (2010), available at Social Science Research Network (SSRN), http://ssrn.com/abstract=1364014.

28. Jorg Oechssler, Andreas Roider, and Patrick W. Schmitz, "Cognitive Abilities and Behavioral Biases." *Institute for the Study of Labor* (2008), working paper, http://www .awi.uni-heidelberg.de/bf/doc/dp3481.pdf.
29. James J. Choi, David Laibson, and Brigitte C. Madrian, "Why Does the Law of One Price Fail? An Experiment on Index Mutual Funds," *Review of Financial Studies* 23, no. 4 (2009): 1405–1432.
30. Jane J. Kim, "U.S. Senators' Stock Picks Outperform the Pros," *Wall Street Journal,* October 26, 2004, http://online.wsj.com/article/SB109874916042455390.html.
31. United States District Court, District of Connecticut, Securities and Exchange Commission v. Pequot Capital Management, Inc. and Arthur J. Samberg, filed May 27, 2010, http://www.sec.gov/litigation/complaints/2010/comp-pr2010–88.pdf.
32. Trond Doskeland and Hans K. Hvide, "Do Individual Investors Have Asymmetric Information Based on Work Experience?, *Journal of Finance* (forthcoming 2010), available at Social Science Research Network (SSRN), http://ssrn.com/ abstract=1413782.
33. Nicholas Varchaver, "What Warren Thinks . . . ," *Fortune,* April 14, 2008, 157, 59–62, http://money.cnn.com/galleries/2008/fortune/0804/gallery.buffett.fortune/index.html.
34. Carol Loomis, "Buffet's Big Bet," *Fortune,* June 23, 2008, 45–51.
35. Ben Stein, "Everybody's Business: Lessons from the Pits of Travel and Investment," *New York Times,* December 9, 2007, http://travel.nytimes.com/2007/12/09/business/09every .html.
36. Deborah Lohse, "Tricks of the Trade: 'Buffet Is Buying This' and Other Sayings of the Cold-Call Crew—Brokers Who Sell Tiny Stocks Reveal Secrets to Rookies in Candid Audio Tapes—How to Seem Like a Big Shot," *Wall Street Journal,* June 1, 1998, A1.
37. PBS, "Betting on the Market," *PBS Frontline* television program, broadcast on January 14, 1997.
38. Ianthe Jeanne Dugan, "Hard Lessons: Copying Peter Lynch, Investors Bought a Stock, Watched It Tank," *Wall Street Journal,* October 15, 2004, A1.
39. *World's Work,* "The War, Wall Street and Water," October 1915, 638–641.
40. Morningstar forum, "Play on Afghanistan Surge," Post # 2741232, December 4, 2009, 12:10 pm, http://socialize.morningstar.com/NewSocialize/forums/274232/Print Thread.aspx.
41. Morningstar forum, reply to Post # 274232, "Play on Afghanistan Surge," Post #2741234, December 4, 2009, 12:13 pm, http://socialize.morningstar.com/ NewSocialize/forums/274232/PrintThread.aspx.

Chapter 2

1. Ravi Dhar and William N. Goetzmann "Bubble Investors: What Were They Thinking?", (2006), available at Social Science Research Network (SSRN),http://ssrn.com/ abstract=683366.
2. Felix Meschke, "CEO Interviews on CNBC," (2004), available at Social Science Research Network (SSRN), http://ssrn.com/abstract=302602 or doi:10.2139/ ssrn.302602.
3. Laura Frieder and Jonathan Zittrain, "Spam Works: Evidence from Stock Touts and Corresponding Market Activity," (2007), available at Social Science Research Network (SSRN): http://ssrn.com/abstract=920553.
4. *Forbes* magazine, July 15, 1931, 32.
5. Cover page of *Fortune,* Special Investor's Issue, June 23, 2008.
6. Joseph D. Goodman, "5 Stocks with Possibilities," *Forbes,* July 1, 1929, 29
7. Andrew Ross Sorkin, "Goldman Acknowledges Conflicts with Clients," *New York Times,* January 12, 2010, http://dealbook.blogs.nytimes.com/2010/01/12/goldman -executive-discloses-conflicts-policy/.

8. Amos Tversky and Daniel Kahneman, "Belief in the Law of Small Numbers," *Psychological Bulletin* 76 (1971): 105–110.
9. Charles Gasparino, "Small-Company Stocks Propelled Fund Winners in Latest Ratings," *Wall Street Journal*, July 3, 1996, R3.
10. John Bowen, Jr. and Meir Statman, "Performance Games," *Journal of Portfolio Management* 23, no. 2 (Winter 1997): 8–15
11. R. J. Herrnstein and Donald Loveland, "Maximizing and Matching on Concurrent Ratio Schedules," *Journal of Experimental Analysis and Behavior* 24, no. 1 (1975): 107–116.
12. Kenneth Fisher and Meir Statman, "Investor Sentiment and Stock Returns," *Financial Analysts Journal* 56, no. 2 (March/April 2000): 16–23.
13. Ibid.; Kenneth Fisher and Meir Statman, "Sentiment, Value, and Market Timing," *Journal of Investing* 13, no. 3 (Fall 2004): 10–21.
14. Travis Proulx and Steven Heine, "Connections from Kafka: Exposure to Meaning Threats Improves Implicit Learning of an Artificial Grammar," *Psychological Science* 20, no. 9 (2009): 1125–1130.
15. Michael Drosnin, *The Bible Code* (New York: Touchstone, 1998).
16. Ibid., 33.
17. Sharon Begley, "Seek and Ye Shall Find," *Newsweek*, June 9, 1997, 51.
18. Maya Bar-Hillel and Avishai Margalit, "Madness in the Method," December 1999, http://www.dartmouth.edu/~chance/teaching_aids/books_articles/Maya.html.
19. Maya Bar-Hillel,Dror Bar-Natan, and Brendan McKay, "The Torah Codes: Puzzle and Solution," *Chance* magazine, May 1998, http://cs.anu.edu.au/people/bdm/dilugim/Chance.pdf.
20. Channelingstocks, "Buy and Sell the Same Stock Again and Again!", June 17 2008, channelingstocks.com.
21. Ravi Dhar and William N. Goetzmann, "Bubble Investors: What Were They Thinking?," (2006), available at Social Science Research Network (SSRN), http://ssrn.com/abstract=683366.
22. Steven Huddart, Mark Lang, and Michelle Yetman,"Volume and Price Patterns around a Stock's 52-Week Highs and Lows: Theory and Evidence," *Management Science* 55, no. 1 (2009): 16–31.
23. Chan-Yang Hwang and Thomas George, "The 52-Week High and Momentum Investing," *Journal of Finance* 59, no. 5 (2005): 2145–2176.
24. Jeanne Long, *Universal Clock: Forecasting Time and Price in the Footsteps of W. D. Gann* (Jacksonville, Florida: PAS Astro-Soft, Inc., 1993).
25. *Galactic Investor,* http://www.galacticinvestor.com/galactic_trader_main.htm.
26. Jeanne Long, ed., *A Trader's Astrologicial Almanac* (quarterly online subscription), http://www.galacticinvestor.com/galactic_trader_main.htm.
27. Long, *Universal Clock*, 5.
28. Quy Toan Do and Tung Duc Phung, "Superstition, Family Planning, and Human Development," World Bank Policy Research, working paper no. 4001 (2009).
29. Associated Press, "Orange County Ex-Official Says He Used Star Charts," *San Jose Mercury News*, July 25, 1998.
30. Rob Curran, "Written in the Stars," *Wall Street Journal*, October 24, 2008.
31. Gabriele M. Lepori, "Dark Omens in the Sky: Do Superstitious Beliefs Affect Investment Decisions?", (2009), available at Social Science Research Network (SSRN), http://ssrn.com/abstract=1428792.
32. Charles T. Clotfelter and Philip J. Cook, "Lotteries in the Real World," *Journal of Risk and Uncertainty* 4, no. 3 (1991): 227–232.
33. Gary Rivlin, "How the Slot Machine Was Remade, and How It Is Remaking America," *New York Times Magazine*, May 9, 2004, 42.

34. Henry W. Chase and Luke Clark, "Gambling Severity Predicts Midbrain Response to Near-Miss Outcomes," *Journal of Neuroscience* 30, no. 18 (May 5, 2010): 6180–6187, doi:10.1523/JNEUROSCI.5758-09.2010.

35. Keith C. Brown, W. V. Harlow, and Laura T. Starks, "Of Tournaments and Temptations: An Analysis of Managerial Incentives in the Mutual Fund Industry," *Journal of Finance* 51 (1996): 85–110

36. Kenneth Chang, "Earthquakes' Many Mysteries Stymie Efforts to Predict Them," *New York Times*, April 14, 2009, http://www.nytimes.com/2009/04/14/science/14quak.html.

37. William J. Broad, "Data Tying Cancer to Electric Power Found to Be False," *New York Times*, July 24, 1999, A1.

38. Benjamin Graham, *The Intelligent Investor*, updated with new commentary by Jason Zweig (New York: Harper Business Essentials, 2003), 368.

39. Roger Lowenstein, *Buffett: The Making of an American Capitalist*. (New York: Random House, 1995), 97.

40. Meir Statman and Jonathan Scheid, "Buffett in Foresight and Hindsight," *Financial Analysis Journal* 58, no. 4 (July/August): 11–18.

41. Carol Loomis, "Hard Times Come to the Hedge Funds," *Fortune*, January 1970, 101.

42. Mary Greenbaum, "Gauging the Market's Prospects," *Fortune*, January 10, 1983, 97–98.

Chapter 3

1. Edward M. Saunders, "Stock Prices and Wall Street Weather," *American Economic Review* 83 (1993): 1337–1345.

2. David Hirshleifer and Tyler Shumway, "Good Day Sunshine: Stock Returns and the Weather," *Journal of Finance* 58 (June 2003): 1009–1032.

3. Mark J. Kamstra, Lisa A. Kramer, and Maurice D. Levi, "Winter Blues: A SAD Stock Market Cycle," *American Economic Review* 93 (2003): 324–343.

4. Marianne Bertrand, Dean Karlan, Sendhil Mullainathan, Eldar Shafir, Jonathan Zinman, "What's Advertising Content Worth? Evidence from a Consumer Credit Marketing Field Experiment," *Quarterly Journal of Economics* 125 (February 2010): 263–305.

5. Enrichetta Ravina, "Love & Loans: The Effect of Beauty and Personal Characteristics in Credit Markets," (2008) available at Social Science Research Network (SSRN), http://ssrn.com/abstract=1101647.

6. Rose Palazzolo, "Is Friday the 13th a Reason to Stay in Bed?," *ABC News,* May 13, 2005, http://abcnews.go.com/Health/story?id=751011&page=1.

7. Thomas Kramer and Lauren Block, "Conscious and Nonconscious Components of Superstitious Beliefs in Judgment and Decision Making," *Journal of Consumer Research* 36, no. 4 (2008): 783–793.

8. Sun Na and Thomas Ervin Schneider, "The Use of 'Lucky' Numbers in the Pricing of Chinese A-Share Initial Public Offerings," available at Social Science Research Network (SSRN): http://ssrn.com/abstract=1588352.

9. James S. Ang , Ansley Chua, and Danling Jiang, "Is A Better than B? How Affect Influences the Marketing and Pricing of Financial Securities," *Financial Analysts Journal* 66, no. 5 (September–October 2010).

10. Terrance Odean, Michal Ann Strahilevitz, and Brad M. Barber, "Once Burned, Twice Shy: How Naive Learning and Counterfactuals Affect the Repurchase of Stocks Previously Sold," (2004), available at Social Science Research Network (SSRN), http://ssrn.com/abstract=611267.

11. Daniel Dorn, "Does Sentiment Drive the Retail Demand for IPOs?," *Journal of Financial and Quantitative Analysis* 44, no. 1 (2009): 85–108.

12. Markku Kaustia, and Samuli Knupfer, "Do Investors Overweight Personal Experience? Evidence from IPO Subscriptions," *Journal of Finance* 63 (2008): 2679–2702.

13. Adam L. Alter and Daniel M. Oppenheimer, "Predicting Short-Term Stock Fluctuations by Using Processing Fluency," *Proceedings of the National Academy of Sciences* 103, no. 24 (2006): 9369–9372.

14. John Burgess, "IBM's $5 Billion Loss Highest in American Corporate History," *Washington Post,* January 20, 1993.

15. Meir Statman, Kenneth Fisher, and Deniz Aginer, "Affect in a Behaviorial Asset Pricing Theory," *Financial Analysts Journal* 64, no. 2 (March/April 2008): 20–29.

16. Viral V. Acharya and Matthew Richardson, "Causes of the Financial Crises," *Critical Review* 21, no. 2–3 (2009): 195–210.

17. *World's Work,* "Imitation 'War-Bride' Stocks," October 1916, 612–614.

18. Quoted in Albert Shaw, "The Worst Mistake an Investor Can Make," *The American Review of Reviews* (November 1908): 631.

19. Jason Zweig, "Baloney.com: Don't Believe the Hype about Internet Stocks and Funds," *Money,* vol. 29, no. 5, May 1, 1999, 63.

20. Hilary Kramer, "Interview with Tom Hudson," *PBS Nightly Business Report,* April 28, 2010.

21. Don Moore, Terri Kurtzberg, Craig Fox, and Max Bazerman, "Positive Illusions and Biases of Prediction in Mutual Fund Investment Decisions," *Organizational Behavior and Human Decision Processes* 79, no. 2 (1999): 95–114.

22. William Goetzmann and Nadav Peles, "Cognitive Dissonance and Mutual Fund Investors," *Journal of Financial Research* 20, no. 2 (1997): 145–58.

23. Shelley Taylor and Jonathon Brown, "Illusion and Well-Being: A Social Psychological Perspective on Mental Health," *Psychological Bulletin* 103 (1988): 193–210.

24. Ibid.

25. Ying Zhang and Ayelet Fishbach, "Counteracting Obstacles with Optimistic Predictions," *Journal of Experimental Psychology* 139, no. 1 (2010): 16–31.

26. Manju Puri and David Robinson, "Optimism and Economic Choice," *Journal of Financial Economics* 86 (2007): 71–99.

27. Charles Clotfelter and Philip Cook, "Lotteries in the Real World," *Journal of Risk and Uncertainty* 4, no. 3 (July 1991): 227–232.

28. Meir Statman, Steven Thorley, and Keith Vorkink, "Investor Overconfidence and Trading Volume," *Review of Financial Studies* 19 (2006): 1531–1565.

29. Federico Nardari and René M. Stulz, "Do Investors Trade More When Stocks Have Performed Well? Evidence from 46 Countries," *Review of Financial Studies* 20 (2007): 905–951.

30. *World's Work,* "His First Bond," July 1912, 274.

31. New York Stock Exchange, "Market Volatility and Investor Confidence: A Report to the Board of Directors of the New York Stock Exchange," 1990, 3.

32. Dan Colarusso, "Investing; Day Trading Takes a Conservative Turn," *New York Times,* March 10, 2002, http://www.nytimes.com/2002/03/10/business/investing-day-trading-takes-a-conservative-turn.html.

33. Patrick McGeehan, "Schwab to Eliminate 2,400 Jobs in New Round of Cuts," *New York Times,* August 23, 2001, http://www.nytimes.com/2001/08/31/business/schwab-to-eliminate-2400-jobs-in-new-round-of-cuts.html?pagewanted=1?pagewanted=1.

34. Utpal Bhattacharya and Hazem Daouk, "The World Price of Insider Trading," *Journal of Finance* 57 (2002): 75–108.

35. Russell Baker, *New York Times,* December 9, 1975, in Philip A. Neher, "The Pure Theory of the Muggery," *The American Economic Review,* 68, no. 3, (June 1978): 437–445.

36. Hui Huang, "An Empirical Study of the Incidence of Insider Trading in China," (2007), available at Social Science Research Network (SSRN), http://ssrn.com/abstract=993341.

37. Jennifer Whitson and Adam Galinsky, "Lacking Control Increases Illusory Pattern Perception," *Science* 3 (October 2008): 115–117.

38. Lysann Damisch, Barbara Stoberock, and Thomas Mussweiler, "Keep Your Fingers Crossed! How Superstition Improves Performance," *Psychological Science* 21, no. 7 (2007): 1014–1020.

39. Mark Fenton-O'Creevy, Nigel Nicholson, Emma Sloane, and Paul Willman, "Trading on Illusions: Unrealistic Perceptions of Control and Trading Performance," *Journal of Occupational and Organizational Psychology* 76 (2003): 53–68.

40. Jennifer S. Lerner and Dacher Keltner, "Fear, Anger, and Risk," *Journal of Personality and Social Psychology* 81, no. 1 (2001): 146–159.

41. Paul Litvak, Jennifer Lerner, Larissa Tiedens, and Katherine Shonk, "Fuel in the Fire: How Anger Impacts Judgment and Decision-Making," in *International Handbook of Anger*, ed. Michael Potegal, Gerhard Stemmler, and Charles Spielberger (New York: Springer, 2010), 287-310.

42. David Segal, "Day Traders 2.0—Wired, Angry and Loving It," *New York Times*, March 26, 2010, accessed June 14, 2010 at http://www.nytimes.com/2010/03/28/business/28trader.html?pagewanted=2&ref=david_segal.

43. Douglas Jordan and David Diltz, "The Profitability of Day Traders," *Financial Analysts Journal* (November/December 2003): 85–94.

44. Atonio Damasio, *Descartes' Error* (New York: HarperCollins, 1994).

45. Baba Shiv, George Loewenstein, Antoine Bechara, Hanna Damasio, and Antonio R. Damasio, "Investment Behavior and the Negative Side of Emotion," *Psychological Science* 16, no. 6 (2005): 435–439.

46. George Loewenstein. Elke U. Weber, Christopher K. Hsee, and Edward L. Welch, "Risk as Feelings," *Psychological Bulletin* 127, no. 2 (2001), 267–286.

47. Guy Kaplanski and Haim Levy, "Sentiment and Stock Prices: The Case of Aviation Disasters," *Journal of Financial Economics* 95 (2010): 174–201.

48. Sebastian Müller and Martin Weber, "Financial Literacy and Mutual Fund Investments: Who Buys Actively Managed Funds?" *Schmalenbach Business Review* 62 (April 2010): 126–153.

Chapter 4

1. W. E. Woodward, *Introduction to "Watch your Margin: An Insider Looks at Wall Street* (New York: Horace Liveright, 1930), 7.

2. Ibid., 8–9.

3. Ibid., 116.

4. Jason Zweig, "A Perk of Power: Trading in Companies You Oversee," *Wall Street Journal*, April 10, 2010, http://online.wsj.com/article/SB10001424052702304703104575174124009720464.html.

5. Arvid O. I. Hoffmann, "Individual Investors' Needs and the Investment Professional: Lessons from Marketing," *The Journal of Investment Consulting* 8, no. 2 (2007): 80–91.

6. Daniel Dorn and Paul Sengmueller, "Trading as Entertainment?" *Management Science* 55, no. 4 (2009): 591–603.

7. Ravi Dhar and William N. Goetzmann "Bubble Investors: What Were They Thinking?," (2006), available at Social Science Research Network (SSRN), http://ssrn.com/abstract=683366.

8. James R Hagy, "Interview with Charles Schwab," *Mutual Funds*, September 1996, 50–55.

9. David L. Babson, "Index Funds: Why Throw in the Towel," *Journal of Portfolio Management* 2, no. 3 (1976): 45–52.

10. John McLaughlin, comment to the article by Meir Statman, "The Mistakes We Make—and Why We Make Them," in the *Wall Street Journal Online* (August 24, 2009), http://online.wsj.com/article/SB10001424052970204313604574326223160094150.html#articleTabs%3Dcomments.

11. Mark Grinblatt and Matti Keloharju, "Sensation Seeking, Overconfidence, and Trading Activity," *Journal of Finance* 64, no. 2 (2009): 549–578.

12. Mihaly Csikszentmihalyi, *Finding Flow: The Psychology of Engagement* (New York: HarperCollins, 1997), 28–29.

13. John F. Kennedy, address at Rice University on the Nation's Space Effort, September 12, 1962, http://www.jfklibrary.org/Historical+Resources/Archives/Reference+Desk/Speeches/JFK/003POF03SpaceEffort09121962.htm.

14. David Funderburke, "Climbing the Wall—My First Marathon," http://www.marathonguide.com/features/FMStories/DavidFunderburke.cfm.

15. Benjamin Scheibehenne, Ranier Greifeneder, and Peter Todd, "Can There Ever Be Too Many Choices? A Meta-analytic Review of Choice Overload," *Journal of Consumer Research* 37, no. 3 (October 2010): 409-425

16. Rebecca Buckman, "Day-Trading Blues," *Wall Street Journal*, March 1, 2000, http://www.press-enterprise.com/newsarchive/2000/03/01/951883091.html.

17. Sonali Shah, "Motivation, Governance, and the Viability of Hybrid Forms in Open Source Software Development," *Management Science* 52, no. 7 (2006): 1000–1014.

18. Lynn Cowan, "Web Enthusiasts Take Up Scam Baiting," *Wall Street Journal*, March 19, 2003.

19. Young Han Lee and Ulrike Malmendier, "The Bidder's Curse," *American Economic Review*, forthcoming.

20. Rebecca Buckman, "Rock on! Stewart Rules as Web Trader," *Wall Street Journal*, December 7, 1999, C1.

21. *Literary Digest*, "German Marks and American 'Gamblers,'" 71 (1921): 50–51.

22. Daniel Dorn, "Investors with Too Many Options?" (2010), available at Social Science Research Network (SSRN), http://ssrn.com/abstract=1571788.

23. Hendrik P. Van Dalen, Kene Henkens, Kees C. G. Koedijk. and Alfred Slager, "Decision Making in the Pension Fund Board Room: An Experiment with Dutch Pension Fund Trustees," (2010), available at Social Science Research Network (SSRN), http://ssrn.com/abstract=1562681

24. John Bowen, Jr. and Meir Statman, "Performance Games," *Journal of Portfolio Management* 23, no. 2 (Winter 1997): 8–15

25. Suzanne Woolley, "Join the Club." *Money*, May 15. 2000, 64.

26. Lynn Cowan, "Web Enthusiasts Take Up Scam Baiting," *Wall Street Journal*, March 19, 2003.

27. N. R. Branscombe, and Daniel L. Wann, "The Positive Social and Self-Concept Consequences of Sports Team Identification," *Journal of Sport & Social Issue* 15 (1991): 115–127.

28. Suresh Ramanthan and Ann L. McGill, "Consuming with Others: Social Influences on Moment-to-Moment and Retrospective Evaluations of an Experience," *Journal of Consumer Research* 34, no. 4 (2007): 506–524.

29. Wal-Mart, Wal-Mart cheer, http://walmartstores.com/AboutUs/320.aspx.

30. Sandy Quadros Bowles, "Investment Club Has Happy Returns, Seniors Pool Money for Stocks," *Telegram and Gazette*, July 26, 2000.

31. Brad M. Barber and Terrance Odean, "Too Many Cooks Spoil the Profits: Investment Club Performance," *Financial Analysts Journal* 56, no. 1 (1999): 17–25.

32. Clare Ansberry, "Investment Club Weighs Future Amid Turmoil," *Wall Street Journal*, October 28, 2008, D1

33. Peter Webb. "Pilgrimage to Omaha," http://www.peterwebb.co.uk/pilgrimage.htm.

34. Graham Bowley, "Morgan Stanley Tries on a New Psyche," *New York Times,* January 17, 2010, BU1.
35. David Firestone, "For Mourners in Atlanta, Some Solace but No Answers," *New York Times,* August 5, 1999, U. S. section,http://www.nytimes.com/1999/08/05/us/for-mourners-in-atlanta-some-solace-but-no-answers.html.
36. Danny Hakim, "Online Investing Clubs Evolve, Thanks to One-Stop Internet Shops," *New York Times,* July 18, 2000, C6.

Chapter 5

1. Kenneth L. Fisher and Meir Statman, "Sentiment, Value, and Market Timing," *Journal of Investing* 13, no. 3 (Fall 2004): 10–21.
2. Message on Yahoo.com's Amazon message board, msg 192149, December 10, 1999.
3. Message on Yahoo.com's Amazon message board, msg #191672, December 9, 1999.
4. Charles P. Kindleberger, "Manias, Panics and Crashes," *A History of Financial Crisis,* 3rd edition (New York: John Wiley and Sons, Inc., 1996)
5. Message on Yahoo.com's Amazon message board, msg # 191300, December 9, 1999.
6. Message on Yahoo.com's Yahoo message board msg #180245, December 9, 1999.
7. Message on Yahoo.com's GE message board, msg #40723, August 24, 2000.
8. Message on Yahoo.com's Home Depot message board, msg # 19554, December 26, 1999.
9. Message on Yahoo.com's Amazon message board, msg # 190850, December 8, 1999.
10. Message on Yahoo.com's Amazon message board, msg #189506, December 4, 1999.
11. Message on Yahoo.com's GE message board, msg #41290, August 28, 2000.
12. Message on Yahoo.com's Home Depot message board, msg # 19734, December 28, 1999.
13. Message on Yahoo.com's GE message board, msg # 188790, July12, 2002.
14. Message on Yahoo.com's GE message board, msg #187329,July 10, 2002.
15. Message on Yahoo.com's GE message board, msg #186651, July 9, 2002.
16. *World's Work,* "When Caution Pays the Investor, December 1908, 10978–10980.
17. Warren Buffett, lecture to a group of students at Columbia University, http://vinvesting.com/buffett/bquotes.html.
18. Message on Yahoo.com's GE message board, msg # 187151, July 10, 2002.
19. Lilian Ng and Fei Wu. "Peer Effects in the Trading Decisions of Individual Investors," *Financial Management* 39 (Summer 2010): 807–831.
20. Daniel Dorn, Gur Humberman, and Paul Sengmueller, "Correlated Trading and Returns," *Journal of Finance* 63, no. 2 (2008): 885–920.
21. Jeffery R. Brown, Zoran Ivković, Paul A. Smith, and Scott Weisbenner, "Neighbors Matter: Causal Community Effects and Stock Market Participation" (May 27, 2007), available at Social Science Research Network (SSRN), http://ssrn.com/abstract=966334.
22. Russell E. Jame and Qing Tong, "Retail Investor Industry Herding, (September 5, 2009), available at Social Science Research Network (SSRN), http://ssrn.com/abstract=1468952.
23. Ajay Khorana, Eric C. Chang, and Joseph W. Cheng, "An Examination of Herd Behavior in Equity Markets: An International Perspective," *Review of Financial Studies* 17, no. 1 (2004): 165–206.
24. Brad M. Barber and Terrance Odean. "Do Retail Trades Move Markets?," *Review of Financial Studies* 22, no. 1 (2009): 151–186.
25. Markku Kaustia and Samuli Knupfer, "Learning from the Outcomes of Others: Evidence from the Stock Market," working paper, *Helsinki School of Economic,* (2009).

26. Mark Grinblatt, Matti Keloharju, and Seppo Ikaheimo, "Interpersonal Effects in Consumption: Evidence from the Automobile Purchases of Neighbors," (September 2004), available at Social Science Research Network (SSRN), http://ssrn.com/abstract=513945.

27. Massimo Massa and Andrei Simonov, "Do Bubbles Have a Birthdate? The Role of College Interaction in Portfolio Choice," (March 2005), available at Social Science Research Network (SSRN), http://ssrn.com/abstract=685923.

28. Esther Duflo and Emmanuel Saez, "Participation and Investment Decision in a Retirement Plan: The Influence of Colleagues' Choices," *Journal of Public Economics* 85 (2002): 121–148.

29. Richard W. Sias, "Institutional Herding," (February 24, 2002), available at Social Science Research Network (SSRN), http://ssrn.com/abstract=307440 or doi:10.2139/ssrn.307440.

30. Markus K. Brunnermeir and Stefan Nagel, "Hedge Funds and the Technology Bubble," *Journal of Finance* 59, no. 5 (2004): 2013–2040.

31. Nerissa C. Brown, Kelsey D. Wei, and Russ R. Wermers, "Analyst Recommendations, Mutual Fund Herding, and Overreaction in Stock Prices," (July 21, 2009), available at Social Science Research Network (SSRN), http://ssrn.com/abstract=1092744.

32. John M. Griffin, Selim Topaloglu, and Jeffrey H. Harris, "The Dynamics of Institutional and Individual Trading," *Journal of Finance* 58, no. 6 (2003): 2285–2320.

33. Woochan Kim and Shang-Jin Wei, "Foreign Portfolio Investors Before and During a Crisis," *Journal of International Economics* 56, no. 1 (2002): 77–96.

34. Jennifer Peltz, "Madoff Scandal Fits Profile of 'Affinity Fraud,' Proves Particularly Wrenching for Jews," *Star Tribune,* December 26, 2008.

35. Avi Issacharoff, "Hezbollah's Madoff Brings Serious Financial Losses to Top Members," Haaretz.com, July 9, 2009.

36. Benjamin Weiser and Mathew Warren, "In This Scheme, Man Is Accused of Fleecing Fellow Churchgoers," *New York Times,* December 26, 2008, http://www.nytimes.com/2008/12/26/nyregion/26ponzi.html.

37. Peter Applebome, "A Mini-Madoff Who Worked the Pews," *New York Times,* January, 14, 2010, A28.

38. The Committee on Energy and Commerce, prepared witness testimony, developments relating to Enron Corp, February 6, 2002, Mr. James S. Chanos, president and founder, Kynikos Associates, Ltd.,http://www.actwin.com/kalostrader/EnronTestimony.htm.

39. Markus K. Brunnermeir and Stefan Nagel, "Hedge Funds and the Technology Bubble," *Journal of Finance* 59, no. 5 (2004): 2013–2040.

40. Wei Xiong and Jialin Yu, "The Chinese Warrants Bubble" (March 17, 2009), available at Social Science Research Network (SSRN), http://papers.ssrn.com/abstract=1361220.

41. David Barboza, "To See a Stock Market Bubble Bursting, Look at Shanghai," *New York Times,* April 2, 2008, http://www.nytimes.com/2008/04/02/business/worldbusiness/02yuan.html.

42. Gene Amromin and Steven A. Sharpe, "Expectations of Risk and Return among Household Investors: Are Their Sharpe Ratios Countercyclical?" (January 15, 2009), available at Social Science Research Network (SSRN): http://ssrn.com/abstract=1327134; Kenneth L. Fisher and Meir Statman, "Consumer Confidence and Stock Returns," *Journal of Portfolio Management* 30, no. 1 (2003): 115–127.

43. George Frederick, "Common Stocks and the Average Man," (New York: *The Business Bourse,* 1930), 17–19.

44. *Literary Digest,* "All Kinds of People Buying Stocks, December 29, 1918, 45,

45. The Gallup Organization, "UBS Index of Investor Optimism." Approximately one-fifth of investors had no opinion of refused to disclose it. (It would have been good to know how investors answered these questions in the six months ending in February 2009,

after the stock market plunged, and more recently. Alas, the survey is not conducted anymore.)

46. Jesse Eisinger and Jake Bernstein, "The Magnetar Trade: How One Hedge Fund Helped Keep the Bubble Going," *Propublica*, April 9, 2010, http://www.propublica.org/feature/the-magnetar-trade-how-one-hedge-fund-helped-keep-the-housing-bubble-going.

47. Gretchen Morgenson and Louise Story, "Banks Bundled Bad Debt, Bet Against It and Won," *New York Times*, December 24, 2009, Business.

48. Landon Thomas Jr., "For Bankers, a Routine Deal Became a $840 Million Mistake," *New York Times*, April 23, 2010, A1.

49. Mary Pilon, Karen Blumenthal, and Jason Zweig, "When 'Stop Loss' Trades Backfire on Investors," *Wall Street Journal*, May 15, 2010, Investing, http://online.wsj.com/article/NA_WSJ_PUB:SB10001424052748703950804575242942496526282.html

50. New York Stock Exchange, "Market Volatility and Investor Confidence: a Report to the Board of Directors of the New York Stock Exchange," 1990, 3.

Chapter 6

1. Cecilie Hoigard and Liv Finstad, *Backstreets: Prostitution, Money and Love* (University Park, PA: Pennsylvania State University Press, 1992), 49.

2. Carl Husemoller, *Nightingale On the Edge: A History of Poor Black Children and Their American Dreams* (New York: Basic Books, 1993), 36.

3. Cletus Coughlin and Thomas Garrett, "Income and Lottery Sales: Transfers Trump Income from Work and Wealth," (January 17, 2008), available at Social Science Research Network (SSRN), http://papers.ssrn.com/s013/papers.cfm?abstract_id=1084183.

4. Jean Lave, *Cognition in Practice* (Cambridge, UK: Cambridge University Press, [first published in 1988]), p. 132.

5. Lee Rainwater, Richard Coleman, and Gerald Handel, *Workingman's Wife. Her Personality, World and Life Style* (New York: Oceana Publications, 1959), 155.

6. Laura Rowley, "Fast Track to Financial Success," May 13, 2010, Yahoo.Finance, http://finance.yahoo.com/retirement/article/109540/fast-track-to-financial-success.

7. Ethan Cohen-Cole and Jonathan Morse, "Your House or Your Credit Card, Which Would You Choose? Personal Delinquency Tradeoffs and Precautionary Liquidity Motives," (2010), available at Social Science Research Network (SSRN), http://ssrn.com/abstract=1411291.

8. PBS, "Secret History of the Credit Card," PBS *Frontline*, November 23, 2004, http://www.pbs.org/wgbh/pages/frontline/shows/credit/.

9. Sumit Agarwal, Paige Marta Skiba, and Jeremy Bruce Tobacman, "Payday Loans and Credit Cards: New Liquidity and Credit Scoring Puzzles?," (January 15, 2009), available at Social Science Research Network (SSRN), http://ssrn.com/abstract=1327125.

10. Alejandro Ponce, Enrique Seira, and Guillermo Zamarripa, "Do Consumers Borrow on Their Cheapest Credit Card? Evidence From Mexico, " (March 18, 2009), available at Social Science Research Network (SSRN), http://ssrn.com/abstract=1364722.

11. Yuichi Shoda, Walter Mischel, and Philip Peak, "Predicting Adolescent Cognitive and Self-Regulatory Competencies from Preschool Delay of Gratification: Identifying Diagnostic Conditions," *Developmental Psychology* 2, no. 6 (1990): 978–986.

12. Stephan Meier and Charles Sprenger, "Present-Biased Preferences and Credit Card Borrowing," (June 1, 2009), available at Social Science Research Network (SSRN, http://ssrn.com/abstract=1412276.

13. John Warner and Saul Pleeter, "The Personal Discount Rate Evidence from Military Downsizing Programs," *American Economic Review* 91, no. 1 (2001): 33–53.

14. thebostonchannel.com and the Associated Press, "Millionaire Lottery Winner Dies in Fire. Gonsalves Still Owed $1 Million From from 1994 Jackpot Win," The Boston

Channel, March 22, 2008, http://www.thebostonchannel.com/news/15677454/detail.html.

15. Scott Hankins, Mark L. Hoekstra, and Paige Marta Skiba, "The Ticket to Easy Street? The Financial Consequences of Winning the Lottery," (January 9, 2009), available at Social Science Research Network (SSRN), http://ssrn.com/abstract=1324845.

16. Annette Vissing-Jorgensen, "Consumer Credit: Learning Your Customer's Default Risk from What (S)He Buys," (2010), available at Social Science Research Network (SSRN), http://ssrn.com/abstract=1570812.

17. Lendol Calder, *Financing the American Dream: A Cultural History of Consumer Credit* (Princeton, NJ: Princeton University Press, 1999), 173.

18. Xavier Giné, Dean S. Karlan, and Jonathan Zinman, "Put Your Money Where Your Butt Is: A Commitment Contract for Smoking Cessation," (2009), available at Social Science Research Network (SSRN), http://ssrn.com/abstract=1429254.

19. Jan-Emmanuel De Neve and James H. Fowler, "The MAOA Gene Predicts Credit Card Debt," (2010), available at Social Science Research Network (SSRN), http://ssrn.com/abstract=1457224.

20. Samuel McClure, David I. Laibson, George Loewenstein, and Jonathan D. Cohenet, "Separate Neural Systems Value Immediate and Delayed Monetary Rewards," *Science* 306, no. 5695 (2004): 503–507.

21. Kris Kirby, Nancy M. Petry, and Warren K. Bickel, "Heroin Addicts Have Higher Discount Rates for Delayed Rewards than Non-Drug-Using Controls," *Journal of Experimental Psychology* 128, no. 1 (1999): 78–87.

22. John Ameriks, Andrew Caplin, and John Leahy, "Wealth Accumulation and the Propensity to Plan," *Quarterly Journal of Economics* 118, (2003): 1007–1047.

23. Arul Mishra and Himanshu Mishra, "We Are What We Consume: The Influence of Food Consumption on Impulsive Choice," *Journal of Marketing Research* (forthcoming 2011), available at Social Science Research Network (SSRN), http://ssrn.com/abstract=1498082.

24. X. T. Wang and Robert D. Dvorak, "Sweet Future: Fluctuating Blood Glucose Levels Affect Future Discounting," *Psychological Science* 21 (2010): 183–188.

25. Margo Wilson and Martin Daly, "Do Pretty Women Inspire Men to Discount the Future?" *Biology Letters* 271 (2004): S177–S179.

26. Ayelet Rishbach and James Shah, "Self Control in Action: Implicit Dispositions toward Goals and Away from Temptations," *Journal of Personality and Social Psychology* 90, no. 5 (2006): 820–832.

27. *World's Work*, "Mr. John G. Shedd on Saving and Investing," December 1917, 129–130.

28. Karen Cheney, "Building $125,000 on $44,000 a year at 35, *Money*, July 1996, 102–111.

29. Michael Barbaro, "Mayor Doesn't Always Live by His Health Rules," *New York Times*, September 22, 2009, Dining & Wine, http://www.nytimes.com/2009/09/23/dining/23bloom.html.

30. David Gal and Wendy Liu, "The Grapes of Wrath: The Implicit Emotional Consequences of Being Virtuous," (working paper, Northwestern University, 2010).

31. Stefano DellaVigna and Ulrike Malmendier, "Paying Not to Go to the Gym," *American Economic Review* 96, no. 3 (June 2006): 694–719.

32. PBS, "The Card Game," *Frontline*, November 24, 2009, http://www.pbs.org/wgbh/pages/frontline/creditcards/etc/script.html.

33. John Ameriks, Andrew Capli., John Leahy, and Tom Tyler, "Measuring Self-Control," *American Economic Review* 97, no. 3 (2007): 966–972.

34. Thomas Stanley and William D. Danko, *The Millionaire Next Door* (New York: Pocket Books, 1996), 9–10

35. Ibid, 203.

36. Scott Rick, Cynthia Cryder, and George F. Loewenstein, "Tightwads and Spendthrifts," *Journal of Consumer Research* 34, no. 6 (2008), 767–782.

37. Brian Knutson, Scott Rick, G. Elliott Wimmer, Drazen Prelec, and George Loewenstein, "Neural Predictors of Purchases," *Neuron* 53 (January 2007): 147–156.

38. W. E. Woodward, *Watch Your Margin: An Insider Looks at Wall Street* (New York: Horace Liveright, 1930), Introduction.

39. Anat Keinan and Ran Kivetz, "Remedying Hyperopia: The Effects of Self-Control Regret on Consumer Behavior," *Journal of Marketing Research* 45 (2008): 676–689.

40. Ran Kivetz and Itamar Simonson, "Self-Control for the Righteous: Toward a Theory of Precommitment to Indulgence," *Journal of Consumer Research* 29 (September 2002): 199–217.

Chapter 7

1. Christine Dugas, "Retirement Crisis Looms as Many Come Up Short," *USA Today*, July 19, 2002, Money section, http://www.usatoday.com/money/perfi/retirement/bw/2002-07-19-usat-cover.htm.

2. Alicia Munnell, Anthony Webb, and Luke Delorme, "Retirements at Risk: A New National Retirement Index," (working paper, Boston College Center for Retirement Research, 2006), http://ideas.repec.org/p/crr/issbrf/ib48.html.

3. Jonathan Skinner, "Are You Sure You're Saving Enough for Retirement?" *Journal of Economic Perspectives* 21, no. 3 (2007): 59–80.

4. Jason Scott, William Sharpe, and John Watson, "The 4% Rule—At What Price?" *Journal of Investment Management* 7, no. 3 (2008): 31–48.

5. Rebecca White, "Format Matters in the Mental Accounting of Funds: The Case of Gift Cards and Cash Gifts," (working paper, University of Waterloo, November 30, 2006), http://papers.ssrn.com/s013/papers.cfm?abstract_id=948587.

6. Hersh Shefrin and Meir Statman, "Explaining Investor Preference for Cash Dividends," *Journal of Financial Economics* 13, (1984): 253–282

7. Annelena Lobb, "Investors Lick Wounds from Dividend Cuts," *Wall Street Journal*, October 7, 2008, C1.

8. Personal correspondence with Jonathan Clements, who shared these e-mails with me.

9. Malcolm Baker, Stefan Nagel, and Jeffrey Wurgler, "The Effects of Dividends on Consumption," *Brookings Papers on Economic Activity* 1 (2007): 231–276.

10. E. S. Browing, "Loyalty Pays a Bitter Dividend," *Wall Street Journal*, October 1, 1008, A1.

11. Donald Rendelmeier and Daniel Kahneman, "Patient Memories of Painful Medical Treatments: Real Time and Retrospective Evaluations of Two Minimally Invasive Procedures," *Pain* 66, no. 1 (1996): 3–8.

12. George Loewenstein and Darzen Prelec, "Preferences for Sequences of Outcomes," *Psychological Review* 100, no. 1 (1993): 91–108.

13. Shane Frederick, George Loewenstein, and Ted O'Donoghue, "Time Discounting and Time Preference: A Critical Review," *Journal of Economic Literature* 40 (2002): 351–401.

14. Dean S. Karlan, Margaret McConnell, Sendhil Mullainathan, and Jonathan Zenman, "Getting to the Top of the Mind: How Reminders Increase Savings" (2010), available at Social Science Research Network (SSRN), http://ssrn.com/abstract=1596281.

15. Sondra Beverly, Peter Tufano, and Daniel J. Schneider, "Splitting Tax Refunds and Building Savings: An Empirical Test," *Tax Policy and the Economy* 20 (2006): 111–162.

16. Alan Schwarz, "Two Ex-Players Leverage Connections in N.F.L. Workers' Comp Cases," *New York Times*, April 7, 2010, Sports, http://www.nytimes.com/2010/04/08/sports/football/08lawyers.html.

17. Villia Jefremovas, "Women are Good with Money: The Impact of Cash Cropping on Class Relations and Gender Ideology in Northern Luzon, Philippines," in *Women*

Farmers and Commercial Ventures: Increasing Food Security in Developing Countries, ed. Anita Spring (Boulder, CO and London: Lynne Reinner, 2000), 131–150.

18. Suzanne A. Brenner, "Why Women Rule the Roost: Rethinking Japanese Ideologies of Gender and Self-Control, in *Bewitching Women, Pious Men: Gender and Body Politics in Southeast Asia,* ed. Aihwa Ong and Michael G. Peletz, (Berkeley, CA: University of California Press, 1995), 19–50.

19. Nava Ashraf, "Spousal Control and Intra-Household Decision Making: An Experimental Study in the Philippines," *American Economic Review* 99, no. 4 (2009): 1245–77.

20. Nava Ashraf, Dean S. Karlan, and Wesley Yin, "Female Empowerment: Impact of a Commitment Savings Product in the Philippines," (World Development, 2009), http://people.hbs.edu/nashraf/FemaleEmpowerment.pdf.

21. Roy Mersland and Oyvind Eggen, "You Cannot Save Alone: Financial and Social Mobilization in Savings and Credit Groups," (2007), available at Social Science Research Network (SSRN), http://ssrn.com/abstract=1032247; Peter Tufano and Daniel Schneider, "Using Financial Innovation to Support Savers: From Coercion to Excitement," (2008), available at Social Science Research Network (SSRN), 2008, http://ssrn.com/abstract=1120382.

22. Dean S. Karlan, "Social Connections and Group Banking," Social Connections and Group Banking," *Economic Journal* 117 (February 2007, 117): F52–84

23. *World's Work,* "The First Thousand Dollars," December 1913, 135.

24. *Business Week,* "Easy Payment Plan for Stocks," December 12, 1953, 121–122.

25. *Literary Digest,* "No Royal Road For the Small Investor," December 14, 1929, 52–55.

26. John Graham and Alok Kumar, "Do Dividend Clienteles Exist? Evidence on Dividend Preferences of Retail Investors," *Journal of Finance* 61, no. 3 (2006): 1305–1336.

27. David Leonhardt and Alex Markel, " What Investors Should Do Now," *New York Times,* August 10, 2003, http://www.nytimes.com/2003/08/10/business/what-investors-should-do-now.html?pagewanted=1?pagewanted=1.

28. Nicholas D. Kristof, "Op-Ed: Sparking a Savings Revolution," *New York Times,* December 31, 2009, http://www.nytimes.com/2009/12/31/opinion/31kristof.html.

29. Jeff Opdyke, "Covered Calls Prove Popular Strategy," *Wall Street Journal,* January 2, 2010, http://online.wsj.com/article/SB100014240527487039163045746323129191 84046.html.

Chapter 8

1. Mylene Mangalindan, "Hoping Is Hard to Do in Silicon Valley," *Wall Street Journal,* July 15, 2002, C1.

2. CBS, "'Down-To-Earth' Couple Wins $270M Jackpot," *The Early Show,* February 25, 2008, http://www.cbsnews.com/stories/2008/02/25/earlyshow/main3872118.shtml.

3. William Goetzmann and Alok Kumar "Equity Portfolio Diversification," *Review of Finance* 12, no. 3 (2008): 433–463; Marshall Blume, Jean Crockett, and Irwin Friend. , "Stock Ownership in the United States: Characteristics and Trends," *Survey of Current Business* 54, no. 11 (November 1974): 16–40.

4. David Moss, *When All Else Fails: Government as the Ultimate Risk Manager* (Cambridge, MA: Harvard University Press, 2002), 180.

5. Fred Schwed, Jr., Where Are the Customers' Yachts? (New York: John Wiley & Sons, 1995), 80.

6. Hersh Shefrin and Meir Statman, "Behavioral Portfolio Theory," *Journal of Financial and Quantitative Analysis* 35, no. 2 (2000): 127–151; Meir Statman, "Foreign Stocks in Behavioral Portfolios," *Financial Analysts Journal* 55, no. 2 (1999): 12–16; Meir

Statman, "The Diversification Puzzle," *Financial Analysts Journal* 60, no. 4 (2004): 44–53; Meir Statman, "Lottery Players, Stock Traders," *Financial Analysis Journal* 58, no. 1 (January/February 2002): 14–21.

7. *Literary Digest*, "No Royal Road for the Small Investor," 103, no. 11, December 14, 1929, 52–55.

8. Arthur Wiesenberger, *Investment Companies* (New York: Arthur Wiesenberger and Company, 1952).

9. Kate Zernike, "Stocks' Slide Is Playing Havoc with Older Americans' Dreams," *New York Times*, (July 14, 2002): A1, A16.

10. David Wessel, David. 1999. "Internet Mania Is Like Lottery, Fed Chief Says." *Wall Street Journal*, January 29, 1999, C1.

11. Sewell Chan, "Online Betting, Barred by U.S., Gets a Second Look," *New York Times*, July 29, 2010, A1.

12. Charles Clotfelter and Philip Cook, *Selling Hope: State Lotteries in America* (Cambridge, MA: Harvard University Press, 1989), 75.

13. "How Americans View Personal Wealth vs. How Financial Planners View This Wealth," press release, Consumer Federation of America, January 9, 2006, http://www.americasaves.org/downloads/www.americasaves.org/01.09.2006.pdf.

14. Lisa Holton, "Redefining the Rainy Day," *American Demographics* 22 (2000): 6.

15. Cade Massey, Joseph Simmons, and David Armor, "Hope Over Experience: Desirability and the Persistence of Optimism," (2010), available at Social Science Research Network (SSRN), http://ssm.com/abstract=1552394.

16. Luis Coelho, Richard Taffer, and Kose John, "Bankrupt Firms: Who's Buying?" (working paper, New York University, 2010)

17. Alok Kumar, "Who Gambles in the Stock Market? *Journal of Finance* 64, no. 4 (2009): 1889–1933.

18. Xiaohui, Gao, and Tse-Chun Lin, "Natural Experiments on Individual Trading: Substitution Effect Between Stock and Lottery," (June 8, 2010), available at SSRN, http://ssrn.com/abstract=1622184.

19. Steve Frank, "Playing the Net," *Wall Street Journal*, March 12, 2000.

20. George Frederick, *Common Stocks and the Average Man* (New York: The Business Bourse, 1930), 356.

21. Christopher Jarvis, "The Rise and Fall of Albania's Pyramid Schemes," *Finance and Development* 37, no. 1 (March 2000), www.imf.org/external/pubs/ft/fandd/2000/03/jarvis.htm.

22. Simon Romero, "Where Officials See Fraud, Colombia's Masses See a Folk Hero," *New York Times*, January 31, 2009, Americas section, http://www.nytimes.com/2009/01/31/world/americas/31murcia.html?_r=1.

23. Garrick Blalock, David Just, and Daniel Simon, "Hitting the Jackpot or Hitting the Skids: Entertainment, Poverty, and the Demand for State Lotteries," *American Journal of Economics and Sociology* 66, no. 3 (July 2007): 545–570.

24. Ruth Simon and E. S. Browning, "Some Online Investors Can't Seem to Say No to Playing the Market," *Wall Street Journal*, August 4, 2000, A1.

25. Emily Haisley, Romel Mustafa, and George Loewenstein, "Subjective Relative Income and Lottery Ticket Purchases," *Journal of Behavioral Decision Making* 21, no. 3 (2008): 283–295.

26. PBS, "Betting on the Market," *Frontline*, January 14, 1997; Derek D. Rucker and Adam D. Galinsky, Desire to Acquire: Powerlessness and Compensatory Consumption," *Journal of Consumer Research* 35, no. 2 (2008): 257–267.

27. Pierre Bourdieu, *The Social Structures of the Economy* (Cambridge, UK: UL Polity Press., 2005).

28. Steve Sanders, "FHA Mortgage Reform—Thanks, but No Thanks, Says MBA," *FHA Mortgage Guide* (October 26, 2007), www.fhaloanpros.com/2007/10 /fha-mortgage-reformthanks-but-no-thanks-says-mba/.

29. Eric Lipton and Stephen Labaton,"A Deregulator Looks Back, Unswayed," *New York Times,* November 17, 2008, A1, http://www.nytimes.com/2008/11/17/business/ worldbusiness/17iht-17gramm.17881800.html.

30. Jonathan Gardner and Andrew J. Oswald, "Money and Mental Well-Being: A Longitudinal Study of Medium-Sized Lottery Wins," (2006), available at Social Science Research Network (SSRN), http://ssrn.com/abstract=923539.

31. Constantijn Panis, "Annuities and Retirement Well-Being," *Pension Design and Structure: New Lessons from Behavioral Finance,* ed. Olivia Mitchell and Stephen Utkus, (Oxford, UK: Oxford University Press, 2004).

32. Peter Tufano and Daniel Schneider, "Using Financial Innovation to Support Savers: From Coercion to Excitement," in *Insufficient Funds: Savings, Assets, Credit, and Banking Among Low-Income Households,* ed. Rebecca Blank and Michael Barr (New York: Russell Sage Foundation, 2008).

33. Nick Maynard, Jan-Emmanuel De Neve, and Peter Tufano, "Consumer Demand for Prize-Linked Savings: A Preliminary Analysis," working paper no. 08–061 (Harvard Business School, Finance, February 8, 2008).

34. There is no magic in indexed annuities. Investors are deprived of any interest that could have accumulated on their $1,000 during the seven years, and they are deprived of any dividends paid by S&P 500 Index companies during these years.

35. *World's Work,* "Trying to Get Rich in a Hurry," January 1909, 11090–11092.

36. Louis H. Ederington and Evgenia V. Golubeva, "The Impact of Risk and Return Perceptions on the Portfolio Reallocation Decisions of Mutual Fund Investors," (March 4, 2010), available at Social Science Research Network (SSRN), http://ssrn.com/ abstract=1570574.

37. Gretchen Morgenson and Jennifer Bayot, "Older Investors More Jittery as U.S. Markets Disappoint," *New York Times,* August 24, 2004. Business Day, http://www.nytimes. com/2004/08/24/business/the-markets-market-place-older-investors-more-jittery-as -us-markets-disappoint.html?sec=&spon=&pagewanted=all.

38. John Leland and Louis Uchitelle, "Retirees Filling the Front Line in Market Fears," *New York Times,* September 23, 2008, Business, http://www.nytimes.com/2008/09/23/ business/23retirees.html.

39. Abhishek Varma and John E. Nofinger, "Pound Wise and Penny Foolish? OTC Stock Investor Demographics and Portfolios," (December 15, 2009), available at Social Science Research Network (SSRN), http://ssrn.com/abstract=1537256.

Chapter 9

1. Glenn Ruffenach, "Confessions of a Scam Artist," *Wall Street Journal,* August 9, 2004, R1.

2. Jonathan Karp, "Deadly Crop: Difficult Times Drive India's Cotton Farmers to Desperate Actions," *Wall Street Journal,* February 18, 1998, A1.

3. Ulrike Malmendier and Stefan Nagel, "Depression Babies: Do Macroeconomic Experiences Affect Risk Taking?", forthcoming, *Quarterly Journal of Economics,* 2010.

4. Meir Statman, "The Cultures of Risk Tolerance," (2010), available at Social Science Research Network (SSRN), http://papers.ssrn.com/s013/papers .cfm?abstract_id=1647086.

5. Carrie Pan and Meir Statman, "Beyond Risk Tolerance: Overconfidence, Regret, Personality and Other Investor Characteristics," (2010), available at Social Science

Research Network (SSRN), http://papers.ssrn.com/s013/papers.cfm?abstract
_id=1549912.

6. Camelia M. Kuhnen and Joan Y. Chiao , "Genetic Determinants of Financial
Risk Taking," *PLoS ONE* 4, no. 2 (February 2009): e4362, http://www.plosone
.org/article/info:doi%2F10.1371%2Fjournal.pone.0004362.

7. David Cesarini, Christopher J. Dawes, Magnus Johannesson, Paul Lichtenstein,
and Björn Wallace, "Genetic Variation in Preferences for Giving and Risk Taking,"
Quarterly Journal of Economics 124, no. 2 (2009): 809–842; Seth A. Eisen, Nong Lin,
Michael J. Lyons, Jeffrey F. Scherrer, Kristin Griffith, William R. True, Jack Goldberg,
and Ming T. Tsuang, "Familial Influences on Gambling Behavior: An Analysis of 3359
Twin Pairs," *Addiction* 93 (1998): 1375–1384.

8. Marvin Zuckerman, *Behavioral Expressions and Biosocial Bases of Sensation Seeking*
(New York: Cambridge University Press, 1994)

9. Meir Statman and Vincent Wood, "Investment Temperament," *Journal of Investment
Consulting* 7, no. 1 (Summer 2004): 55–66.

10. Thomas Dohmen, Armin Falk, David Huffman, Uwe Sunde, "The Intergenerational
Transmission of Risk and Trust Attitudes," (May 2008), available at Social Science
Research Network (SSRN), http://papers.ssrn.com/s013/papers.cfm?abstract_
id=941116.

11. Carrie Pan and Meir Statman, "Beyond Risk Tolerance: Overconfidence, Regret,
Personality and Other Investor Characteristics (2010), available at Social Science
Research Network (SSRN), http://papers.ssrn.com/s013/papers.cfm?abstract
_id=1549912.

12. Robert McCrae and Antonio Terracciano, "Personality Profiles of Culture: Aggregate
Personality Traits," *Journal of Personality and Social Psychology* 89, no. 3 (September
2005): 407–425.

13. Geert Hofstede, *Culture's Consequences: Comparing Values, Behaviors, Institutions and
Organizations Across Nations*, 2nd ed. (Thousand Oaks, CA: Sage Publications, 2001).

14. Ibid.

15. PBS, "Daughter from Danang" *PBS American Experience,* 2002, http://www.pbs.org/
wgbh/amex/daughter/filmmore/pt.html.

16. Cnn.com, "Gambler: Roulette Play 'Just a Mad Thing to Do,'" April 12, 2004, http://
www.cnn.com/2004/SHOWBIZ/TV/04/12/roulette.win/.

17. Sumit Agarwal, Souphala Chomsisengphet, and Chunlin Liu, "Consumer Bankruptcy
and Default: The Role of Individual Social Capital" (2009), available at Social Science
Research Network (SSRN), http://papers.ssrn.com/s013/papers.cfm?abstract
_id=1408757.

18. Meir Statman, "The Cultures of Risk Tolerance," (2010), available at Social Science
Research Network (SSRN), http://papers.ssrn.com/s013/papers
.cfm?abstract_id=1647086; Christopher Hsee and Elke Weber, "Cross-National
Differences in Risk Preferences and Lay Predictions," *Journal of Behavioral Decision
Making* 12, no. 2 (May 1999): 165–179.

19. Statman, "The Cultures of Risk Tolerance."

20. S. H. Schwartz, "Beyond Individualism/Collectivism: New Cultural Dimensions of
Values," in *Individualism and Collectivism: Theory, Method, and Applications*, ed. Uichol
Kim, Harry C. Triandis, Ciqdem Kagitcibasi, Sang-Chin Choi, and Gene Yoonet,
(Newbury Park, CA: Sage Publications, 1994).

21. Robyn A. LeBoeuf, Eldar Shafir, and Julia B. Bayuk, "The Conflicting Choices of
Alternating Selves," *Organizational Behavior and Human Decision Processes* 111, no. 1
(2010): 48–61.

22. Meir Statman and Jessica Weng , "Investments Across Cultures: Investment Attitudes
of Chinese-Americans," *Journal of Investment Consulting* (2010), available at Social

Science Research Network (SSRN), http://papers.ssrn.com/s013/papers
.cfm?abstract_id=1647087.

23. David Hillier, David, Paul Draper, and Robert W. Faff, "Do Precious Metals Shine?
An Investment Perspective," *Financial Analysts Journal* 62, no. 2 (2006): 98–106; C.
Mitchell Conover, Gerald R. Jensen, Robert R. Johnson, and Jeffrey M. Mercer, "Can
Precious Metals Make Your Portfolio Shine?" *Journal of Investing* 18, no. 1 (2007):
75–86.

24. Gary Painter, Gary, Lihong Yang, and Zhou Yu, "Home Ownership Determinants for
Chinese Americans: Assimilation, Ethnic Concentration, and Nativity," (Lusk Center
Working Paper No. 2003–1001, 2003).

25. Michael Pettis, "What Makes Mr. Zhang Save?" *The Wilson Quarterly* 33, no. 3
(Summer 2009): 49.

26. Statman and Weng, "Investments Across Cultures," http://papers.ssrn.com/s013/papers
.cfm?abstract_id=1647087.

Chapter 10

1. Meir Statman, "Martha Stewart's Lessons in Behavioral Finance," *Journal of Investment
Consulting* 7, no. 2 (2005): 52–60.

2. Kevin Delaney and Ann Grimes, "For Some Who Passed on Google Long Ago, Wistful
Thinking," *Wall Street Journal,* August 23, 2004, A1.

3. Hersh Shefrin and Meir Statman, "The Disposition to Sell Winners Too Early and
Ride Losers Too Long: Theory and Evidence," *Journal of Finance* 40, no. 3, (July 1985):
777–790; Terrance Odean, "Are Investors Reluctant to Realize Their Losses?," *Journal of
Finance* LIII, no. 5 (October 1998): 1775–1798.

4. Ravi Dhar and Ning Zhu, "Up Close and Personal: Investor Sophistication and the
Disposition Effect," *Management Science* 52, no. 5 (May 2006): 726–740.

5. Zur Shapira and Yitzhak Venezia, "Patterns of Behavior of Professionally Managed
and Independent Investors," *Journal of Banking and Finance* 25, no. 8 (August 2001):
1573–1587.

6. Mark Grinblatt and Matti Keloharju, "What Makes Investors Trade?", *Journal of
Finance* 56, no. 2 (2001), 589–616.

7. Andrew Jackson, "The Aggregate Behaviour of Individual Investors," (July 29, 2003),
available at Social Science Research Network (SSRN), http://papers.ssrn.com/s013/
papers.cfm?abstract_id=536942.

8. Cristiana C. Leal, Manuel J. Rocha Armada, and Joao Duque, "Are All Individual
Investors Equally Prone to the Disposition Effect All the Time? New Evidence from
a Small Market," (2008), available at Social Science Research Network (SSRN), http://
papers.ssrn.com/s013/papers.cfm?abstract_id=1024763.

9. Lei Feng and Mark Seasholes, "Do Investor Sophistication and Trading Experience
Eliminate Behavioral Biases in Financial Markets?" *Review of Finance* 9 (2005):
305–351.

10. Robert McGough and Michael Siconolfi, "Buy and Fold: Their Money's Fleeing, but
Some Investors Just Keep Hanging On," *Wall Street Journal,* June 18, 1997, A1.

11. Jonathan Berk and Ian Tonks, "Return Persistence and Fund Flows in the Worst
Performing Mutual Funds," (2007), available at Social Science Research Network
(SSRN), http://ssrn.com/abstract=980430.

12. Humphrey Neill, *Tape Reading and Market Tactics: Three Steps to Successful Stock
Trading* (New York: B. C. Forbes Publishing Company, 1931), dedication.

13. Ibid., 173–174.

14. Hal R. Arkes, David Hirshleifer, Danling Jiang, and Sonya S. Lim, "A Cross-Cultural Study of Reference Point Adaptation: Evidence from China, Korea, and the U.S.," *Organizational Behavior and Human Decision Processes* 112, no. 2 (2007): 99–111.

15. Carmen Lee, Rjoman Kräussl, Andre Lucas, and Leo Paas, "Dynamic Model of Investor Decision-Making: How Adaptation to Losses Affect Future Selling Decisions," (June 18 , 2009), available at Social Science Research Network (SSRN), http://ssrn.com/abstract=1304644.

16. David Leonhardt, "The Capital of Slumping Home Sales," *New York Times,* December 12, 2007, Business.

17. David Genesove and Christopher Mayer, "Loss Aversion and Seller Behavior: Evidence from the Housing Market," *The Quarterly Journal of Economics* 116, no. 4 (2001): 1233–1260.

18. Charles T. Clotfelter and Philip J. Cook, "Lotteries in the Real World," *Journal of Risk and Uncertainty* 4, no. 3 (1991): 227–232.

19. Mitchell Zuckoff, "The Perfect Mark: How a Massachusetts Psychotherapist Fell for a Nigerian E-mail Scam," *The New Yorker,* May 15, 2006, 36-42, http://www.newyorker.com/archive/2006/05/15/060515fa_fact?currentPage=1

20. LeRoy Gross, *The Art of Selling Intangibles: How to Make Your Millions by Investing Other People's Money* (New York: New York Institute of Finance, 1982): 150.

21. Martin Jacob, "Why Do Some Realize Capital Gains and Others Losses?—Evidence from German Income Tax Data," (2010), available at Social Science Research Network (SSRN), http://ssrn.com/abstract=1474862.

22. Jennifer Levitz, Ilan Brat, and Nicholas Casey, "Wall Street Ills Seep into Everyday Life," *Wall Street Journal,* September 19, 2008, A1.

23. Niklas Karlsson, George Loewenstein, and Duane J. Seppi, "The Ostrich Effect: Selective Attention to Information," *Journal of Risk and Uncertainty* 38 (2009): 95–115.

24. Dan Galai, and Orly Sade, "The Ostrich Effect and the Relationship between Liquidity and the Yields of Financial Assets," *Journal of Business* 79, no. 5 (2006): 2741–2759.

25. Diya Gullapalli, Shefali Ananad, and Daisy Maxey, "Money Fund, Hurt by Debt Tied to Lehman, Breaks the Buck," *Wall Street Journal,* September 17, 2008, C1.

26. Jena McGregor, Steve Hamm, and David Kiley, "Sweet Revenge," *Business Week,* January 22, 2007, cover story, http://www.businessweek.com/magazine/content/07_04/b4018001.htm.

27. Tanjim Hossain and John A. List, "The Behavioralist Visits the Factory: Increasing Productivity Using Simple Framing Manipulations," (December 2009), available at Social Science Research Network (SSRN), http://papers.ssrn.com/s013/papers.cfm?abstract_id=1530079.

28. Jennifer S. Lerner, Deborah Small, and George Loewenstein, "Heart Strings and Purse Strings: Carry-Over Effects of Emotions on Economic Decision," *Psychological Science* 15, no. 5 (2004): 337–341.

29. Seunghee Han, Jennifer S. Lerner, and Richard J. Zeckhauser, "Disgust Promotes Disposal: Souring the Status Quo," (June 2010) , available at Social Science Research Network (SSRN), http://papers.ssrn.com/s013/papers.cfm?abstract_id=1624889.

30. Sonny Kleinfield, *The Traders* (New York: Holt, Reinhart and Winston, 1983), 17, 18, 30.

31. Anna D. Scherbina and Jin Li, "Inheriting Losers," forthcoming, *Review of Financial Studies,* 2010.

32. Dara Doyle and James Ludden, "Leeson, Who Ruined Barings, May Return to Trading," Bloomberg.com, March 7, 2007.

33. Katherine Burton, Katherine and Jenny Strasburg, "Amaranth's $6.6 Billion Slide Began With Trader's Bid to Quit," Bloomberg.com, December 6, 2006, http://www.bloomberg .com/apps/news?pid=20601082&sid=aRJS57CQQbeE&refer=canada; Jenny Anderson, "Hedge Fund with Big Loss Says It Will Close," New York Times, June 15, 2010, http:// www.nytimes.com/2006/09/30/business/30hedge.html?ex=1317268800&en=28145791 1aace1af&ei=5088&partner=rssnyt&emc=rss.
34. Martin Fackler, "Toshiba Concedes Defeat in the DVD Battle," New York Times, February 20, 2008, http://www.nytimes.com/2008/02/20/technology/20newdisc.html? _r=1&ref=martin_fackler.
35. Yukari Iwatani Kane, " Toshiba's Plan for Life After HD DVD," Wall Street Journal, March 3, 2008, Boss Talk, http://online.wsj.com/article/NA_WSJ_PUB: SB120450428955606405.html.

Chapter 11

1. Michael Brick, "Man Crashes Plane into Texas I.R.S. Office," New York Times, February 19, 2010, http://www.nytimes.com/2010/02/19/us/19crash.html.
2. Comments to an article by Laura Sanders, "Rich Cling to Live to Beat Tax Man," Wall Street Journal, December, 30, 2009, http://online.wsj.com/article/ SB126213588339309657.html.
3. Abigail B. Sussman and Christopher Y. Olivola, "Axe the Tax: Taxes Are Disliked More than Equal Costs," (presented at the 1st Annual Boulder Summer Conference on Consumer Financial Decision Making, June 27–29 2010).
4. Monica Langley, "Generosity Pays: A Popular Tax Shelter for the 'Angry Effluents,'" Wall Street Journal, January 22, 1999, A1.
5. Edvard Pettersson and David Voreacos. "Ex-UBS Client McCarthy Avoids Prison in U.S. Tax Case (Update1)," Business Week Online, March 22, 2010, http://www .businessweek.com/news/2010-03-22/ex-ubs-client-mccarthy-avoids-prison-in-u -s-tax-case-update1-.html. (The case is USA v. McCarthy, 09-cr-00784, U.S. District Court, Central District of California [Los Angeles]).
6. Megan Barnett, "Leona Helmsley," US News & World Report, August, 8, 2004, http:// www.usnews.com/usnews/biztech/articles/040816/16eewhere.htm.
7. Laura Sanders, "Rich Cling to Live to Beat Tax Man," Wall Street Journal, December 30, 2009, http://online.wsj.com/article/SB126213588339309657.html.
8. Robert J. Yetman and Michelle Yetman, "How Does the Incentive Effect of the Charitable Deduction Vary Across Charities?" (2010), available at Social Science Research Network (SSRN), http://ssrn.com/abstract=1435150.
9. David Cay Johnston, "New Guidance on Getting the Most Out of Giving," New York Times, December 21, 2003, BU6.
10. Lynnley Browning, "Suicide Victim May Have Hidden Millions Abroad," New York Times, September 16, 2009, http://www.nytimes.com/2009/09/16/business/16suicide .html.
11. Joel Slemrod, "Cheating Ourselves: The Economics of Tax Evasion," Journal of Economic Perspectives 21 (Winter 2007): 25–48.
12. Henrik Kleven, Martin Knudsen, Claus Thustrup Kreiner, Løren Lønstrup Pederson, Emmanuel Sae, "Unwilling or Unable to Cheat? Evidence from a Randomized Tax Audit Experiment in Denmark," (February 2010), available at Social Science Research Network (SSRN), http://ssrn.com/abstract=1556132.
13. Dubner, Stephen J. and Steven D. Levitt, 2006. "Filling in the Tax Gap." New York Times Magazine, April 2, 2006, 28–30.
14. Marcus Walker, "Tragic Flaw: Graft Feeds Greek Crisis," Wall Street Journal, April 15, 2010, Economy, http://online.wsj.com/article/NA_WSJ_PUB:SB1000142405270230382 8304575179921909783864.html.

15. *World's Work,* "Of Buying Stocks to Dodge Taxes, May 1914, 20–21.
16. IRS—1.B, *Abusive Tax Shelter History,* 1–9, http://www.irs.gov/pub/irs-utl/i.b
    _-_history_of_shelters.pdf.
17. Marlys Harris, "I'm 24 and Earn $23,000. How Can I Invest $10,000 So I Can Quit
    Work at 45?" *Money* 25, no. 8 (September 1996): 153.
18. Andrew Ross Sorkin, "Bobbing as the Taxman Weaves," *New York Times,* May 17, 2010,
    page B1, http://www.nytimes.com/2010/05/18/business/18sorkin.html.
19. Lynnley Browning, "KPMG Developed New Version of Tax Shelter IRS Had
    Disallowed," *New York Times,* August 26, 2004, http://www.nytimes.com/2004/08/26/
    business/kpmg-developed-new-version-of-tax-shelter-irs-had-disallowed.html.
20. David Cay Johnston, "Skeptical Hearing for Audit Firm," *New York Times,* November
    19, 2003, 3.
21. Cassel Bryan-Low, "KPMG Didn't Register Strategy: Former Partner's Memo Says Fees
    Reaped from Sales of Tax Shelter Far Outweigh Potential Penalties." *Wall Street Journal,*
    November 17, 2003, C1.
22. Ryan J. Donmoyer and Jeff Feeley, "EMC Founder Egan Cheated IRS While Envoy,
    Judge Says," *Business Week Online,* May 18, 2010, http://www.businessweek.com/
    news/2010–05–18/emc-founder-egan-cheated-irs-while-envoy-judge-says-update1
    -.html.
23. Todd Wallack, "EMC Founder's Son Not Sure He'll Fight Tax-Shelter Ruling," *Boston
    Globe Online,* May 19, 2010, http://www.boston.com/business/articles/2010/05/19/
    emc_founders_son_not_sure_hell_fight_tax_shelter_ruling/.
24. KPMG, "Tax Shelter Regime for Audio-Visual Work," http://www.kpmg.com/BE/en/
    Whatwedo/Interests/TaxShelter/Pages/Default.aspx.

Chapter 12

1. J. Brooks, *The Go-Go Years: The Drama and Crashing Finale of Wall Street's Bullish 60s*
   (New York: Wiley Investment Classics, 1999), 144.
2. Jenny Anderson, "Pension Funds Still Waiting for Big Payoff From Private Equity," *New
   York Times,* April 2, 2010, http://www.nytimes.com/2010/04/03/business/03equity
   .html.
3. Steven N. Kaplan and Antoinette Schoar, "Private Equity Performance: Returns,
   Persistence and Capital Flows," *Journal of Finance* 60, no. 4 (August 2005): 1791–1823.
4. Ludovic Phalippou and Oliver Gottschalg, "Performance of Private Equity Funds,"
   2009, *Review of Financial Studies* 22, no. 4 (2009): 1747–1776.
5. Ilia D. Dichev and Gwen Yu, "Higher Risk, Lower Returns: What Hedge Fund
   Investors Really Earn," (2009), available at Social Science Research Network (SSRN),
   http://ssrn.com/abstract=1354070.
6. The Vintage Wine Fund, "Targeting Superior Capital Appreciation by Investing in Fine
   Wines," 2010, http://www.vintagewinefund.com/
7. Amanda Hesser, "Why Wine Costs What It Does," *New York Times,* April 9, 2003, D1.
8. Kickstarter.com, *Person of Interest: Off the Grid Film Tour Independent Cinema: Driven
   by Community,* a project by Gregory Bayne, http://www.kickstarter.com/projects/
   gregorybayne/person-of-interest-off-the-grid-film-tour-independ?pos=6&ref=
   recommended.
9. Peter Landesman, "A 20th-Century Master Scam," *New York Times Magazine,*
   July 18, 1999.
10. Lisa Jardine, *Worldly Goods: A New History of the Renaissance* (New York: W.W.
    Norton and Company, 1996), 11–12.
11. William N. Goetzmann, Luc Renneboog, and Christophe Spaenjers, "Art and Money,"
    (2010), available at Social Science Research Network (SSRN), http://ssrn.com/
    abstract=1501171.

12. Luc Renneboog and Christophe Spaenjers, "The Iconic Boom in Modern Russian Art," (2010), available at Social Science Research Network (SSRN), http://ssrn.com/abstract=1466792.

13. Agnes Crane and Rob Cox, "The Long Reach of a Foreign Crisis," *Business Day*, May 5, 2010, Economy, http://www.nytimes.com/2010/05/06/business/economy/06views.html.

14. Carpl Vogel, "Works by Johns and de Kooning Sell for $143.5 Million." *New York Times*, October 12, 2006, Art and Design, http://www.nytimes.com/2006/10/12/arts/design/12geff.html.

15. The Fine Art Group, 2010, http://www.thefineartfund.com/.

16. Lisa Gubernick, "Buying Your Way onto a Board," *Wall Street Journal*, May 7, 1999, W1.

17. Susanne Craig and Kelly Crow, "Fallen Tycoon to Auction Prized Works," *Wall Street Journal*, September 26, 2008, W1.

18. Sara Justine Solnick and David Hemenway, "Is More Always Better?: A Survey on Positional Concerns," *Journal of Economic Behavior and Organization* 37, no. 3 (1998): 373–383; Sara Justine Solnick and David Hemenway, "Are Positional Concerns Stronger in Some Domains than in Others?", *American Economic Review* 95, no. 2 (2005): 147–151.

19. Karen E. Dynan and Enrichetta Ravina, "Increasing Income Inequality, External Habits, and Self-Reported Happiness," *American Economic Review* 97, no. 2 (2007): 226–231.

20. Andrew Oswald and Daniel Zizzo, "Are People Willing to Pay to Reduce Others' Incomes?" *Annales D'Economie et de Statistique*, Special ed 64 (2002): 39–65.

21. James Ang, Gregory Nagel, and Jun Yang, "The Effect of Social Pressures on CEO Compensation (2009), available at Social Science Research Network (SSRN), http://papers.ssrn.com/s013/papers.cfm?abstract_id=1107280.

22. Christoper D. Carroll, "Why Do the Rich Save So Much?," in *Does Atlas Shrug? The Economic Consequences of Taxing the Rich*, ed. Joel B. Slemrod. (New York: Harvard University Press, 2000), 463–485.

23. Xinyue Zhou, Kathleen D. Vohs, and Roy F. Baumeister "The Symbolic Power of Money: Reminders of Money Alter Social Distress and Physical Pain," *Psychological Science* 20, no. 6 (2009): 700–706.

24. Carnie Mellon Tepper School of Business, "Meet the Man Behind the Gift," Carnegie Mellon, Tepper School of Business, news release, November 17, 2004, http://www.tepper.cmu.edu/news-multimedia/news/news-detail/index.aspx?nid=119

25. Warren St. John and Alexandria Wolfe, "What Do Peacocks Say? ACK," *New York Times*, July 31, 2005, Fashion and Style.

26. Francesca Gino and Lamar Pierce, "Robin Hood Under the Hood: Wealth-Based Discrimination in Illicit Customer Help," (2008), available at Social Science Research Network (SSRN), http://ssrn.com/abstract=1157083.

27. Lisa Bannon and Bob Davis, "Spendthrift to Penny Pincher: A Vision of the New Consumer," *Wall Street Journal*, December 18, 2009, http://online.wsj.com/article/SB126100996572894719.html.

28. Yael Zemack-Rugar, Lisa Cavanaugh, and Gavan J. Fitzsimons, "Wanting What I Shouldn't Have and Finding a Way to Get It: When Guilt Increases Hedonic Consumption" (paper presented at the Association for Consumer Research Annual Conference, Pittsburgh, PA, October, 22–25, 2009).

29. Amy Kazmin, "Montblanc: Perils of Blundering into India's Cultural Minefield," *Financial Times*, March 18, 2010.

30. Richard H. Smith, Terence J. Turner, Ron Garonzik, Colin W. Leach, Vanessa Urch-Druskat, and Christine M. Weston, "Envy and Schadenfreud, " *Personality and Social Psychology Bulletin* 22, no. 2 (1996): 158–168.

31. Will Swarts, "In the End, Stewart's Friends Were Her Undoing," (March 5, 2004), http://www.thestreet.com/pf/markets/willswarts/10147349.html.
32. Tuba Ustuner and Douglas B. Holt, "Toward a Theory of Status Consumption in Less Industrialized Countries," *Journal of Consumer Research* 37, no. 1 (2010): 37–56.
33. Vivi Alatas, Abhijit V. Banerjee, Rema Hana, Benjamin A. Olken, and Julia Tobias, "Targeting the Poor: Evidence from a Field Experiment in Indonesia," (2010), available at Social Science Research Network (SSRN): http://ssrn.com/abstract=1607470.
34. Lucia van der Post, "Little Time for the Second-Rate," *Financial Times,* August 30, 1999, 6.
35. David Neumark and Andrew Postlewaite "Relative Income Concerns and the Rise in Married Women's Employment," (2000), available at Social Science Research Network (SSRN), http://ssrn.com/abstract=225823.
36. Gary Rivlin, "The Millionaires Who Don't Feel Rich," *New York Times,* August 5, 2007, A1.
37. Katie Hafner, "In Web World, Rich Now Envy the Superrich," *New York Times,* Technology, November 21, 2006, http://www.nytimes.com/2006/11/21/technology/21envy.html.
38. Kerwin Kofi Charles, Erik Hurst, and Nikolai Roussanov, "Conspicuous Consumption and Race," *Quarterly Journal of Economics* 124, no. 2 (2009): 425–67.
39. Jennifer L. Romich, Sarah Gordon, and Eric N. Waithaka ,"A Tool for Getting by or Getting Ahead? Consumers' Views on Prepaid Cards," (2009), available at Social Science Research Network (SSRN), http://ssrn.com/abstract=1491645.
40. Rod Nordland, "Iraqis Snap Up Hummers, Seeing Them as Icons of Power," *New York Times,* March 30, 2009, A6.
41. Gretchen Morgenson, "Fair Game: Hedge Funds and the Little People," *New York Times,* September 2, 2007,Your Money, http://select.nytimes.com/2007/09/02/business/yourmoney/02gret.html.
42. George Quattrone and Amos Tversky, (1984) "Causal Versus Diagnostic Contingencies: On Self-Deception and on the Voter's Illusion," *Journal of Personality and Social Psychology* 46, no. 2 (1984): 237–248.
43. Peter Damisch, Monish Kumar, Anna Zakrzewski, and Natalia Zhiglinskaya, "Leveling the Playing Field: Upgrading the Wealth Management Experience for Women," Boston Consulting Group, July 2010, http://www.bcg.com/documents/file56704.pdf.
44. *World's Work,* "The Nervous Investor and The News," March 1917, 14081–14083.
45. *World's Work,* "The Financial Mistakes of Women," September 1917, 14805–14808.
46. J. George Frederick, *Common Stocks and the Average Man* (New York: Business Bourse, 1930), 284.
47. Ibid., 289.
48. *Business Week,* "To Sell Securities, Educate a Market," February 21, 1953, 64–65.
49. Kathryn Welling, "Women and Money '77: You've Come a Long Way, Baby—Further than Brokers Think," *Barron's,* October 10, 1977, 9–12.
50. Martin Fackler, "Japanese Housewives Sweat in Secret as Markets Reel," *New York Times,* September 16, 2007, World Business, http://www.nytimes.com/2007/09/16/business/worldbusiness/16housewives.html.
51. Kara Scannell, "On the Outside of Hedge Funds Looking In," *Wall Street Journal,* September 1–2, 2007, B1.
52. Susanne Craig, "Goldman's Trading Tips Reward Its Biggest Clients," *Wall Street Journal,* August 24, 2009, Markets, http://online.wsj.com/article/NA_WSJ_PUB:SB125107135585052521.html.
53. N. R. Kleinfield, "Coping with Homework and a Bear Market," *New York Times,* June 21, 2001,N.Y./Region, http://www.nytimes.com/2001/06/21/nyregion/coping-with-homework-and-a-bear-market.html?pagewanted=4.

Chapter 13

1. Jessica E. Vascellaro, "Brin Drove Google to Pull Back in China," *Wall Street Journal,* March 24, 2010, Technology, http://online.wsj.com/article/SB10001424052748704266504575141064259998090.html.
2. Ilana Polyak, "Do Blue Chips Belong in Social Purist's Portfolio?," *New York Times,* May 1, 2005, BU8.
3. Phil Thompson, "Mutual Funds," *Consumer Reports,* May 2004, 10.
4. Carl Goldstein, "Letters: How Socially Responsible?" *New York Times,* May 8, 2005, BU9.
5. Meir Statman, "Quiet Conversations: The Expressive Nature of Socially Responsible Investors," *Journal of Financial Planning* 21, no. 2 (2008): 40–46.
6. Social Investment Forum, "1999 Report on Socially Responsible Investing Trends in the United States," 7.
7. Becky Yerak, "Faith-Based Funds Start Making Noise," *Chicago Tribune,* September 16, 2006, Business.
8. Matthew Hood, John Nofsinger, and Abhishek Varma "Sin Stocks and the Religious Investor," working paper, January 2009, Washington State University.
9. Rodney Wilson, "Islamic Economics and Finance," *World Economics* 9, no. 1 (January–March 2008): 193.
10. Noah Efron, *Real Jews: Secular vs. Ultra-Orthodox* (New York: Basic Books, 2003), 162.
11. Mark Schwartz, Meir Tamari, and Daniel Schwab, "Capital Markets and Jewish Teachings," working paper, 2002, 1–21, http://www.kayema.com/docs/Capital%20Markets%20and%20Jewish%20Teachings.pdf.
12. Nati Toker, "Rabbinical Court Forbids Haredim from Investing in Israeli Companies," *Haaretz,* May 7, 2010, http://www.haaretz.com/print-edition/business/rabbinical-court-forbids-haredim-from-investing-in-israeli-companies-1.288841.
13. Mennonite Mutual Aid (MMA) Stewardship Solutions, "The Ethical Issues Report: What Matters to Religious Investors: MMA's National Survey of Religious Americans and How Business Ethics Affects Their Attitudes About Investing," MMA, November 2003, http://www.mmapraxis.com/stewardship_investing/investing_survey/index.html.
14. Danny Hakim, "On Wall St., More Investors Push Social Goals," *New York Times,* February 11, 2001, Business Day, http://www.nytimes.com/2001/02/11/business/on-wall-st-more-investors-push-social-goals.html.
15. Nicolas P. B. Bollen, "Mutual Fund Attributes and Investor Behavior," *Journal of Financial and Quantitative Analysis* 42, no. 3 (September 2007): 683–708.
16. Barbara Krumsiek, "The Emergence of a New Era in Mutual Fund Investing: Socially Responsible Investing Comes of Age," *Journal of Investing* 6 (Winter 1997): 25.
17. Jonas Nilsson, "Segmenting Socially Responsible Mutual Fund Investors: The Influence of Financial Return and Social Responsibility," *International Journal of Bank Marketing* 27, no. 1 (2009): 5–31.
18. Evan Halper and Michael Rothfeld, "Whitman's Funds Could Pose Conflicts," *Los Angeles Times,* March 12, 2010, http://articles.latimes.com/2010/mar/12/local/la-me-whitman-wealth12–2010mar12.
19. Charles Piller, Edmund Sanders and Robyn Dixon, "Dark Cloud over Good Works of Gates Foundation," *Los Angeles Times,* January 7, 2007, http://articles.latimes.com/2007/jan/07/nation/na-gatesx07.
20. Rob Walker, "Hummer Love," *New York Times Magazine,* November 1, 2009, http://www.nytimes.com/2009/11/01/magazine/01fob-consumed-t.html; Marius K. Luedicke, Craig J. Thompson, and Markus Giesler, "Consumer Identity Work as Moral Protagonism: How Myth and Ideology Animate a Brand-Mediated Moral Conflict," *Journal of Consumer Research* 36, no. 6 (2010): 1016–33.

21. Timothy Middleton, "Mutual Funds: Social Responsibility Is Out; 'Sin-Vesting' Is In," MSN Money, April 2005, http://moneycentral.msn.com.

22. Jamie Heller, "Calpers Rule Would Limit Evictions at Investments," *Wall Street Journal,* April 15, 2010, Business, http://online.wsj.com/article/NA_WSJ_PUB:SB10001424052 7023033485045751843814057233 18.html.

23. Christopher Palmeri ,"Commentary: CalPERS May Not Do as Well by Doing Good," *Business Week,* June 19, 2000, Management, http://www.businessweek.com/archives/2000/b3686148.arc.htm.

24. Mary Wells, "Public Investing: Conscience vs. Profit," letter to BusinessWeek editor July 10, 2000.

25. Harrison Hong and Marcin Kacperczyk, "The Price of Sin: The Effects of Social Norms on Stock Markets," *Journal of Financial Economics* 93 (2009): 15–36.

26. Karen Damato, "AMA Wants Tobacco-Free Mutual Funds," *Wall Street Journal,* April 24, 1996, Fund Track.

27. Meir Statman and Denys Glushkov, "The Wages of Social Responsibility," *Financial Analysts Journal* 65, no. 4 (2009): 33–46.

28. Matt Richtel, "A Thaw in Investment Prospects for Sex-Related Businesses? Maybe," *New York Times,* July 27, 2007, C7.

29. *Literary Digest,* "Is Good Business Always Ethical?", June 11, 1927, 34.

30. Ibid.

31. Nancy Hass. "Scholarly Investments," *New York Times,* December 6, 2009, Fashion and Style, http://www.nytimes.com/2009/12/06/fashion/06charter.html.

32. Dean Karlan and Jonathan Zinman, "Expanding Credit Access: Using Randomized Supply Decisions to Estimate the Impacts," *Review of Financial Studies* 23, no. 1 (2009): 433–464.

33. Neil MacFarquhar, "Big Banks Draw Big Profits from Microloans to Poor," *New York Times,* April 13, 2010, World, http://www.nytimes.com/2010/04/14/world/14microfinance.html.

34. Peter G. Peterson, "Why I'm Giving Away $1 Billion—The Moment Is Overdue for Us to Become Moral and Worthy Ancestors," *Newsweek,* June 8, 2009, 21.

35. Betsey Stevenson and Justin Wolfers , "Economic Growth and Subjective Well-Being: Reassessing the Easterlin Paradox," *Brookings Papers on Economic Activity,* Spring 2008, 1–87.

36. Elizabeth W. Dunn, Lara B. Aknin, and Michael I. Norton, "Spending Money on Others Promotes Happiness," *Science* 21, 319, no. 5870 (March 2008): 1687–1688.

37. Lalin Anik, Lara B. Aknin, Michael I. Norton, and Elizabeth W. Dunn, "Feeling Good About Giving: The Benefits (and Costs) of Self-Interested Charitable Behavior," (2009), available at Social Science Research Network (SSRN), http://papers.ssrn.com/s013/papers.cfm?abstract_id=1444831.

38. Graham Bowley and Michael J. de la Merced, "Small Investors May Be Enlisted in Bank Bailout, *New York Times,* April 9, 2009, A1.

39. A. G. Sulzberger, "At Military Contractor's Trial, a $100,000 Buckle," *New York Times,* July 26, 2010, N.Y. Region, http://www.nytimes.com/2010/07/27/nyregion/27fraud .html.

40. *American Review of Reviews,* "The Benefits of Personal Investment" (December 1908): 751–752.

41. Joseph Goodman, "5 stocks with possibilities," *Forbes,* July 1, 1939, 29.

42. John Straley, *What About Mutual Funds?* (New York: Harper & Brother, 1954), 123.

43. Tapen Sinha and Jayavel Sounderpandian, "Pride and Prejudice: Links Between the Nominal Exchange Rates of Indian and Pakistani Currencies During 1957–1997," *Ritsumeikan Journal of Asia Pacific Studies* 15 (January 2005): 65–82.

44. *Literary Digest,* "Eight Investment Precepts," August 9, 1930, 43–44.
45. Lisa Holton,"Redefining the Rainy Day," *American Demographics* 22 (2000): 6.
46. Adair Morse and Sophie Shive, "Patriotism in Your Portfolio, *Journal of Financial Markets* (forthcoming, 2010).
47. Evangelos Benos and Marek Jochec, "Patriotic Name Bias and Stock Returns," (2007), available at Social Science Research Network (SSRN), http://papers.ssrn.com/s013/papers.cfm?abstract_id=993289.
48. Evangelos Benos and Marek Jochec, "Liberalism and Home Equity Bias," (2009), available at Social Science Research Network (SSRN), http://papers.ssrn.com/s013/papers.cfm?abstract_id=1325857.
49. Eric Lawrence, John Sides and Henry Farrell, "Self-Segregation or Deliberation? Blog Readership, Participation and Polarization in American Politics," *Perspectives on Politics* 8, no. 1 (2010): 141–157.
50. Harrison G. Hong and Leonard Kostovetsky, "Red and Blue Investing: Values and Finance,"(2010), available at Social Science Research Network (SSRN), http://papers.ssrn.com/s013/papers.cfm?abstract_id=1214382.
51. Amanda Y. M. Chin and Jerry T. Parwada, "Red-Blooded Republican or True-Blue Democrat? The Influence of Political Preferences on Money Managers' Portfolio Decisions," (2009), available at Social Science Research Network (SSRN), http://papers.ssrn.com/s013/papers.cfm?abstract_id=1339725.
52. Yosef Bonaparte, Alok Kumar, and Jeremy K. Page, "Political Climate, Optimism, and Investment Decisions," (2010), available at Social Science Research Network (SSRN), http://papers.ssrn.com/s013/papers.cfm?abstract_id=1509168.
53. Sami Torstila, "Stock Market Aversion? Political Preferences and Stock Market Participation," (2010), available at Social Science Research Network (SSRN), http://papers.ssrn.com/s013/papers.cfm?abstract_id=966254.
54. Alan Greenspan, "Gold and Economic Freedom," in Ayn Rand, *Capitalism: The Unknown Ideal* (New York: Signet Classics Centennial Edition, First Signet printing, 1967), 107.

Chapter 14

1. Larry Rohter, "Brazilians May Be Accustomed to Corrupt Officials, but Draw the Line at Soccer Referees," *New York Times,* October 11, 2005, World, http://query.nytimes.com/gst/fullpage.html?res=9D0DE7D9163FF932A25753C1A9639C8B63.
2. Ernst Fehr and Simon Gächter, "Cooperation and Punishment in Public Goods Experiments," *American Economic Review* 90 (2000): 980–994
3. PBS, "Bank Chiefs Take Heat on Capitol Hill over Foreclosure Crisis," PBS *Newshour* April 13, 2010.
4. Nick Timiraos, "Fannie Set to Penalize Defaulters," *Wall Street Journal,* June 24, 2010, Loans and Credits, http://online.wsj.com/article/NA_WSJ_PUB:SB10001424052748704629804575325113962811380.html.
5. Luigi Guiso, Paola Sapienza, and Luigi Zingales, "Moral and Social Constraints to Strategic Default on Mortgages," (2010), available at Social Science Research Network (SSRN), http://papers.ssrn.com/s013/papers.cfm?abstract_id=1573328.
6. Manny Fernandez, "Drive-By A.I.G. Protest on Fairfield's Elite Streets" *New York Times,* March 21, 2009, N.Y./Region, http://www.nytimes.com/2009/03/22/nyregion/22working.html.
7. David Jackson, "Obama: 'Fat-Cat' Bankers Owe Help to U.S. Taxpayers, *USA Today,* Money, December 18, 2009.

8. *New York Times*,"Taming the Fat Cats," December 19, 2009, Opinion.
9. Stevenson Jacobs, "CEO Gets Lower-than-Normal Stock Bonus," *Washington Times*, News, February 6, 2010, http://www.washingtontimes.com/news/2010/feb/06/ goldman-ceo-lower-normal-stock-bonus-09.
10. Camelia Kuhnen and Alexandra Niessen, "Public Opinion and Executive Compensation," (2010), available at Social Science Research Network (SSRN), http:// papers.ssrn.com/s013/papers.cfm?abstract_id=1612201.
11. Arthur Levitt, *Taking on the Street* (New York: Pantheon, 2002), 93.
12. Ibid., 87.
13. Alexander Cappelen, Astri Drange Hole, Erik Sørensøn, and Bertil Tungodden, "The Pluralism of Fairness Ideals: An Experimental Approach," *American Economic Review* 97, no. 3 (June 2007): 818–827.
14. Arthur Levitt, "Don't Set Speed Limits on Trading: Why Penalize Efficiency? It Creates Deep and Liquid Markets." *Wall Street Journal* opinion section, August 17, 2009.
15. John C. Bogle, Jr., letter to the *Wall Street Journal* editor, September 4, 2009, responding to an article by Arthur Levitt, "Don't Set Speed Limits on Trading: Why Penalize Efficiency? It Creates Deep and Liquid Markets." *Wall Street Journal* opinion section, August 17, 2009.
16. Michael Siconolfi, "The Spin Desk: Underwriters Set Aside IPO Stock for Officials of Potential Clients," *Wall Street Journal*, November 12, 1997, A1.
17. James Penrose, "Letters to the Editor," *Wall Street Journal*, December 3, 1997, A23.
18. Andy Kessler, "Let's Be Frank." *Wall Street Journal*, May 6, 2004, A18.
19. A video of comments by President Barack Obama at the signing the Credit Card Reform Act, May 2009, http://www.whitehouse.gov/videos/2009/May/20090522 _Credit_Card_Reform.mp4.
20. P. F. Christian, "New Law on Bank Overdraft Fees & the 'Courtesy' Overdraft Protection," January 20, 2010, http://www.christianpf.com/new-law-on-bank -overdraft-fees-the-courtesy-overdraft-protection/.
21. Andrew Martin, "Bank of America to End Debit Overdraft Fees," *New York Times*, March 9, 2010, Credit and Debit, http://www.nytimes.com/2010/03/10/your-money/ credit-and-debit-cards/10overdraft.html.
22. Richard A. Oppel Jr., "Enron Traders on Grandma Millie and Making Out Like Bandits," *New York Times*, June 13, 2004, Weekend.
23. Linda Babcock and George Loewenstein, "Explaining Bargaining Impasse: The Role of Self-Serving Biases," *Journal of Economic Perspectives* 11, no. 1 (Winter 1997): 109–126.
24. Lisa Belkin, "Just Money," *New York Times Magazine*, December 8, 2002.
25. Alberto Alesina and George-Marios Angeletos, "Fairness and Redistribution," *American Economic Review* 95, no. 4 (September 2005): 960–980.
26. Alberto Alesina and Edward L. Glaeser, *Fighting Poverty in the U.S. and Europe: A World of Difference* (Oxford: Oxford University Press, 2004).
27. Lisa E Bolton, Hean Tat Keh, and Joseph W. Alba, "How Do Price Fairness Perceptions Differ Across Culture?" *Journal of Marketing Research*, forthcoming 2010.
28. Luigi Guiso, Paola Sapienza, and Luigi Zingales, "Trusting the Stock Market," *Journal of Finance* 63, no. 6 (January 2008): 2557–2600.
29. Stephan Knack and Philip Keefer, "Does Social Capital Have an Economic Payoff? A Cross Country Investigation," *Quarterly Journal of Economics* 112, no. 4 (November 1997): 1251–1288.
30. Meir Statman, "Is It Fair?: Perceptions of Fair Investment Behavior Across Countries," *Journal of Investment Consulting* (forthcoming 2011).

Chapter 15

1. Charles Gasparino, "Ghosts of E-Mails Continue to Haunt Wall Street," *Wall Street Journal*, November 18, 2002, C1, C13.
2. Advertisement in *Literary Digest*, December 28, 1929, 45.
3. Paul Halsall, ed., *Medieval Sourcebook: Jewish Ethical Wills, 12th and 14th Centuries*, (New York: Fordham University Center for Medieval Studies, 2006), http://www .fordham.edu/halsall/source/jewish-wills.html.
4. Advertisement by Tiffany & Co., *The New York Times* April 19, 2003, A3.
5. Peter Tufano, "Just Keep My Money! Supporting Tax-Time Savings with US Savings Bonds" (August 13, 2010), Harvard Business School Finance Working Paper No. 09–059, available at Social Science Research Network (SSRN), http://ssrn.com/ abstract=1285385.
6. Mead Johnson, "Parents Can Start Saving for Their Children's Education When Purchasing Enfamil Formulas," press release, Mead Johnson Nutritional, September 18, 2000.
7. Peter Tufano and Daniel Schneider, "Using Financial Innovation to Support Savers: From Coercion to Excitement," (2008), available at Social Science Research Network (SSRN), http://papers.ssrn.com/s013/papers.cfm?abstract_id=11203824.
8. John Laitner and F. Thomas Juster, "New Evidence on Altruism: A Study of TIAA -CREF Retirees," *American Economic Review* 86, no. 4 (September 1996): 893–908.
9. Wojciech Kopczuk and Joseph Lupton, "To Leave or Not to Leave: The Distribution of Bequest Motives," *Review of Economic Studies* 74, no. 1 (2007): 207–235.
10. Villia Jefremovas, "Women Are Good with Money: The Impact of Cash Cropping on Class Relations and Gender Ideology in Northern Luzon, Philippines," in *Women Farmers and Commercial Ventures: Increasing Food Security in Developing Countries*, ed. Anita Spring (Boulder and London: Lynne Reinner 2000), 131–150.
11. Suzanne A. Brenner,"Why Women Rule the Roost: Rethinking Japanese Ideologies of Gender and Self-Control," in *Bewitching Women, Pious Men: Gender and Body Politics in Southeast Asia*, ed. Aihwa Ong and Michael G. Peletz (Berkeley: University of California Press, 1995): 19–50.
12. Esther Duflo, "Grandmothers and Granddaughters: Old Age Pension and Intra-household Allocation in South Africa," *World Bank Economic Review* 17, no. 1 (2003): 1–25.
13. Elain Kurtenbach, "Chinese Turning to Business Icons from America," *San Jose Mercury News*, April 28, 2002, 5F
14. Advertisement in the *New York Times Book Review*, April 18, 2004, 23.
15. Carolyn Starks, "Parents Saving Less for Kids' College Cost, National Survey Finds," *Chicago Tribune*, September 24, 2008, http://articles.chicagotribune.com/2008–09–24/ news/0809240975_1_kids-college-costs-college-tuition-four-year-public-college.
16. Diana B. Henriques, "Determined to Share the Wealth." *New York Times*, November 29, 1998, Business Day, http://www.nytimes.com/1998/11/29/business/personal-business -determined-to-share-the-wealth.html.
17. David Cay Johnston, "Learning to Share," *New York Times,* September 10, 2008, Business, http://www.nytimes.com/2008/09/10/business/businessspecia13/10FAMILY .html.
18. Ilho Yoo and InHyouk Koo, "Do Children Support Their Parents' Application for the Reverse Mortgage?: A Korean Case," (2008), available at Social Science Research Network (SSRN), http://papers.ssrn.com/s013/papers.cfm?abstract_id=1095549.
19. Richard A. Settersten, "Becoming Adult: Meanings and Markers for Young Americans," in *Coming of Age in America*, ed. Patrick Carr and Maria Kefalas, March 2006, available at Transitions to Adulthood Research Network, http://www.transad .pop.upenn.edu/downloads/Settersten%20Becoming%20Adult%20final%203–06).pdf.
20. Robert Schoeni and Karen Ross. "Material Assistance from Families During the Transition to Adulthood," in *On the Frontier of Adulthood: Theory, Research, and Public*

Policy, ed. Richard A. Settersten, Jr., Frank F. Furstenberg, Jr., and Rubén G. Rumbaut (Chicago: University of Chicago Press, 2005): 396–416.

21. Angel Jennings, "Nest Eggs Emptying, Not the Nests," *New York Times,* July 14, 2007, B1.
22. John Jurgensen, "Allowance 2.0," *Wall Street Journal,* January 6, 2007, 1.
23. Kid's Money, "Parents' Allowance Pieces," kidsmoney.org/allpar.htm.
24. Jennifer C. Lee and Jeylan T. Mortimer, "Family Socialization, Economic Self-Efficacy, and the Attainment of Financial Independence in Early Adulthood," *Longitudinal and Life Course Studies* 1, no. 1 (2009): 45–62.
25. Kerwin Kofi Charles and Erik Hurst, "The Correlation of Wealth Across Generations," *Journal of Political Economy* 111, no. 6 (December 2003): 1155–1182
26. Geng Li, "Information Sharing and Stock Market Participation: Evidence from Extended Families, working paper, The Federal Reserve Board (2009), http://www .federalreserve.gov/PUBS/FEDS/2009/200947/200947pap.pdf.
27. CBS, "Tom Perkins: The Captain of Capitalism, *60 Minutes,*" January 23, 2009. http:// www.cbsnews.com/stories/2007/11/01/60minutes/main3442193_page4.shtml.
28. D. H. Lawrence, "The Rocking Horse Winner," *The Complete Short Stories of D.H. Lawrence,* vol III (New York: Compass Books edition, fourth printing, October 1966), 790–804. (Originally issued in 1961 by Viking Press, Inc.)
29. Stephan Manes, *Make Four Million Dollar$ by Next Thur$day!* (New York: Bantam Doubleday Dell Books for Young Readers, 1996).
30. Ibid., 47–48.
31. Lewis Mandell, "Financial Education in High School," ed. Annamaria Lusardi, *Overcoming the Saving Slump: How to Increase the Effectiveness of Financial Education and Saving Programs* (Buffalo, NY: State University of New York-Buffalo Press, 2007).
32. Tanya Schevitz, "Students Swept Up in Stock-Market Mania/Nasdaq Drop Teaches Real-Life Lesson," *San Francisco Chronicle,* February 25, 2001, http://articles.sfgate .com/2001-02-25/business/17584680_1_real-life-lesson-stock-market-college -students.
33. Jennifer Levitz, "Playing the Market, These Kids Are Losing a Lot of Play Money," *Wall Street Journal,* October 29, 2008, A1.
34. Make Love, Not Debt: A Relationship Finance Blog, "Raise Your Children to Rely on Them—Asian Culture and Finances," posted on May 8 by Him, http://www.make lovenotdebt.com/2007/05/raise_your_children_to_rely_on_them_asian_culture_and _finances.php.
35. Jane Gross, "Elder-Care Costs Deplete Savings of a Generation," *New York Times,* December 30, 2006, A1.
36. Alvin Ang, Shikha Jha, and Guntur Sugiyarto, "Remittances and Household Behavior in the Philippines," (2009), available at Social Science Research Network (SSRN), http://papers.ssrn.com/s013/papers.cfm?abstract_id=1618125.
37. Albert Bollard, David McKenzie, and Melanie Morten, "The Remitting Patterns of African Migrants in the OECD," (2010), available at Social Science Research Network (SSRN), http://papers.ssrn.com/s013/papers.cfm?abstract_id=1585039.
38. Carlos Vargas-Silva, "The Global Crisis and the Impact on Remittances to Developing Asia," (2009) available at Social Science Research Network (SSRN), http://papers.ssrn .com/s013/papers.cfm?abstract_id=1618088.
39. Rolf Engelbrecht, *The Hernia–Amusing Anecdotes and Cultural Insights from Missionary Life in Guinea, West Africa* (self-published, 2005).
40. Peter Tufano and Daniel Schneider, "Using Financial Innovation to Support Savers: From Coercion to Excitement," (2008), available at Social Science Research Network (SSRN), http://papers.ssrn.com/s013/papers.cfm?abstract_id=1120382.
41. Michael Luo, "Jobless Turn to Family for Help," *New York Times,* January 30, 2010, US section, http://www.nytimes.com/2010/01/30/us/30borrow.html.

42. Jennie Green, "Leaning on Their Parents, Again, *New York Times,* July 20, 2003, Business Day, http://www.nytimes.com/2003/07/20/business/leaning-on-their-parents-again.html?pagewanted=all.
43. Robert Brodrick, Mukhtar Karim, and Rami Cheblak, "An Introduction to Shari'a Succession," *Trowers & Hamlins Trusts & Trustees* 14, no. 7 (2008): 475–479, doi:10.1093/tandt/ttn064.
44. Jere Behrman and Mark Rosenzweig, "Parental Allocations to Children: New Evidence on Bequest Differences among Siblings," *Review of Economics and Statistics* 86, no. 2 (2004): 637–640.
45. Sachiko Miyamoto, "Bequests and Household Assets," *Nomura Capital Market Review* 9, no. 4 (2006), available at Social Science Research Network (SSRN), http://papers.ssrn.com/s013/papers.cfm?abstract_id=968529.
46. Ann Perry, "How to Handle 'Heirloom' Stocks," TheStreet.com, September 9, 2003.
47. E. S. Browning, "Loyalty Pays a Bitter Dividend," *Wall Street Journal,* October 1, 2008, A1.
48. Gay Jervey, "A Legacy of Rancor: Estate Fights Rising," *New York Times,* March 28, 2004, BU7.

Chapter 16

1. Yahoo! Message Boards, Praecis Pharmaceuticals (PRCS), "Deer Caught in. Headlights!" Msg: 7580, July 20, 2004.
2. Patrick McGeehan, "Do-It-Yourself Stock Trades Drop as Fast as the Markets," *Wall Street Journal,* March 15, 2001, Technology, http://www.nytimes.com/2001/03/15/technology/15BROK.html.
3. Lisa Gibbs, "Chuck Would Like a Word with You," *Money,* January–February, 2010, 98–103.
4. Annamaria Lusardi and Olivia Mitchell, "How Ordinary Consumers Make Complex Economic Decisions: Financial Literacy and Retirement Readiness," (2009), available at Social Science Research Network (SSRN), http://papers.ssrn.com/s013/papers.cfm?abstract_id=1472288.
5. Annamaria Lusardi, Olivia Mitchell, and Vilsa Curto, "Financial Literacy and Financial Sophistication Among Older Americans," (2009), available at Social Science Research Network (SSRN), http://papers.ssrn.com/s013/papers.cfm?abstract_id=1501454.
6. Tara Siegel Bernard, "Working Financial Literacy in with the Three R's," *New York Times,* April 9, 2010, Your Money.
7. Annamaria Lusardi, Olivia Mitchell, and Vilsa Curto, "Financial Literacy Among the Young: Evidence and Implications for Consumer Policy," (2009), available at Social Science Research Network (SSRN), http://papers.ssrn.com/s013/papers.cfm?abstract_id=1459141.
8. Catherine J. Bell, Dan R. Gorin, and Jeanne M. Hogarth, "Does Financial Education Affect Soldiers' Financial Behavior?", (2009), available at Social Science Research Network (SSRN), http://papers.ssrn.com/s013/papers.cfm?abstract_id=1445635.
9. Fernanda Santos, "Free Advice on Money for Those with Little," *New York Times,* March 28, 2010, N.Y./Region, http://www.nytimes.com/2010/03/29/nyregion/29money.html.
10. Daniel Bergstresser and John Beshears, "Who Selected Adjustable-Rate Mortgages? Evidence from the 1989–2007 Surveys of Consumer Finances," (2010), available at Social Science Research Network (SSRN), http://papers.ssrn.com/s013/papers.cfm?abstract_id=1573625.

11. Kristopher Gerardi, Lorenz Goette, and Stephan Meier, "Financial Literacy and Subprime Mortgage Delinquency: Evidence from a Survey Matched to Administrative Data," (2010), available at Social Science Research Network (SSRN), http://papers.ssrn.com/s013/papers.cfm?abstract_id=1600905.

12. James Lacko and Janis Pappalardo, "The Failure and Promise of Mandated Consumer Mortgage Disclosures: Evidence from Qualitative Interviews and a Controlled Experiment with Mortgage Borrowers," *American Economic Review* 100, no. 2 (May 2010): 516–521.

13. Sumit Agarwal, Gene Amromin, Itzhak Ben-David, Souphala Chomsisengphet, and Douglas D. Evanoff, "Learning to Cope: Voluntary Financial Education and Loan Performance during the Housing Crisis, *American Economic Review* 100, no. 2 (May 2010): 495–500.

14. Vincent Carosso, *Investment Banking in America: A History* (Cambridge, MA, Harvard University Press, 1970), 160.

15. Ibid., 49

16. Peter S. Goodman, "Taking Hard New Look at a Greenspan Legacy," *New York Times,* October 9, 2008, A1.

17. Meir Statman, "Regulating Financial Markets: Protecting Us from Ourselves and Others," *Financial Analysts Journal* 65 (May/June 2009): 22–31.

18. Arvid E. Roach, II. 1978. "The Suitability Obligations of Brokers: Present Law and the Proposed Federal Securities Code." *Hastings Law Journal* 29 (1978): 1069–1159.

19. J. S. Ellenberger and Ellen Mahar, *Legislative History of the Securities Act of 1933 and Securities Exchange Act of 1934,* vol. 5 (South Hackensack, NJ: Law Librarians' Society of Washington, DC, Fred B. Rothman and Co., 1973), 2.

20. *World's Work,* "An Architect's 'Investment' in Stocks," July 1913, 276–277.

21. George Stigler, "The Theory of Economic Regulation." *The Bell Journal of Economics and Management Science* 2, no. 1 (1971): 3–21.

22. Binyamin Appelbaum, "Financial Bill to Close Regulator of Fading Industry," *New York Times,* July 14, 2010, B1.

23. Warren St. John, "Making Sure Hollywood's Nouveau Riche Stay Riche." *New York Times,* August 22. 2004, Fashion and Style, http://www.nytimes.com/2004/08/22/fashion/22SPEN.html.

24. Carrie Kirby, "Inside Look at a Billionaire's Budget/Larry Ellison's Spending Worries His Accountant," SFGate.com, January 31, 2006, http://articles.sfgate.com/2006-01-31/news/17279373_1_oracle-stock-larry-ellison-shareholder-lawsuit.

25. N. R. Kleinfield, "Counseling, Consoling, and Staying Calm," *New York Times,* October 11, 2008. N.Y./Region, http://www.nytimes.com/2008/10/11/nyregion/11planner.html.

26. BBC News," German Pensioners Kidnapped Financial Adviser," February 8, 2010, http://news.bbc.co.uk/2/hi/europe/8505090.stm.

27. Edward Wyatt, "S.E.C. Seeks Mutual Fund Fee Overhaul," *New York Times,* July 21, 2010, Business Day, http://www.nytimes.com/2010/07/22/business/22sec.html.

28. *World's Work,* "Splitting Up Funds for Safety," May 1911, 14319–14321.

29. *World's Work,* "Mr. Marsden J. Perry on Investments," September 1917, 484–485.

30. Message on Yahoo.com finance section, http://messages.finance.yahoo.com/Business_%26_Finance/Investments/Stocks_(A_to_Z)/Stocks_E/threadview?bn=5996&tid=165920&mid=165938.

31. Message on Yahoo.com finance section, http://messages.finance.yahoo.com/Business_%26_Finance/Investments/Stocks_(A_to_Z)/Stocks_E/threadview?bn=5996&tid=165920&mid=165940.

32. *World's Work,* "Emerson McMillin on Business and Investment," November 1917, 16–18.

33. Ibid.
34. Humphrey B. Neill, *Tape Reading and Market Tactics: Three Steps to Successful Stock Trading,* (New York: B. C. Forbes Publishing Company, 1931), 197–198.
35. A. Wolinsky, "Competition in the Market for Informed Experts' Services." *Rand Journal of Economics* 24 (1993): 380–398; A. Wolinsky, "Competition in Markets for Credence Goods," *Journal of Institutional and Theoretical Economics* 151 (1995): 117–131.
36. Susan Woodward and Robert Hall, "Consumer Confusion in the Mortgage Market: Evidence of Less than a Perfectly Transparent and Competitive Market," *American Economic Review* 100, no. 2 (May 2010): 511–515.
37. Claire Cain Miller, "Lose Confidence in Your Bank? Turn to the Web," *New York Times,* December 20, 2008, Your Money, http://www.nytimes.com/2008/12/20/your-money/20mint.html.
38. Alex Williams, "Not-So-Personal Finance," *New York Times,* April 27, 2008, Fashion and Style, http://www.nytimes.com/2008/04/27/fashion/27salary.html.
39. Morningstar.com, "How Many People Bought at or Near the March Low?, Morningstar forums, January 11, 2010, 12:36 pm, post #2756752.
40. Morningstar.com, "Super Newbie Needs Some Direction," post #2726827, November 2, 2009.
41. Ibid., 5:44 PM, Post #2756934 .
42. Morningstar.com, "Are Expense Ratios That Important?, Morningstar forums, January 23, 2010, Post #2763069.
43. Australian Securities & Investments Commissions, (ASIC), "International Cold Calling Investment Scams," June 2002, Table 1, 1–64, http://www.asic.gov.au/fido/fido.nsf/by headline/02%2F218+International+cold+calling+investment+scams+report?open Document.

Conclusion

1. Robert Powell, "Retirement-Savings Rewind: Obama's Plan Seen as Going Only So Far in Offering Workplace-Based Initiatives," *Wall Street Journal,* January 30, 2010, Markets, http://online.wsj.com/article/NA_WSJ_PUB:SB10001424052748704343104575033540551357582.html.
2. Walter H. Inge, *Wall Street Journal,* letter to the editor, February 7, 2010.
3. Sumit Agarwal, John C. Driscoll, Xavier Gabaix, and David Laibson October 19, 2009 "The Age of Reason: Financial Decisions over the Life-Cycle with Implications for Regulation," *Brookings Papers on Economic Activity,* 2009, no. 2 (Fall 2009): 51–117.
4. Karen Blumenthal, "A Family's Fight to Save an Elder From Scammers: When the Patriarch Fell Prey to Thieves, Relatives Took Matters Into Their Own Hands," *Wall Street Journal,* June 17, 2009, Family Money, http://online.wsj.com/article/NA_WSJ_PUB:SB124520056162621509.html.
5. Sewell Chan, "Online Betting, Barred by U.S., Gets a Second Look, *New York Times,* July 29, 2010, A1.
6. Response to a blog by John Ameriks, Vanguard blog, http://www.vanguardblog.com/2010.05.05/when-to-start-spending.html.
7. Response to a blog by Nicholas Kristoff, "How About a Beer," On the Ground blog, *New York Times,* May 22, 2010, http://community.nytimes.com/comments/kristof.blogs.nytimes.com/2010/05/22/how-about-a-beer/?sort=oldest&offset=2.
8. Richard Thaler and Cass Sunstein, *Nudge* (New Haven, Yale University Press, 2008)
9. Response to a blog by John Ameriks, Vanguard blog, http://www.vanguardblog.com/2010.05.05/when-to-start-spending.html.

Index

Rotating savings and credit
associations, 100–101
Roth, Bradford, 144
Royal Bank of Scotland
(R.B.S.), 79
Royal Dutch Petroleum, 42
Rubenstein, Joshua, 153

S
SafeScript Pharmacies, 13
Safety nets
of family and friends,
126–27
public, 127
zero-coupon Treasury
bonds as, 144–45
Sage, Russell, 92
Samberg, Arthur, 9
Sanders, Steve, 114
Santa Clara University, 186
Satin Bags investment club, 64
Satisficers, 122
Saving (*See also* Retirement
saving)
in China *vs.* United States,
130–31
lifetime sequence of
spending and, 98–102
rotating savings and credit
associations, 100–101
self-control for, 89–90
transmitting habits of, 214
Savings accounts
money market funds *vs.*,
145
prizes for, 116
Saylor, Dennis Saylor, 159
Scams, 5–6, 119, 140–41
Schadenfreude, 168–69
Schiff, Jacob, 227
Schwab, Charles, 56–57
Schwatz, Shalom, 128
Schwed, Fred, Jr., 108–9
Seals, Gregory G., 237
Sebbag, Yonni, 8–9
*Secret History of the Credit
Card, The* (documentary),
84
Securities and Exchange
Commission, 74
Self-control, 85–92
excessive, 91–92

mastering, 86–87
mental accounting
combined with, 92
and pride, guilt, and anger,
89–90
and realization of loss, 135
in resisting temptation,
88–89
and voices of "should" and
"want," 90–91
Self-esteem, 172
Self-respect, 176
Sentiment (*See* Emotions)
Seth, Suhel, 168
Shanghai Composite Index, 76
Shannon, Brian, 52
Shedd, John, 89
Shell Transport and Trading, 42
Sherman Brad, 111
Shoulds, xvi–xvii, 90–91
Shur, Muhammed, 72
Sibling rivalry, 221–22
Sierra Club, 178
Sies, Catharina Kitty, 5
Signals, status, 171–73
Similarity information, 22, 23
Sin stocks, 184–85
Sladich, Marcia, 72
Small investors, respect desired
by, 175–76 (*See also*
Individual investors)
Small numbers, law of, 22
Social capital, 205
Social Security, 99–100, 108,
111
Socialism, 192
Socially responsible investing,
177–91
balance between investors,
185–88
benefits of, xii, 179–80
civil rights origins of, 182
in philanthropy, 188–90
reasons for avoiding,
190–91
religious values in, 181–82
utilitarian benefits from,
182–84
values in, 178–79
Solman, Paul, 44
Son of BOSS tax shelter, 158,
159

Sonic Trading, 47
South Africa
loan rates in, 38
social pension program
in, 211
South America, rotating
savings and credit
associations in, 100
S&P 500 Index, 11, 34
Spammers, stocks touted by,
19–20
Speculation, 112
Spending, lifetime sequence of
saving and, 98–102
Spendthrifts, 92
Spinning, fairness of, 201
Split-capital funds, 104
Stack, Andrew Joseph, III, 151
Stahl, Lesley, 215
Starbucks, 185
Status, 161–73
of art investments, 164–66
competitions based on,
170–71
desire for, xvi
displays of, 166–70
investing for, 162
of movie investments,
163–64
and *schadenfreude,* 168–69
signaling, 171–73
of wine investments,
162–63
Stawarz, Erin, 211
Steadman Funds, 138
Stein, Ben, 11–12
Stein, Eric, 119
Stewart, Martha, 134, 143, 169
Stock dividends, 98, 102–3, 118
Stocks
Internet, 112
as lottery tickets, 107–13
margin on, 228
war, 13–15
Stop-loss orders, 79–80
Strategic defaults, 197
Strong (company), 30
Structured products, 116
Subprime mortgages, 41–42,
78, 114
Success Charter Network, 189
Sugar, self-control and, 87, 88